THE
DEFIANT

THE
DEFIANT

CHRIS LEE

A HISTORY OF FOOTBALL
AGAINST FASCISM

First published by Pitch Publishing, 2022
Reprinted 2024
2

Pitch Publishing
9 Donnington Park,
85 Birdham Road,
Chichester,
West Sussex,
PO20 7AJ
www.pitchpublishing.co.uk
info@pitchpublishing.co.uk

ISBN 978 1 80150 185 9

Typesetting and origination by Pitch Publishing
Printed and bound in India by Replika Press Pvt. Ltd.

Contents

Introduction

THE 1981 film *Escape to Victory* sees a host of film stars and footballers, supported by extras from Ipswich Town FC, acting as a team of Allied prisoners of war. The POWs take on a Nazi football team in an exhibition match set in the Colombes Stadium in Paris, with plans to escape after the match via a tunnel in the changing room into the Paris sewage network. *Escape to Victory* was inspired by real-life events, not in Paris, but in far-flung Kyiv, capital of Ukraine, and a game that has since become known as the 'Death Match'. After reneging on a pact of non-aggression with Stalin during World War II, Hitler set his sights on occupying the Soviet Union (USSR) and on 22 June 1941, Operation Barbarossa began. Initially, the Germans made swift advances, taking Kyiv by mid-September. The Nazis imposed horrific conditions on the Ukrainians, whose lands they occupied, deporting many to labour camps and committing atrocities against the Jewish population. Those who remained behind were never far from starvation and under constant threat of arrest for the smallest act of defiance.

In Kyiv on 6 August 1942, a team drawn from the *Luftwaffe* (German Air Force) called *Flakelf* (The Flak Eleven) took on a team formed out of a local bakery, known as FC Start. FC Start drew players from established Kyiv clubs – predominantly Dynamo and Lokomotiv – who had survived the conflict thus far and the inhumane conditions of Nazi occupation. Football in occupied Kyiv was initially designed as a distraction for the impoverished local population. Yet, despite the FC Start players' weakened state, the team won all its nine matches during the summer of 1942, including the 6 August match against *Flakelf* by five goals to one. Apparently, the Germans demanded a rematch, which became known as the infamous 'Death Match', held at the Zenit Stadium in Kyiv on 9 August 1942 in front of 2,000 spectators. Reportedly, FC Start defied orders to show the Nazi salute before the match, thus upsetting the referee, who had been drawn from the Nazi SS (*Schutzstaffel* – Protection Squads). I've read conflicting reports; I've heard the referee let a number of rough and targeted tackles from the *Flakelf* team against the FC Start players go unpunished. I've also heard the match was relatively cordial; the players certainly posed smiling for the cameras in the post-match photo. After falling behind, FC Start regrouped and levelled with a long-range shot. The Ukrainians had been used to playing together in a system, so grew into the game and began to take control, despite the rough treatment of their opponents and the apparent bias of the referee.

FC Start left the pitch 3-1 ahead at half time with the delighted cheers of the Ukrainian crowd in their ears. At this point, the post-war Soviet accounts suggest that the SS visited the dressing room to remind the players of the situation; the Germans were to win, or there would be repercussions. As it was, the *Flakelf* side appeared intimidated by the baying crowd in the second half, despite enhanced security, and the tackles were less fierce than in the first half. FC Start won the match 5-3. The German humiliation was exacerbated by the fact that their supposed allies – Hungarian soldiers – had joined in with the locals' jeering of the Nazi high command in the grandstand. However, there were no immediate consequences. The Ukrainian players went back to work in the bakery as before and even played another fixture in the coming days. However, any false sense of security was soon dispelled. The Nazis had merely been letting things calm down before taking action. On 18 August, the Gestapo visited the bakery and called out several FC Start players. One of them, Nikolai Korotkykh, had been denounced as having worked for the Soviet secret police, the NKVD. He was the first to die, his heart giving up after 20 days of torture. The others were transferred to the notorious Siretz work camp or made to work for Nazi officials.[1] Three other FC Start players would die at the hands of the Nazis, but not until several months after the 5-3 victory. There is no clear evidence that any punishments were related to the FC Start v *Flakelf* matches.

It was only in 1946, long after the Soviets had recovered Kyiv, that the legend of the 'Death Match' was pushed as part of post-war Stalinist propaganda. The team – and its victims during the war – are commemorated with statues across the city. A Russian-made film, *Match*, which came out in 2012 to coincide with Ukraine's joint hosting of the European Championship and the 70th anniversary of the 'Death Match', caused uproar in Ukraine, where many felt the film portrayed negative depictions of Ukrainians.[2] So how do Ukrainians view the 'Death Match' now, 80 years on? Denys Nachornyy is a football blogger and Dynamo Kyiv fan. 'The correct information is widely available, and everyone who has any interest knows the truth,' Nachornyy tells me. 'There is quite an amount of people – especially among the older generation – who still believe the propaganda myth simply because of how widespread this was during the Soviet times. The "Death Match" was one of *the* biggest war-time propaganda stories – all of them were later debunked – and anyone of a certain age heard it a million times.' Nachornyy believes we need to take the simple view that the 'Death Match' is really just a story about people who tried to survive the war and just wanted to play football – to keep their sanity, to entertain themselves, to escape the grim working conditions or maybe even earn a bit of money. 'So, essentially, it is a story about football and people who played it. And revealing the real truth is the best way to commemorate the fallen and those who had to live the rest of their lives hiding in the shadow of the myth,' he adds. 'That's why most of us – Dynamo fans and even the general public – are against the propaganda story so much, even though it paints such a heroic picture. Those people were not Soviet heroes, they were professional footballers who could really play the game, and that's it.'*

Four FC Start players died at Nazi hands during the war, and they are now immortalised in stone. Beyond the myth, the reality is that the 'Death Match' is one of the most famous examples of football against fascism. One of the reasons I chose the topic of the history of football against fascism was because one of the most popular posts on my football culture blog *Outside Write* is an article on the world's left-wing football clubs. At the same time, I observed an increase in the interest in, and study of, *ultrà* (extreme fan) groups, many of which have extreme political views. Clearly, there is an interest in football against fascism and the far right, and it's not even a new thing, as we will discover during this book. As long as there has been fascism, there has been opposition to it on the football field, around the stadium and in wider society.

This interview was conducted long before the invasion of Ukraine by Russian forces in February 2022

What is 'fascism' and the far right?

Fascism as a political ideology emerged after the devastation of World War I. A *fascio* in Italian means 'bundle' – effectively, a group of people. On 23 March 1919, the future dictator of Italy, Benito Mussolini, launched his *Fasci Italiani di Combattimento* (Italian Combat Groups) in Milan. Its name was a reference to the *fasces* of imperial Rome, and Mussolini installed the first fascist regime in Italy after his 'March on Rome' in October 1922. His initial success inspired extreme right movements in other countries, most notably in Germany. Political theorist Cas Mudde describes extremism as that which 'rejects the essence of democracy, that is, popular sovereignty and majority rule'.[3] The standout characteristics of fascism include opposition to liberals, left-wingers and independent trade unions, and disdain for the free press and parliamentary democracy. Other traits of fascism include extreme nationalism and the othering of immigrant groups or minorities, which often leads to violence.

While Mussolini and Hitler's fascist regimes were destroyed in World War II, along with those of many of their Eastern European sympathisers, fascism lived on in Europe in Franco's Spain and Salazar's Portugal until the 1970s. New far-right dictatorships emerged in the 1960s and '70s in Brazil, Argentina, Paraguay, Uruguay and Chile. In recent decades, a new far right has made its presence known on European terraces. When hooliganism really became an issue in Britain in the late 1970s, its growth mirrored that of the far-right National Front party and elements of the skinhead movement. Mudde tells me that while the British hooligan scene became increasingly multicultural and less political, in Europe – which often looked to the UK for cultural trends – hooliganism remained as it had arrived, associated with the far right. 'Hooliganism came to Europe at a time when it was primarily defined as very violent and far right, so you saw various groups in Western Europe adopting it,' he explains. 'Football being the most popular sport is still a very attractive vehicle for political ambitions.'

Where there's a platform, there is an opportunity to influence the masses and the media, and that is true from the earliest days of football until the present day. So, what attracts the far right in particular to football in order for it to become a platform? Dr

Stuart Whigham is a senior lecturer in Sport, Coaching and Physical Education at Oxford Brookes University in England, and has written extensively on the relationship between national identity and football. Whigham explains that it is a complex relationship to define because it is fluid and dependent on the individual national context. However, broadly speaking, football provides for a nation's population to gather around an event or phenomena, and overtly express their national identity in a comparatively acceptable domain, something that is not always possible in other fields such as politics, economics or culture. Football's near-universal appeal also means that it is the best example of the link between national identity and sport, more so than rugby, cricket or athletics. According to Whigham, this makes football particularly attractive to the far right. 'Football offers a domain in which it is both feasible and, in some ways, condoned as part of football fan culture to express nationalist sentiments without fear of repercussion,' he tells me. 'Football crowds offer an opportunity for the "de-individuation" of the self, whereby an individual can form part of a larger group mentality to express particular sentiments without being concerned about any potential repercussions. This leads to a sort of "group-think" whereby far-right groups can foster support from a larger proportion in the context of football crowds or stadiums, whereas organising such *en masse* expressions would be difficult in other settings – such as mass demonstrations or protests – due to likely counter-protests, prosecution and/ or violence. Furthermore, football supporters often attempt to reproduce a set club identity in their fan groups, which leads to the re-perpetuation of a specific political ideology, hence the strong associations with particular clubs with far-right or other political ideologies. It becomes part of the expression of fanhood of a particular club in turn to align with far-right or discriminatory ideologies.'

In this book, we'll explore football's role in challenging fascism and the far right for more than a century. We look at football's role in opposing the fascist regimes of Mussolini, Franco, Hitler and Salazar in Europe, to football against the authoritarian dictatorships in the Cold War theatre of Latin America (1960s–80s). We discover how, time and again, dictators viewed visiting teams as an endorsement of the legitimacy of their regime and took advantage of politicians and administrators from democratic countries who believed – perhaps naïvely – that sports and politics should not mix. We will hear stories of footballers who made the absolute sacrifice as partisans in the fight against fascism. We will see examples of football matches as key morale-building and propaganda exercises to rally the masses during times of war, and we will see how socio-political culture wars are still fought on the terraces in the form of fan activism deep into the 21st century. According to the United Nations, far-right attacks tripled between 2015 and 2020,[4] so the topic seems particularly relevant in an increasingly divided world. However, in this book we also meet the people behind modern progressive football movements and clubs that are challenging the beliefs, activities and influence of the far right in their country, and striving for positive change.

Author's note

The relationship between politics and football has always fascinated me. In the late 1990s, when I was at university, I wrote my dissertation on Spanish regional identity as expressed through football. It really opened my eyes to the enormous impact politics has had on the game and how the sport has been a platform for political expression, protest and propaganda. My interest in football's history and culture led me to explore the early development of association football, which was the focus of my first book, *Origin Stories: The Pioneers Who Took Football to the World.* During my research for *Origin Stories,* I discovered more about the impact social and political landscapes have had on football across Europe and beyond. I also argue that association rules football has been political since the very beginning. This is really when the idea for my second book, *The Defiant,* began to form. I wanted to dig further into the complex history of football, politics and propaganda.

There has always been so much more to football than purely a sporting contest. In Britain, football was the platform for a social struggle between the upper-class gentlemen who laid down the rules and the working-class men and women who eventually made the game their own. When association rules football arrived in Ireland in the late 1870s, sport became a key point of contention among the Irish nationalists who were keen to preserve and promote Irish sports, like Gaelic football and hurling, ahead of British imports like soccer, rugby and cricket. Similarly, football became part of the national awakenings of Portugal, Egypt, Turkey, India, Uruguay and many other places.

In this book, I meet the fan groups, organisations and clubs in the modern era that are seeking to tackle the challenges presented by the modern far right around football, such as xenophobia, racism, sexism, antisemitism and misogyny, both inside and outside the stadium. For some – especially in Europe in the 1930s and '40s, and much of Latin America during the Cold War period – football against fascism and the extreme right could be a matter of life or death. Politics, fascism and extremism are sensitive subjects to write about, so I am keen to emphasise that this book is a historical exploration of a particular and prominent aspect of football, and not a political statement or a reflection of my own personal political views. The views expressed by my interviewees are based on their own personal experiences or research. And while personally I gravitate towards more progressive and inclusive clubs, I certainly don't agree with everything that some left-wing fan groups engage in, for example, those that sing songs in praise of Stalin, who was responsible for the deaths of millions of people.

While some football clubs have a clear political identity influenced by the club's directorship itself, many others are defined or perceived politically by the activities of their most vocal fan groups. While it is tempting to stereotype or label a certain club's fans as being of a certain political persuasion, it's essential to remember that the vast majority of spectators go to a stadium simply to watch the unscripted drama of a football match and to support their local club. However, for a notable and vocal percentage of some crowds at certain clubs, politics is a core part of their identity. As we see in the first chapter, within the Italian *ultrà* scene, the terraces are often big enough to support a spectrum of various and often conflicting political viewpoints, so we have to take a nuanced approach to defining a club's fans' political leaning. What the terraces do reveal, however, is something of a microcosm of the society of that time and place.

This book was published around the same time as the centenary of Mussolini's March on Rome in October 1922 to establish the world's first fascist state. From the very beginning, football has been a platform to stand in opposition to the extreme right, so let's explore a century of football against fascism and the far right and, as the western world faces extreme social, economic and political divisions not seen in decades, we ask what it tells us about the future relationship between football and politics.

1 Dougan, Andy; *Dynamo: Defending the Honour of Kiev* (London: Fourth Estate, 2001, p187)

2 http://content.time.com/time/world/article/0,8599,2116038,00.html (retrieved 13/09/21)

3 Mudde, Cas; *The Far Right Today* (Cambridge: Polity Press, 2019, p7)

4 https://www.economist.com/international/2021/03/01/how-far-right-extremism-is-becoming-a-global-threat (retrieved 08/09/21)

Chapter One

Italy

BENITO MUSSOLINI – *Il Duce* – was Italy's authoritarian leader for 21 years, from his 'March on Rome' in October 1922 until he was ousted from power in July 1943. He established the world's first fascist state, and sport was a core ingredient of his reign. His impact on defining football as Italy's national sport is absolutely key to the country's early success in the sport. Under him, a nationwide league – *Serie A* – was founded in 1929 along with the peninsula-wide expansion of the *Coppa Italia* knockout competition. The *Carta di Viareggio* (Charter of Viareggio) in 1926 set out many of the rules that the Italian game would follow, including the legalisation of professionalism and the limiting of foreign players.

All sport was politicised under *Il Duce*. The Italian Football Association, the *Federazione Italiana Giuoco Calcio* (FIGC – Italian Football Federation) was headed up by the politician Leandro Arpinati, who was a friend of Mussolini's and would also head up Italy's Olympic committee during his career. New football clubs were formed to strengthen competition between cities. In Florence, the Club Sportivo Firenze and Palestra Ginnastica Libertas clubs were merged in 1926 to form Associazione Calcio (AC) Fiorentina. The following summer in Rome, Associazione Sportiva (AS) Roma was established through the merger of three clubs from the capital, Fortitudo-ProRoma, Football Club di Roma and Alba-Audace. SS Lazio refused to join the AS Roma project, a move that teed up one of world football's biggest cross-city rivalries. New stadia were also established, like Arpinati's impressive Stadio Littoriale complex in Bologna (now the Stadio Renato Dall'Ara) and the Foro Italico complex in Rome – formerly the Foro Mussolini – which holds the Stadio Olimpico. Even the language changed under Mussolini. Traces of Englishness were removed. Football would now be known as *Calcio* (kick), a nod to the violent medieval Florentine ball game of *Calcio Fiorentino*. English-founded Genoa Cricket and Football Club became Genova 1893 Circolo del Calcio in 1928; in Milan, Internazionale was renamed Società Sportiva Ambrosiana, while Milan Cricket and Football Club became Associazione Calcio Milano. Mussolini even presented Italy as the source of modern football; for him, the English had merely rediscovered the game.

During Mussolini's reign, Italy would host and win the second FIFA World Cup tournament in 1934, claim Olympic football gold in Berlin in 1936 and retain the World Cup in Paris in 1938. However, Mussolini's support for sport was not a benevolent policy; its aims were to prove the Italians' superiority and provide a sense of unity in a country divided by language, politics and economics that had only been created a few decades prior. Rival political parties were outlawed and the death penalty reintroduced. Yet, the fascists' grip on Italian football institutions was not without opponents, both at home and abroad. The Italian national side, the *Azzurri* (Blues), and other Italian clubs would become lightning rods for protests against the Mussolini regime from exiled Italians overseas. As John Foot writes in *Calcio*, his seminal history of Italian football, 'Fascism was good for Italian football, and football was good for fascism.'[1] Foot tells me that there was very little open opposition to Mussolini or the regime during the 1930s. 'In part, that's because of a very effective secret police that's crushed any kind of organised opposition, and anybody who was in organised opposition was massively underground or was abroad,' he explains. 'There's no open opposition at all, either at the games or on the streets. You would get arrested and thrown in jail for five years. It just wasn't worth it.'

Even before Italian fascists marched on Rome, football was caught up in the fast-evolving dynamic within Italy. English club Burnley was due to play a match in Bologna in June 1922 as part of its Italian tour when the city fell to the *Fascisti* along with neighbouring Modena and Ferrara. In 1928, football and fascist politics were already showing themselves abroad when an Italian student team won a tournament in Paris against French, Hungarian and Czechoslovakian teams. At the final whistle, the Italian fans antagonised local supporters with their fascist songs and cheering, which led to a fight in the stands. Police had to break up the scuffles.[2]

Italian rebels

Within Italy, the 'Roman salute' – or fascist salute of the raised right arm outstretched in front – was introduced in 1925 by Lando Ferretti, a prominent fascist and journalist who also served as president of the Italian Olympic Committee (CONI – *Comitato Olimpico Nazionale Italiano*). Players were expected to raise their arm pre-match in an act that would court controversy at home and abroad throughout the 1930s. One player who very publicly refused to perform the salute was Bruno Neri. Neri was a midfielder from Faenza, east of Bologna. In 1929, aged 19, he signed for Fiorentina, where he spent seven years of his career. During this time, Fiorentina moved into its new Stadio Giovanni Berta (now the Stadio Artemio Franchi) designed by famed stadium architect Pier Luigi Nervi. The Florentine club's new stadium was named after a local fascist militant killed by communists during clashes in the city a decade earlier. Berta was attacked by socialists and thrown from the Ponte Sospeso to his death. It appears he may have clung on to the bridge before the mob cut off his hand, sending the rest of his body plummeting into the River Arno.[3]

Italian fascists considered Berta a martyr. Neri, however, had no time for fascism. A famous photo taken on 13 September 1931 shows the Fiorentina team lining up for an inaugural match against Admira from Vienna at the Stadio Giovanni Berta. The only man in the line-up conspicuously holding his hands at his side while the rest of his team-mates raise theirs is Bruno Neri. There were 12,000 spectators in the ground, which was still unfinished, including leading local fascists.[4] Neri would go on to die fighting fascism. Having joined partisan fighters in 1943, he died in a shootout after being ambushed by German troops on 10 July 1944 on a path in the Apennine Mountains. A plaque marks the spot where Neri and his comrade Vittorio Bellenghi were gunned down. Faenza's stadium – where Neri had returned to finish his career as player-coach – was named after him in 1946.

The chances for players who showed dissent or held leftist political beliefs were limited. Lucchese's Hungarian Jewish manager Ernö Egri Erbstein was only too keen to take on players whose chances had been restricted elsewhere due to their anti-fascist stances. He snapped up Neri when Fiorentina made him available, along with midfielder Bruno Scher, another committed anti-fascist who refused to Italianise his Yugoslav name. Erbstein's biographer is Dominic Bliss. He tells me that while at Lecce, Scher had been linked with both Milan giants and was likely to have been called up to the Italian national side before his personal anti-fascist viewpoints became known publicly. So, instead of a glittering international career at one of Italy's top clubs, Scher ended up in the country's third tier with

Erbstein's Lucchese. 'Erbstein was known as someone who would overlook the political norms and was courageous in his decisions in that respect,' Bliss tells me. 'He liked characters, he liked people who believed in their own way, and that were progressive.'

Another Erbstein signing was Gino Callegari, brought in from the *Genovese* club Sampierdarenese. Callegari's anarchist views were so well known that when he was introduced to Mussolini pre-match during a short spell at AS Roma in the 1933/34 season, *Il Duce* reputedly commented, 'Ah, the anarchist'.[5] For some players, this meant striking a compromise if they were to enjoy a successful career. One such player was *Il Gatto Magico* (The Magic Cat), Aldo Olivieri, who won 24 caps and the World Cup with the *Azzurri*. Olivieri had never been a fascist and had been spoken to for failing to show the salute in domestic games. On the international stage, however, he went along with the protocol that national team coach Vittorio Pozzo was keen to instil. Indeed, Olivieri was singled out by Mussolini as a national hero for his heroics in Italy's successful retention of its World Cup in 1938.[6] Lucchese could probably claim to be the most rebellious of Italian football clubs during the 1930s, as far as resistance was possible.

Domestic resistance to fascist sporting doctrine was not restricted to men's sport; women footballers also played on despite the regime's disapproval. In Milan in 1933, a group of friends led by Losanna Strigaro and Ninì Zanetti, and including Luisa and Rosetta Boccalini, plus the Lucchese sisters, formed the *Gruppo Femminile Calcistico* (GFC – Women's Football Group). In a global context, the Football Association in England had banned women's football at FA-affiliated grounds in 1921 on apparent health grounds. In Italy, women's *calcio* also faced a struggle for acceptance. The regime had a traditional view of women's roles as good wives and mothers, but on the other hand girls started receiving physical education in schools. Physical health was a key feature of womanhood in the eyes of Mussolini's regime, which was obsessed with Italy's declining birth rate, so women's non-contact sports – such as swimming, tennis and basketball – were promoted within Italy, particularly in the northern and more industrialised cities.

For girls who grew up under Mussolini, their experience of – and exposure to – sport differed from those of their mothers' generation. Marco Giani is a member of the *Società Italiana di Storia dello Sport* (SISS – Italian Society for Sports History). He has researched the GFC extensively and even interviewed members of their families. Giani tells me that attending football matches was a normal activity for girls in Milan, so the natural next step was to organise their own games. The GFC wrote to Leandro Arpinati, who headed up Italian sport at the time, for permission to play, and he said yes. Arpinati, an old friend of Mussolini's, had been the fascist chief of Bologna during the 1920s, yet he was very open-minded about women's sports.

After a couple of matches, the two internal GFC teams decided to play with a 13-year-old boy in goal to avoid any potential criticism of their game being overly physical and, above all, dangerous for their reproductive capacity. In the summer of 1933, the GFC played without any problems. Then, they bravely decided *not* to follow one of Arpinati's conditions – that football was played behind closed doors. The team's second public match at Campo Isotta Fraschini in Milan attracted a crowd of 1,000, including some players and staff from Ambrosiana (Inter Milan's name during this period) and Czechoslovakian side Sparta Prague, who were in town for the semi-finals of the Mitropa Cup. Stories about the *calciatrici* (women footballers) were even carried in the Italian press, including *La Gazzetta dello Sport*.[7]

Attitudes towards women's football changed when Arpinati was succeeded as head of the Italian Olympic Committee by Achille Starace. Italian sports policy was now directed exclusively towards achieving international success and recognition. 'Starace was really cynical, he was really against women's football and any kind of female sports,' Giani tells me. 'Starace was only interested in developing female athletes in sports that would bring prestige to Italy on the international stage in the form of Olympic medals, for example.'

The authorities stopped the first proposed national-level match between the GFC from Milan and a team from nearby Alessandria in October 1933. The GFC kept playing in secret until the spring of 1934, despite losing its president Ugo Cardosi. During these months, the club was led by the new secretary, Giovanna Boccalini Barcellona. Giani describes the ban on women's football as a 'soft ban'; there were no arrests, but the obstacles became too great, and the women stopped playing. GFC co-founder Rosetta Boccalini went on to enjoy a successful career in basketball, including appearances for the Italian national side. Rosetta was one of seven children. One of her older sisters, Giovanna, was a co-founder of the first female partisan group in World War II, *Gruppi di Difesa della Donna* (Women's Defence Group). Some other GFC players were redirected to athletics: the Lucchese sisters became two of the best Italian 800-metre runners of the 1930s, while sprinter Franca Agorni, who was one of the last girls to join the GFC before the boycott, went to the 1936 Summer Olympics as a reserve in the 4x100-metre relay team.

The story of the *Gruppo Femminile di Calcio* was largely unknown until Giani discovered it while researching the history of women's football in Italy at the school where he was teaching in 2014. He published his first two academic articles about GFC in 2017. The story was retold as a novel in Italian by journalist Federica Seneghini in 2020, titled *Giovinette: Le Calciatrici Che Sfidarono Il Duce* (*Giovinette: The Female Footballers Who Challenged the Duce*). In 2021, the Municipality of Milan named a street after the GFC – *Via Calciatrici del '33*. 'On one hand, the *Gruppo Femminile di Calcio* played against prejudice and sexism by going against the accepted tradition of the role of women, but on the other hand, they were daughters of the fascist regime. It's something of a paradox,' Giani concludes. 'The regime destroyed any kind of memory of them; there was no further press coverage. But also, speaking to members of the footballers' families, it appears they didn't fully realise the importance of what they were doing just by playing football at that time. Like many of the women partisans in the war, they didn't seem to think their acts were significant because they were women.'

Political Football: World Cup 1934

FIFA awarded Italy the right to host the 1934 World Cup at its Stockholm summit in October 1932, getting the nod over the Swedish bid. It was the organisation's second tournament and the first to be held in Europe. Despite being hosts, Italy was still required to qualify for its own tournament – the first and only time this has happened in World Cup history. Italy ran out 4-0 winners at home to Greece in March 1934, only for the Greeks to withdraw ahead of the return leg. Seeing the propaganda value of a World Cup win, Mussolini reminded FIGC head, Giorgio Vaccaro, that 'Italy must win the World Cup'.[8] Italy's path to glory was made somewhat easier by some noticeable absentees. The football associations of England, Wales and Scotland still refused to participate in FIFA tournaments. Meanwhile, 1930 hosts and world champions Uruguay also declined the invitation to take part, apparently still sore from so few European sides making the journey to its tournament four years earlier.

To strengthen the national and domestic game while staying relatively true to the Mussolini government's anti-foreigner policy, the regime enabled foreign-born players of Italian descent to play in Italy and, crucially, *for* Italy. Many foreign-born players, known as *oriundi* or *rimpatriati* (returnees), originated in South America, where football was already established to the highest standard. Uruguay won the first World Cup in 1930, building on Olympic gold success in 1928 in Amsterdam and 1924 in Paris. The Uruguayans' opponents in both the 1930 and 1928 tournament finals was Argentina. Italy's 1934 squad included Luis Monti, who featured in Argentina's losing side in the 1930 World Cup Final, and Attilio Demaría, another member of Argentina's 1930 squad. Fellow Argentines Enrique Guaita and Raimundo Orsi, a veteran of Argentina's 1928 Olympic final defeat, were joined by Brazilian-born Anfilogino Guarisi. In all, 47 South American footballers moved to Italy to become *oriundi* in the Italian leagues between the wars, a handful playing at the highest level for the national side. So significant was the exodus that the Argentine FA complained directly to the FIGC, arguing that the fascist Italian government was wanting Argentina's leading players to make Italian football the best in the world.[9]

The man charged with delivering international glory was Vittorio Pozzo. The cultured Piedmontese manager had played football in Switzerland with Grasshopper of Zurich and been a founder member of Torino FC. He had coached the Italian football team as early as the Stockholm Olympics of 1912 before serving in Italy's Alpine division during World War I. Pozzo took charge of the Italian Olympic team in Paris in 1924 while also working as a journalist for *La Stampa*. In 1929, Leandro Arpinati approached Pozzo to take over the reins as Italy's national coach permanently, a post he held for 19 years. During this period, Pozzo brought his *Metodo* (Method) system of play, which increased the focus on defence in a 2-3-2-3 formation.

As the organisers had promised in their bidding process, no expense was spared. Foreign visitors were enticed with offers, overseas fans enjoyed subsidies of up to 70 per cent and the cost of travel between games within Italy itself was also reduced.[10]

Mussolini ordered the creation of an alternative trophy, the *Coppa del Duce* (The Duce Trophy). It was six times the size of FIFA's Jules Rimet trophy and would also be presented to the eventual winner. Football writer Aidan Williams has studied Mussolini-era football extensively and asserts that while hosting a successful tournament was essential for how Italy was perceived abroad, it would not have been quite as beneficial for the regime had the *Azzurri* not won the trophy. 'While Mussolini wasn't massively into football himself, he recognised the political value that a successful national side could provide,' Williams tells me. 'Pozzo also claimed that he was only able to select party members for the 1934 squad.'

After sweeping aside the USA 7-1 in its opening game, Italy scored controversial victories over Spain and Austria's *Wunderteam* to reach the final. Various question marks remain over the quality and impartiality of the officiating in those fixtures. In the final, held at the Stadio Nazionale PNF – the fascist party stadium in Rome – the Italians would face Czechoslovakia. 'Much to the chagrin of Mussolini, on the day of the final itself, the Czechoslovakian government decided that this was the day to announce that it was to ally with the Soviet Union,' Williams explains. 'This communist pact was very much seen as an anti-fascist move, and to announce it on the day of the final was seen by Mussolini – and probably correctly – as a hugely symbolic gesture.' Italian communists had suffered greatly in the 12 years that Mussolini had been in power, and Williams believes that many communists viewed the final as a mirror of the clash of ideologies between communism and fascism. Williams adds that just four days after Italy's 2-1 extra-time victory over the Czechs, Mussolini and Hitler met for the first time in Venice. The future fascist Axis was founded that would ultimately lead to conflict in Europe.

In 1934, there had been no real opposition to Italy hosting the World Cup. Perhaps the world had not yet been woken up to the expansionist designs of fascism to consider it a threat. The first real test for the League of Nations, a forerunner to the United Nations, came in October 1935 when Mussolini flexed his muscles abroad and invaded Abyssinia, modern-day Ethiopia. Italian forces advanced from Somaliland, using air support and even poison gas against the vastly technically inferior Abyssinian defenders. Italy succeeded where it had failed in the 1890s in its first attempt to invade Abyssinia and conquered the country within six months. Abyssinian Emperor Haile Selassie fled into exile. Vittorio Pozzo had previously said of the foreign-born *oriundi* that 'if they can die for Italy, they can play for Italy'[11] as they were eligible for national service, yet Enrique Guaita along with Argentine compatriots, AS Roma players Alejandro Scopelli and Andrés Stagnaro, were discovered sneaking over the Swiss border rather than face a military call-up.[12]

The lack of international response to the Italian invasion emboldened Mussolini, and straight after the successful takeover of Abyssinia in the summer of 1936, he was happy to support General Francisco Franco's fascist *coup d'etat* against the democratically elected Second Republic in Spain. Under this cloud of international tension in both Africa and Europe, Italy sent its amateur footballers drawn from various universities to the Berlin Olympics held during August. Rome itself had been a potential host before withdrawing from the selection process in 1931. Notably, the student team representing fascist Italy wore all black – not the traditional *Azzurro* (blue) – on its way to the gold medal, a look that would return to feature controversially for the national side just two years later in France. Another of Erbstein's Lucchese players, Libero Marchini, had been called up to the Olympic squad. The 21-year-old midfielder played in all of Italy's games in the run to the gold medal and came from an anti-fascist family. After the Olympic final victory against Austria, while his team-mates performed the obligatory Roman salute, Marchini is

27

photographed scratching his left thigh, therefore avoiding having to make the gesture. But while the Italians enjoyed a sympathetic crowd in Nazi Germany, tensions were rising in Europe, and ideological divisions were about to enter the field of play.

Tensions abroad

In March 1937, the *Azzurri* were in Vienna to take on Austria's *Wunderteam*. The match had a political edge from the off. The Austrians were conscious of Nazi Germany's ambitions of *Anschluss* – a unification of the German-speaking peoples of Germany and Austria – which would eventually happen the following year. On seeing the Italian side perform the fascist salute at the start of the match, the 50,000-strong Viennese crowd turned on the visitors, booing them vehemently. Some Austrians grabbed hold of Italian flags and tore them up. With echoes of Highbury three years earlier, when Italy lost a bruising encounter with England, the game appears to have descended into violence. Three Italians and two Austrian players were forced to retire, and an Austrian player was sent off. When the Italians refused to allow a free kick to be taken, the referee abandoned the match after 74 minutes, with Austria 2-0 up. The Italians needed a motorised police escort to leave the ground.[13] According to a British United Press report, the match had 'turned into one of the biggest anti-Italian demonstrations seen in the Austrian capital', and the news reached Mussolini himself.[14]

The abandoned Vienna match would have repercussions in Paris just a month later. Tensions between France and Italy had been ratcheting up since the outbreak of the Spanish Civil War the previous summer. A Spanish military *coup d'etat* led by General Francisco Franco was launched in July 1936 against the progressive Republican government. The resulting civil war would rage for three years, and Franco's fascist uprising received support from Mussolini. The war displaced thousands of Spaniards, many of whom fled across the Pyrenees to neighbouring France. Like Britain, France remained neutral in the face of nationalist uprisings in Europe, favouring appeasement over confrontation. A friendly match between France and Italy, scheduled at the Parc des Princes for 11 April 1937, was cancelled by Mussolini after news reached Rome that French communists and Italian anti-fascists exiled in Paris were planning to protest against the Italian side. The Italian football authorities sought assurances that 'ample protection would be afforded to Italian players in case of possible political demonstrations'.[15] French authorities were mindful of crowd trouble following the recent Vienna abandonment and are reported to have informed the Italians that neither the Italian anthem nor the fascist salute would be allowed.[16] The match cancellation followed accusations from Italy that France had been providing military assistance to Spain in contravention of non-intervention agreements. France denied the allegations. Later that month, Italian aircraft were involved in the bombing of the Basque market town of Guernica, which inflamed international outrage at Mussolini's regime.

Tensions against Italian teams continued throughout the summer. Once more, Vienna was the scene of controversy as a 'free fight' broke out between home side Admira and Genoa (Genova) in a Mitropa Cup match on 4 July. 'From the start, the Austrian antipathy to the Italians showed itself in an unfriendly attitude on the part of the 45,000 spectators towards the visitors,' the *Belfast Telegraph* reported.[17] While the game was relatively calm, things changed when an Austrian player converted a penalty near the end and apparently celebrated by 'making a long nose'[18] at the Italians. The nearest Genoa player punched the offending Austrian, and all hell broke loose. One Italian lost several teeth after being kicked in the mouth, and the police were required to keep the two sides apart. Four Italians were injured. In response, when Admira travelled to Italy for the return leg the following week, Mussolini called the game off and gave the Austrians 24 hours to leave the country.[19] Both Admira and Genoa were expelled from the tournament.

The fascists controlled the media, so the only way an Italian could read, hear or see news around *calcio* was through the filter of the regime. Understanding the role of the media early on, in 1933 Italian exiles in Belgium managed to grab hold of radio commentator Nicolò Carosio's microphone at a match and speak to the population at home.[20] Italian exiles would go on to badger the regime abroad wherever possible, most notably in France during the World Cup of 1938. When Italy returned to France to defend its title, it stepped into hostile territory. Many political opponents of Mussolini had fled across the border to France to escape his regime, including Professor Carlo Rosselli, an influential scholar and anti-fascist activist. Rosselli had been interned on the island of Lipari in 1929, but escaped and made his way to France, where he edited the anti-Mussolini paper, *Giustizia E Libertà* (*Justice and Liberty*). He also helped organise Italians fighting for the Republicans in the Spanish Civil War. In June 1937, Rosselli and his brother Sabatino – an esteemed historian also known as 'Nello' – were found stabbed to death in the grounds of a chateau in rural Normandy. An estimated 200,000 people lined the streets of Paris for the brothers' funerals.

When the World Cup came around, protests began as soon as the *Azzurri* arrived in Marseille to take on the Norwegians at Le Stade Velodrome. Six of Norway's starting XI had faced Italy in the Olympic semi-finals two years earlier, which Italy had won 2-1 *en route* to gold. Crowds of 3,000 or more French and Italian anti-fascists had to be contained by mounted police, according to Ambrosiana (Inter Milan) player Ugo Locatelli.[21] In the stadium itself, the fascist salute was greeted with boos, whistles and jeers. The outcry angered Italy coach Vittorio Pozzo so much that he ordered his team to perform the salute twice even after the crowd had quietened down to show them that his side was not intimidated. Despite the world champions getting off to a flying start with a second-minute goal from Pietro Ferraris of Ambrosiana, the Norwegians equalised seven minutes from time, having already hit the woodwork three times. Norway then had a goal ruled out for off side. Olivieri also tipped a goal-bound shot over to keep Italy in the tournament, before Lazio's Silvio Piola bagged the winner in extra time to send the *Azzurri* through.

The Italians progressed to the quarter-final in Paris to take on the hosts at the Stade Olympique de Colombes. As both sides' first-choice shirt was blue, a draw was made to decide colours. France won, and Italy donned an all-black kit with the fascist *Fascio Littorio* crest for the first and only time in a full international.[22] The order to wear black was rumoured to have come from Mussolini himself and, combined with the performing of the fascist salute, sent a message to the home crowd and the wider world. The Parisian crowd was three times the size of that in Marseille, nearing 59,000. The game was so hotly anticipated that gate receipts hit a record 876,000 francs.[23] Yet the playing of the fascist anthem *La Giovinezza* was not received with anywhere near the same hostility as in Marseille. 'Marseille is not Paris,' an Italian journalist said of the difference in reception between the crowds in the two cities.[24] Piola was on target twice to seal a surprisingly easy 3-1 win for the team in black as Italy eliminated the hosts from their own World Cup.

Italy returned to Marseille for the semi-final against an overly confident Brazil side, with the anti-Mussolini Italian and Spanish diasporas in the stands firmly in favour of the South Americans. Anticipating a straightforward victory, Brazil made eight changes, including resting star striker Leônidas. It proved costly as Italy won 2-1 to return to Paris for the final against Hungary, where two goals apiece from Gino Colaussi and Piola (again) secured a 4-2 win for Pozzo's side. Unlike 1934, there was no question mark against Italy's 1938 World Cup triumph. 'Regardless of how those two World Cup triumphs came about, they were won under the fascist flag, they were won in the name of the fascist state and, frankly, they would not have happened without the fascist state in various ways influencing them,' Aidan Williams concludes.

What had changed between 1934 and 1938? John Foot describes 1935, when Italy invaded Abyssinia, as the 'peak of consent' for the Italian public, and by 1938 observers across Europe realised that Mussolini's government was a dangerous, imperialist regime. In 1934, Mussolini was not all that interested in football; he had not even attended the victory after-party and cycling – Italy's most popular sport – pushed the World Cup win off some front pages. Yet by 1938, Mussolini was much more associated with football, Foot says. Taking place in France, Italy's neighbour with a large anti-fascist Italian community in exile, the World Cup became a hotbed for hostility. 'When the 1938 World Cup comes along, that becomes a lightning rod for a series of open anti-fascist demonstrations. This is the first time that Mussolini's regime is openly contested in a public sphere, in that kind of forum, which is a really interesting moment,' Foot tells me. 'But then what Italian propaganda does is turn that on its head to make it into a trial, blaming it on the French mainly, so that despite the hostile atmosphere of the French, we stood firm, we kept our salutes in the air. That kind of propaganda was very clever, turning it on its head and making themselves into victims, like they did with the Highbury game [against England in 1934].'

The team Italy wanted to beat was England, who had still refused to take part in World Cup tournaments in the 1930s. A friendly was arranged for May 1939 in Milan – the first time the two sides had faced each other since the infamous 'Battle of Highbury' five years earlier. Vittorio Pozzo took the fixture against England so seriously that he had his team prepared one month ahead. The match itself drew 60,000 fans to the San Siro, a record for an Italian international fixture at that time. England continued an appeasement mission that almost exactly a year earlier had seen the team issue a fascist salute before a match against Germany in Berlin, sparking a heated debate at home. Again, the England team performed a fascist salute at the San Siro, which this time went largely unnoticed by the press back home. The England team held their arms aloft even though Benito Mussolini himself was not present, although his children were. Similarly, Adolf Hitler had also not been at the Berlin match a year earlier.

The decision for the England team to show the salute during the playing of *La Giovinezza* appears to have been agreed by Football Association secretary Stanley Rous after talking to the new British Ambassador in Rome, Sir Percy Loraine.[25] Some of the British public were upset by the gesture. A *Falkirk Herald* columnist was keen to alert 'hyper-sensitive' people to the 'unwritten laws of courtesy' of guests towards their hosts.[26] In the end, match witnesses recorded that neither the English nor the Italian team appeared quite sure of the protocol. 'It seems that we shall never get this saluting business right,' Clifford Webb lamented in his match report for the *Daily Herald* as he observed 'comic handwaving'.[27] The game itself finished 2-2 with Silvio Piola bagging Italy's controversial second, awarded by the German referee despite English appeals for handball, before a late England equaliser from Willie Hall of Spurs.

England moved on to Belgrade, where the FA side lost 2-1 to the Kingdom of Yugoslavia. Yugoslavia's next opponents ten days later, on 29 May, were the *Azzurri*. The young country of Yugoslavia, two decades in the making after the break-up of the Austro-Hungarian Empire, was in something of a tight spot. Due to the merger of Austria and Germany in the *Anschluss* of 1938, the country now shared borders with both fascist Italy to the west and Nazi Germany in the north. Since Italy's Milan encounter with England, Mussolini had signed a 'Pact of Steel' with Adolf Hitler on 22 May, reinforcing previous accords and aligning the two fascist states militarily, politically and economically in case of war. To make matters worse for Yugoslavia, in April 1939 Italy had invaded Albania to the south, securing naval control of the Adriatic Sea and forcing Albania's King Zog into exile. Yugoslavia's vital sea corridor was now at the mercy of the Italians, and it was in this tense environment that Italy's team arrived in Belgrade. As in France the year before, Italy's footballers were jeered when they presented the fascist salute. Some Yugoslav supporters even threw stones at the Italians.[28] Italy ran out 2-1 winners.

Football resistance in Italy during World War II

Mussolini watched events unfold after Germany invaded Poland in September 1939, which brought about Europe-wide conflict. It was only in June 1940, with France facing capitulation, that Mussolini finally committed Italy militarily to Germany's war effort. In October, Italian forces attacked Greece from their Albanian bases, which turned into a disaster. The Greek campaign and the many Greek footballers that helped force Mussolini and Hitler's forces back are covered in depth in Chapter Four. As men of fighting age, many footballers were called up to serve in the Italian military. Many would later defect to become partisans to fight against the Nazis. Italian activity during World War II was disastrous; with failure on the Greek offensive, defeat in North Africa and Ethiopia, and a huge loss of Italian life supporting the Germans on the Eastern Front. The war created food shortages at home, and opposition movements began collaborating to overthrow Mussolini.

On 10 July 1943, Allied forces led by British Field Marshal Montgomery and American General Patton landed on Sicily. It was the beginning of the end of Mussolini. Two weeks later, on 25 July, the Fascist Grand Council demanded Mussolini resign and *Il Duce*'s reign was over. He was arrested later that day. On hearing of his arrest, anti-fascists in Bologna entered the Stadio Littoriale and attempted to tear down the bronze statue of Mussolini on horseback that stood under the Maratona tower. They succeeded in taking down *Il Duce*, but his legs and the horse remained in place for another four years.[29] On 8 September, the new Italian government struck a truce without the occupying Germans' knowledge, and Italy had, in effect, switched sides. The Allies began pushing northwards up the country. Mussolini was broken out of his prison in a German commando raid and made leader of a puppet state in the Nazi-occupied north of the country called 'the Italian Social Republic', also known as the Republic of Salò.

With the Nazis desperately trying to stem the Allied advance through Italy, fighting became bogged down and morale was low among the troops. Like other parts of occupied Europe, football became a distraction. As in Kyiv earlier in the conflict, a legendary match took place between the occupying Nazis and local men. The small town of Sarnano sits on the eastern shadow of the Monti Sibillini National Park in the region of Marche. The mountain range was crawling with Italian partisans keen to subvert the German occupation. One such partisan, Decio Filipponi, had been executed by the Nazis. His body was left to hang in the town square for a week to send a message to the locals. Here in Sarnano, in the spring of 1944, Nazi officers knocked on the door of a local resident, Mario Maurelli – a former referee in *Serie A*. They asked him if he could raise a team of men aged between 17 and 22 for a match against the younger German soldiers.[30] The Nazi officers promised Maurelli, whose brother Mimmo was among the partisans, that no harm would come to the players.

Mario sent word and raised a team. He would referee the match on 1 April. The Italian XI, dressed in blue shirts, found themselves on a pitch surrounded by German soldiers. Mario Maurelli had briefed the team to go easy on the occupying team so as not to upset them. Yet the Italians played their natural game, were far superior to the German side, and a partisan named Grattini headed them in front. Not quite sure how to play it, the Italians took their foot off the pedal in the second half to allow the Germans to equalise towards the end. With the game tied at 1-1, Mario Maurelli blew for full time, at which point the partisan XI sprinted off the pitch and disappeared back into the Sibillini mountains.

After July 1943, some footballers who had been mobilised as part of the Italian army joined the partisans fighting the Nazis. One such player was American-born Armando Frigo, who had won the *Coppa Italia* with Fiorentina in the 1939/40 season. Frigo was born in Clinton, Indiana to Italian parents, but the family moved back to Vicenza when he was eight. He became an *oriundo* – a foreign-born player of Italian descent who was permitted to play in Italy on grounds of his heritage. Frigo had been based on the Dalmatian Coast in Croatia when the armistice was signed. He immediately joined local partisans in defending the roads around the town of Crkvice but was rounded up and shot. When sifting through Frigo's belongings, his captors found his Fiorentina membership card that he had kept with him throughout his active service.

In the far north-eastern fringes of Italy, the region of Friuli shares borders with Austria to the north and Slovenia to the east, part of the former Yugoslavia. Here, promising footballer Antonio Bacchetti, who had stints during the war at Potenza, Savoia and Cormonese, was active with Italy's resistance. At the time in the spring of 1945, partisans were sourcing food from local farmers to supply to resistance fighters hiding in the mountains. This supply was being hindered by local agricultural sector officials. Bacchetti and his group were commissioned to bring one of the agriculture officials to trial by the *Comitato di Liberazione Nazionale* (CLN – National Liberation Committee) in the town of Pradamano. However, increased German round-ups in the area made it difficult to escort the official to trial without being caught. At some point in transit, the captive official was shot dead. Six years later, while Bacchetti was enjoying a successful period of his career at Napoli, the dead official's family accused the members of the party of kidnapping and killing him. Bacchetti, his brother Germano and three other members of his division were called to trial in Udine, but the process ended in amnesty.[31] Bacchetti returned to Udine to turn out for Udinese before enjoying other short stints at Torino and Crotone.

Resistance did not need to be military; it could be found in the workplace too. Former Fiorentina midfielder Vittorio Staccione is one example. Staccione had long been known for his socialist views right back to the 1920s. As a Torino player, he had missed the opening of the new Stadio Filadelfia because he was recovering from an attack during which two fascists had broken a couple of his ribs. After hanging up his boots in 1935, he held various factory jobs in Turin and was known to authorities as politically anti-fascist. He was regularly tracked and harassed by the Italian secret police. In March 1944, workers went on strike across northern Italy, and Staccione was arrested. It appears the local commissioner may have warned Staccione that he would be deported. Still, he did not flee and instead reported to the police station the next day. He was packed on a train to Gusen, a sub-camp of the Mauthausen concentration camp, where he survived a year before succumbing to septicaemia and gangrene.[32] Also sent to Gusen and Mauthausen for his support for the general strike was former Seregno and Milan midfielder Ferdinando Valletti. Valletti was deported from the infamous underground

Platform 21 at Milano Centrale railway station, where political prisoners and Jews were deported to labour and death camps. At Mauthausen – which is covered in more detail in Chapter Three – football kept Valletti alive. He was forced to turn out for the SS team and given work in the kitchen, which gave him access to food. He survived 18 months of internment and returned to his wife and daughter, who the Vallettis had been expecting when he was arrested.[33] After the war, Valletti returned to work at car maker Alfa Romeo. Valletti's former club AC Milan organises educational visits to the *Memoriale della Shoah* (Holocaust Memorial) at Milano Centrale station.[34]

La Spezia – Italy's wartime champion

By the summer of 1944, the Nazis and Italian fascist forces had been forced to dig in, defending the 'Gothic Line' that ran from the naval base of La Spezia in the west to Pesaro on the eastern Adriatic coast. Conscripted Italian labour was drafted in to build defences to delay the Allied advance from the south. North of the Gothic Line, competitive football continued. The FIGC based itself in Milan and created a mixed division championship split into six regional groups – the *Campionato Alta Italia* – the Northern Italian Championship. Regional group winners and some runners-up would qualify for the semi-final group stage, with the final held in Milan.

As a significant naval base, the Ligurian port of La Spezia was a key target for Allied bombing. The bridges north out of the city were destroyed, breaking road links to Genoa. The port's football club, Spezia Calcio, which had finished sixth in *Serie B* in the 1942/43 season, was also in crisis. Its president, Coriolano Perioli, had been deported to Germany, and six members of the squad were out of reach, south of the Gothic Line. To produce a team, the head of La Spezia's fire department, Luigi Gandino, created a squad formed out of the available Spezia Calcio team along with players from Genoa, Livorno and Napoli. They were all registered as firemen and – as players – excused from military service. The team was named the 42° Corpo Vigili del Fuoco di La Spezia (42nd La Spezia Fire Brigade) and managed by Ottavio Barbieri, who had won the *Scudetto* twice as a winger at Genoa and represented Italy in the 1920s. A fire engine was adapted specially to transport the team and the players all lived together at the fire station.

Vigili del Fuoco won its first group in the Emilia Zone Group D unbeaten, having faced Suzzara, Fidentina, Parma and Busseto. Progressing to the Emilia region semi-finals, the firefighters again topped their group, which featured Suzzara again, along with Carpi and Modena. Vigili del Fuoco travelled to Bologna, where they were a goal up before the match was suspended in the 79th minute due to a pitch invasion by home fans. Vigili del Fuoco were awarded a 2-0 victory to take into the second leg. With La Spezia being too dangerous to hold the return match, the venue was switched to Carpi. Bologna protested and withdrew, meaning the firefighters from La Spezia had made it through to the final round. In Milan, the final was a three-team round-robin featuring the reigning champions Torino, managed by Vittorio Pozzo, and Venezia. Many spectators avoided going to the arena because they feared being rounded up by Germans. The firefighters drew their opening match with Venezia 1-1. Pozzo's Torino side had only lost once in the tournament. Featuring superstars Silvio Piola (on loan from Lazio) and Valentino Mazzola, the side was the overwhelming favourite. However, Barbieri's tactics thwarted the Torino side, and Sergio Angelini scored twice to give Vigili del Fuoco a 2-1 win. Four days later, Torino beat Venezia 5-2, meaning the makeshift firefighter side of La Spezia had become wartime champions of Italy. The FIGC did not recognise the title until in 2002, after a lot of campaigning.[35]

Off the pitch, four members of Spezia Calcio were active Italian partisans – Astorre Tanca, Roberto Fusco, and the Incerti Vecchi brothers, Walter and Riccardo. Tanca had been a distinguished member of the Italian military in North Africa prior to the armistice before being arrested by the Germans. He escaped to join the partisans, where he headed up a brigade and spent much of his time disrupting Nazi supply routes. He died in March 1945, pinning down a German advance until his machine gun jammed, earning enough time for many of his comrades to escape.[36] Tanca now has a sporting campus named after him in La Spezia. The Incerti Vecchi brothers died fighting in the hills of Reggio Emilia in 1944. Fusco had represented Parma in the *Campionato Alta Italia*, where his side was eliminated from Vigili del Fuoco's group, before he joined the partisans in August 1944. He also died in April 1945 in a reprisal attack.[37]

Benito Mussolini was shot dead on 28 April 1945. Among those present in the final moments of *Il Duce*'s life was the former Comense (Como) full-back Michele Moretti. Moretti had played in *Serie B* and *C* and was once considered by Pozzo for a national call-up. Born into a socialist family, he was known to have refused to conduct the pre-match Roman salute in the 1930s before joining the *Partito Comunista d'Italia* (PCI – Italian Communist Party) later that decade. During the war, he helped organise strikes and even escaped from a transport to a Nazi camp before joining up with partisans around Lake Como. There, he took the *nom de guerre* 'Pietro Gatti'. In April 1945, Moretti was involved in the guarding of Mussolini, his lover Clara Petacci, and other leaders of the Republic of Salò. Accounts vary, but partisan Walter Audisio claimed to be the one who dispatched the shots that killed Mussolini and Petacci, potentially using Moretti's gun after his own had jammed.[38] Mussolini's body was taken to Milan and left in the Piazza Loreto along with those of his entourage and former Italian Olympic Committee president

Achille Starace. The locals strung the bodies up and threw stones at them. Mussolini's leading sports minister, Leandro Arpinati, met a similar fate, assassinated by a communist group in Emilia-Romagna shortly after Bologna fell to the Allies.

After the war, many clubs returned to their original names and rebranded their stadiums. Virtus Entella's ground is named after the partisan Aldo Gastaldi, and Carpi plays at the Stadio Sandro Cabassi. Cabassi joined the partisans aged just 18 and was captured and tortured by fascists before dying at the hands of a firing squad. At Sarzana near La Spezia, the Stadio Miro Luperi takes its name from a former ASD Sarzana goalkeeper-turned-partisan. Luperi had escaped to the mountains to join the Garibaldi Brigades and died on 28 November 1944 while holding off a German advance, buying his comrades time to escape. Luperi was awarded the Gold Medal for Military Valor posthumously for his bravery.

Italy's ultrà scene emerges

After the war, Italy's long road to recovery resulted in *il miracolo economico* – the economic miracle – that lasted from the 1950s up to the 1970s. The new consumer world wanted what Italy produced – raw materials, cars, electronics – leading to some of the strongest growth rates in Europe. But the Italian economic miracle was not without its challenges. Despite the strong economic performance, Italy's political scene was descending into violence. By the late 1960s, disillusioned with pay and conditions and inspired by the radical actions in neighbouring France in May 1968, many Italian workers went on strike. Extreme guerrilla groups on the left and the right weighed in, and the period from the late 1960s until the early 1980s are commonly referred to as the *Anni di piombo* (the years of lead) in Italy. There were bombings and even political assassinations. In Italy, political tensions on the street were transferring to the stadium. The emergence and growth of the *ultrà* or 'ultra' correlates with the years of lead. Organised groups of fans with a hierarchy, a belief system and an identity congregated in the *curve* (stands) behind goals at stadiums across Italy. Inspired by British hooligan culture and fashion, along with the influence of the vocal ultra scene that had taken hold in neighbouring Yugoslavia, Italian ultras established their own brand of extreme fandom. The new fan culture absorbed the violence of Italian society and brought it into the football world.

Ultrà just means 'to go beyond', and what constitutes an 'ultra' in the football sense is open to interpretation. James Montague is a writer who has spent time with some of the world's most extreme ultra groups. For him, ultra life is a culture that has developed its own rules and norms. 'Many of the things we see – the choreography, pyro, climactic public displays, political messaging, twinning of ultra groups – all come from Italy, but then there's so much that's taken up from culture from Brazil, or Argentina, or England, and it's all mashed together, so today when you see ultras around the world, it's a globalised product, a globalised culture,' he tells me. According to Montague, ultra culture has developed its own code of honour, purpose and hierarchy and a very organised political identity. 'The terraces reflect the political upheaval that's happening at that time. By understanding fan culture, you really understand a place better than almost any mirror you can hold up to society,' Montague adds.

In Italy, ultra culture emerged in the late 1960s with the *Fossa Dei Leoni* (Lion's Den) group of AC Milan fans, although the term 'ultra' itself was not used until 1970.[39] Groups would take on military-style names, such as *Brigate* (Brigade), Corps, Fighters, Boys and Commandos. The *curva* – the terracing behind the home team's goal – was also a prime recruitment ground for young men looking for identity and belonging. The *curva* became a space where fans – mostly, but not exclusively, men – could come together, sing, wave flags and create choreographed displays. Emboldened, many started becoming active outside the stadium too. Group leaders emerged and developed almost cult-like status. Luca Hodges-Ramon is managing editor of the Italian football website *The Gentleman Ultra* and has studied Italian *ultrà* movements. 'There is undoubtedly an established culture of far-right politics within the ultra movement, and you can trace that back to the unrest of the 1970s and the clashes between the neo-fascist black shirts and the Red Brigades,' he tells me.

In the capital, the Nazi occupation of Rome during World War II has a legacy in the modern left-wing ultra scene. The south-eastern working-class neighbourhood of Quadraro was home to many partisans and left-wing opponents, and even referred to by the SS's chief commander in Rome, Herbert Kappler, as the 'Wasp's Nest'. Tensions were high after the Fosse Ardeatine massacre in March 1944. Here, more than 330 Italian partisans and civilians were murdered in former ash quarries by the Nazis in reprisal for a partisan attack that took 32 German lives. In April 1944, two months before Rome was captured by the Allies, the Nazis launched *Unternehmen Walfisch* (Operation Whale), a dawn raid on Quadraro that saw around 2,000 men arrested. Estimates vary, but it is thought more than 900 of them were deported to concentration camps deep in Germany and Poland. One of the first AS Roma ultra groups to emerge in the 1970s was named *Fedayn* after the Palestinian group. 'Fedayn have their roots on the left,' explains football writer Wayne Girard. 'Fedayn's founder, Roberto Rulli, came from Quadraro, bringing his neighbourhood's identity with him. Fedayn is still highly active in the *curva*, as well as the street.'

Arguably, nowhere in the world is football more political on the terraces than in Italy, certainly at a club and fanbase level.

Italian *curve* often have room for a broad spectrum of political alignments. Since AS Roma's ultra groups emerged in the 1970s, left-leaning *Fedayn* have shared the terraces with the far-right *Boys Roma* group.[40] Girard tells me that Boys Roma dominate the Curva Sud end of the Stadio Olimpico in Rome, but the dynamic is far less political and tumultuous than in the 1970s or '80s. 'When you think of the drums, megaphones and flares, it started with Boys,' he adds. 'Today, they are still the most dominant group with the highest number of members. When you see the large banners in the crowd today, they're typically coming from Boys. They're relatively uncommercialised, and membership spreads through word of mouth.'

Italy was only unified in the 1860s, a process known as the *Risorgimento*. Despite unification and the promotion of one universal Italian language, Italians still feel distinct and strong connections with their own region or town. This attachment is known as *campanilismo* – from the Italian word for a bell tower, *campanile*. This loyal regionalism remains, and often the *curva* is where this loyalty is displayed. Despite the phenomenon of *campanilismo*, many Italian *ultrà* groups will form a friendly bond with like-minded ultras from other clubs. This is known as *gemellaggio*, or twinning. 'Gemellaggio manifests itself in a number of different ways,' explains Tom Griffiths, who blogs about Italian football at *CalcioEngland.com*. 'The most obvious examples are banners, choreography, chanting in mutual respect between the fans from different clubs. There are three reasons why they exist: the first and most dominant is probably along political lines. In *Serie A*, the most prominent is Inter and Lazio, who both have right-wing fan groups. There are friendships that cut across political lines. Common rivalries and shared enemies are the second reason for twinning – for example, Fiorentina and Torino share a well-documented rivalry with Juventus. The third reason is usually based around a particular match that sparked a friendship; for example, Empoli and Parma are twinned due to a famous match played in thick fog.'

Modern Italy's left-wing ultras

While much of Italy's ultra scene originally sprang out of the left, by the 1990s things looked very different on the *curve*, with many of Italy's ultra groups leaning to the right, often to the extreme. Tobias Jones is the author of *Ultra: The Underworld of Italian Football*, in which he explores the history and role of the ultra in modern Italian football and society. I asked him what changed between the 1970s and the 1990s and whether Italy's ultra movement was a reflection of Italian society as a whole. 'It's obviously hard to summarise a subculture made up of tens of thousands of people, but various events happened in the early 1990s which flipped certain *curve* from far left to far right,' he explains. 'The national political situation – with the collapse of the First Republic and Silvio Berlusconi going into alliance with what was then the neo-fascist *Movimento Sociale Italiano* [MSI – Italian Social Movement] – meant there was suddenly no taboo about fascist iconography.'

Jones tells me that in Italy it became common to scorn what had once been central ultra points of reference, like the Resistance in World War II. 'Ultras have always claimed to be extremists, and certainly it felt in the 1990s more transgressive to announce yourself as a *Fascista*,' he continues. 'So fascism was both rehabilitated as a concept in national politics, but also seen as a far more valid fortress for violent insurgents than the far left. The coincidence of the beginnings of mass immigration to Italy, which until the early 1990s had seen only trace levels compared to France or the UK, meant that certain fan groups suddenly felt that the best way to defend the territory – another founding philosophy of ultra-dom – was to scorn all outsiders. That bled, very quickly, into support for far-right parties and slogans, especially since certain movements – *Forza Nuova* [New Force] especially – deliberately and strategically sent young men into the terraces to mingle and agitate.'

Yet, the left still had voices on the *curve*. Nowhere is modern Italy's left-wing anti-fascist football culture more apparent than in the Tuscan port city of Livorno. It's here that the Italian Communist Party (PCI) was formed in 1921, a year before Mussolini marched on Rome. In 1926, fascists arrested one of the leading lights of the PCI, Antonio Gramsci, and imprisoned him for 11 years until his death in 1937. As a multicultural port city, Livorno has a long left-wing tradition, which extends to its football culture as the most visible representation of the city. AS Livorno Calcio's Stadio Comunale Armando Picchi was completed in 1933 and has a wonderful *Art Deco* frontage. The stadium was named after Benito Mussolini's daughter, Edda Ciano Mussolini, for its first decade until the dictator's death in 1945. Now the club's fans – and even some players – will proudly rail against the far right on the peninsula. On match day, you can expect to spot communist insignia in the crowd, such as the hammer and sickle, or images of Che Guevara, and hear the *Bandiera Rossa* (Red Flag) sung alongside the World War II partisan song, *Bella Ciao*. Anti-globalisation is also a key theme of the Livorno *ultrà* scene, and targets of the fans' ire have included former AC Milan owner, politician and media mogul Silvio Berlusconi.

Mark Doidge is a principal research fellow at the University of Brighton in the UK and has studied Livorno's ultras extensively. He tells me that the communist paraphernalia in the *Curva Nord* (North Curve stand) at the Armando Picchi reinforce the political element of the fans' local identity. The Livorno ultras' displays, along with the voracity of their singing, will increase significantly when visiting teams have fans with openly fascist sympathies, such as Lazio or Hellas Verona. Livorno fans also twinned with left-leaning Virtus Verona to provide support in a city where Virtus Verona is the third club after Hellas and Chievo. 'Marxism and communism are significant to the identity of many Livorno fans and ultras. It helps them articulate their difference from other clubs in Italy,' Doidge explains. 'This belief is a product of their history and the wider national political and social context.' Doidge adds that football is a space to articulate specific localised identity – *campanilismo* – and put it into performative action. 'Livorno's Marxist identity frames their understandings of themselves and their interactions with others. It defines their rivals and their allies, as well as guiding their actions,' Doidge tells me. 'Through this, Livorno fans have performed a variety of political protests which both raise awareness of specific issues and reaffirm their identity.' Arguably, no player has embodied this identity more than Cristiano Lucarelli. Lucarelli took a pay cut in 2003 to join his home-town club AS Livorno from Torino. Here, he chose to wear the number 99 as a tribute to the foundation year of the Livorno *ultrà* group, *Brigate Autonome Livornesi* (BAL – Autonomous Livornese Brigade). One of Lucarelli's goal celebrations – the clenched left fist of the communist salute – would earn him a hefty fine. It was the latest in a long line of infamous celebrations from Lucarelli; in an Italy Under-21 match in 1997, he had also revealed a Che Guevara t-shirt under his national team *Azzurri* shirt to the watching *Livornesi* crowd after scoring.[41] In season 2020/21, Lucarelli took up the reins at Umbrian club Ternana, which also has a left-leaning fan base.

The antithesis of AS Livorno fans can be found at Rome-based SS Lazio. Back in the 1920s, Rome's oldest football club resisted fascist moves to merge with three other associations to form a leading club in the capital; that entity is now AS Roma. However, in recent decades many within Lazio's fanbase have been closely associated with the far right, most notably during the time of *Gli Irriducibili* (The Die Hards) ultra group. For more than three decades until its dissolution in February 2020, *Gli Irriducibili* dominated the *Curva Nord* (North Curve) of Rome's Stadio Olimpico. During this time, far-right emblems appeared on the *curva*, including swastikas, Celtic crosses, images of Mussolini and, in a home game against Bari in 2000, a banner hailing indicted Serbian war criminal Arkan.[42] That same year, Italian clubs committed to supporting government incentives to stop play when offensive banners appeared. In 2018, Lazio was fined €50,000 and 13 fans were banned from stadiums for between five to eight years after stickers appeared of Anne Frank in an AS Roma shirt, describing *Giallorossi* fans as 'Jews', intended as an insult. The club was swift to respond, and its players walked out to its next match against Bologna wearing t-shirts featuring Anne Frank's image with the message *'No All' Antisemitismo'* (No to antisemitism). Many Lazio fans at the match snubbed the 'No to antisemitism' messaging, arriving at the ground late, and some were reported to sing *'Me ne frego'* (I don't care).[43] In August 2019, the former leader of *Gli Irriducibili*, Fabrizio 'Diabolik' Piscitelli, who had many enemies from his connections in the criminal underworld, was shot dead with a single bullet while he sat on a park bench in Rome. In 2005, Lazio forward Paolo Di Canio, who had been in *Gli Irriducibili* as a youth, was fined €10,000 by the Italian FA for performing the Roman salute to Lazio fans. He appeared to perform the salute again versus AS Livorno in a game in which Lazio fans reportedly waved swastikas, a symbol that is banned in Italian stadiums.[44]

In 2013, when Di Canio took the manager's job at Sunderland, the club's vice-chairman, former Labour Party minister David Miliband, resigned. Three years later, Di Canio appeared on screen as a pundit in Italy with a short-sleeve t-shirt that revealed a tattoo of the word 'DUX', which could be associated with Mussolini. Following complaints, he was released by the broadcaster.[45] In a 2017 interview with *Correire Della Sera*, Di

Canio expressed regret for his tattoos, the salute and some other actions during his career.[46]

Across Tuscany, there is a strong tradition of left-wing football fan bases, from Livorno to Carrarese and Empoli. Pisa's *curva* has largely depoliticised, while in Florence Fiorentina's *curva* is apolitical. Still, they have both had progressive elements in the past. So why do Tuscan fans go against the grain of much of Italian football by leaning towards the left? Empoli-based journalist Francesco Sani tells me that Tuscany has traditionally been a progressive part of the peninsula, even before the *Risorgimento* brought Italy together. The Grand Duchy of Tuscany was the first state in the world to abolish the death penalty in 1776, and a tolerant society enabled Jews and Armenians to take refuge in the region, especially in Livorno, Sani explains. 'Tuscany is not a place of landowners, but of lively entrepreneurship and commerce; this made it easily permeable to socialist ideals. My region was particularly hostile to the fascist regime – the Italian Communist Party [PCI] was founded in Livorno in 1921, born from a split from the Socialist party – and for this it paid a very high price in terms of deaths during World War II,' Sani says.

The Gothic Line passed through the Apennine Mountains, so the area between Florence and Bologna saw a lot of fighting between Nazi troops and partisans during the war. Sani emphasises that the Resistance was not a political movement, but a generational one. The partisans were above all Communists but also Catholics, Liberals and Republicans, all united and driven by the desire to found a new democratic and free Italy. After the war, liberal parties dominated Tuscan politics and the Livorno-founded PCI still enjoyed strong support in the region in the 1970s. This is when the first ultra movements became active on the Tuscan terraces, including at Empoli, where the *Rangers Empoli* ultra group was formed in 1976. They were inspired by

London club Queens Park Rangers, which had just enjoyed its best league season ever, finishing second in the First Division to Liverpool. However, Sani explains that while Empoli has a strong trade union and anti-fascist culture, it is important to view the emergence of the city's ultra movement in the context of the time, with Italy having experienced its economic miracle. 'I believe that the ultras movement was born on the left more inspired by the climate of the time rather than by the "myth of the resistance" and the social classification in the PCI,' he adds. 'In those years, movements of the extra-parliamentary left such as *Lotta Continua* [The Struggle Continues – a far-left student movement from Turin] were born; they were years of great political ferment and social change in Italy from the economic boom. The ultras are certainly also young people who participate in demonstrations and political initiatives, therefore, in Tuscany, that cultural and social climate of the left manifested itself in the *curve*.'

Empoli's municipal stadium is named after former player Carlo Castellani, who hung up his boots for the club in 1939. Not only was Castellani Empoli's record goalscorer for 70 years after two stints with the club, he was also a victim of Nazi oppression. The club now known as Empoli Calcio was formed in 1920, with Castellani joining as a 17-year-old in 1926. His talent for finding the net helped lift Empoli from the Tuscan Third Division to the Second, before securing a transfer to AS Livorno in *Serie A* under Hungarian coach Vilmos Rady. The Castellani family, based in Fibbiana to the east of Empoli, helped fund Empoli's football club during the early part of World War II. In keeping with fascist policy across Italy, Empoli Football Club was forced to change its name to *Associazione Sportiva Fascista Empoli* (Empoli Fascist Sporting Association) during this period. Locally, the patriarch of the Castellani family, David Castellani, was a known anti-fascist. On 3 March 1944, the *Comitato di Liberazione Nazionale* (CLN – National Liberation

Committee), the leading political body that represented the Italian resistance, called for a general strike across the fascist-run sector of Italy. It was the same strike action that led to the arrest of Vittorio Staccione. Confronted with this mass act of insubordination, the fascists decided to round up those suspected of having connections with the resistance, including David. In a dawn raid on 8 March 1944, the police knocked at the door of the Castellani household. It was David they were after, but his son Carlo opened the door. He offered to go to the station to answer the fascists' questions instead of his father, believing the matter would be resolved swiftly. However, Carlo Castellani would never return. Together with many suspected political dissenters, he was packed on to a train bound for the infamous Nazi concentration camp of Mauthausen in Austria. He died of dysentery at the camp just five months later, on 11 August, aged 35.[47] Empoli Calcio's ground was dedicated to Castellani in 1965 and there is a memorial plaque to him at the ground. Many Empoli fans have visited the Mauthausen camp and left blue scarves in memory of Castellani.

Down the road in Florence, Centro Storico (CS) Lebowski was formed as a response to the disillusion many fans felt with modern football.[48] CS Lebowski, named after the lead character in the Coen Brothers film, *The Big Lebowski*, is a non-profit organisation run by the fans. The club's statute promotes solidarity and co-operation, anti-fascism and anti-sexism.[49] In August 2021, the sixth-tier club secured the services of former Spain international and Fiorentina star Borja Valero. Matthias Moretti heads up communications at CS Lebowski. He first started coming to the club as a student when it was still called AC Lebowski and not yet run by the fans. 'What initially attracted me was the great quality of the *tifo*, and also the great fun and taste for the absurd that the fans had when the team still lost almost all its games,' Moretti tells me. 'In the second phase, when

I came back, I appreciated the seriousness of the sports project managed collectively by its community, which therefore combines cheering in the stands with a real challenge to capitalist football, in which it is possible to play quality sport and also to win on the pitch with a model that does not involve bosses or investment funds, but only the efforts of its community.'

Moretti says that CS Lebowski receives compliments from fans of other teams and has even inspired the creation of fan groups at other clubs in the lower leagues it has featured in. 'Sometimes they were very young guys who somehow took inspiration from us, and we are pleased about that because a return of popular passion in the lower leagues would be a fantastic thing,' Moretti enthuses. 'If we continue to move up a category, it will happen more often to us to meet rival fans, even historical and important ones, and maybe it could also happen that someone will not like us. After all, we are a project that wants to revolutionise football, so we will certainly have some enemies.' CS Lebowski's ultras have *gemellaggi* with fans of Juve Stabia from *Serie C*, and FC Köln's *Coloniacs*. The club also has a friendship with Frazione Calcistica Dal Pozzo, a similar member-run project from near Milan. 'With like-minded clubs we cultivate relationships of collaboration and continuous comparison, because by exchanging skills and experiences we can certainly grow better,' Moretti concludes. 'Surely a growth of all these experiences would be a good thing, if we hope for a real change in the world of football.'

Berlin-based FC Köln fan Alex has been a CS Lebowski member since 2019, having heard about the club via magazines and online articles. He tells me he was attracted to the club because of its ethos. 'Their strongest argument is equality and transparency,' he explains. 'Everyone is equal, it doesn't matter where you're from, how many shares you have, race, gender, etc. On top of the equality and the voice everyone has is transparency. Nothing is hidden and everything is on the table. Being there and with them feels like a big family. I've never seen so many people smile. They established a kids' football school in the old part of Florence, have a women's team and a juniors' team.' Alex adds that CS Lebowski runs a lot of social activities and due to the club's popularity outside Florence, these have included a 'Long Distance Member' weekend, when all members were invited to Florence. So does he believe that community clubs like CS Lebowski are the future of football? 'I think community football is the alternative to money-driven football, which is needed, and we can hope that it will just spread more and more. I'm not sure if it is the future; for me it is the football I was looking for, for many, many, many years. I'm glad I found it, even it is in Italy, but it actually doesn't matter.'

Italy's young progressive football clubs

Meanwhile, in the north of Italy, in Verona, there are three football clubs. The most famous are Hellas Verona and Chievo Verona. Both have competed regularly in Italy's top two divisions. Hellas ultras, in particular, have gained a reputation for far-right behaviour. During the 1990s, there were reports that swastikas were displayed at games and a group of fans even dangled a black mannequin in the blue and yellow of Hellas from the *curva* to send a message that they would not accept a black player at the club.[50] In 2019, Brescia striker Mario Balotelli was on the receiving end of monkey chants and other racist abuse from Hellas fans, and threatened to walk off the pitch.[51] In stark contrast, Verona's third club – Virtus Verona from the eastern suburb of Borgo Venezia – is starting to push for prominence and its politics could not be more different. Despite being formed in 1921, the club has spent much of its century of existence in Italy's lower divisions until in recent seasons it started pushing up the *Serie C* (Third Division) table. Its name comes from the Latin word for 'virtue' and, according to Tom Griffiths, stays true to its community and left-leaning foundations. 'Virtus Verona identifies as anti-racist, anti-fascist, anti-sexist and anti-homophobic,' Griffiths tells me. 'The club sees its purpose extending far beyond the white lines of the football pitch and their success is measured not only in victories but in the social values they hold dear.' Griffiths explains that the club runs a community trust, called *Vita Virtus* ('Virtuous Life'), which helps migrants in the city. Such is the antipathy felt by many Virtus fans towards Hellas that when Virtus was forced to relocate games to Hellas' Stadio Bentegodi in 2014, many refused to go. The club has *gemellaggi* with fellow left-wing fans at AS Livorno and FC St Pauli from Hamburg.

In Milan, St Ambroeus FC was founded in 2018 and named after the city's patron saint. St Ambroeus FC became the first all-refugee team in the city to become affiliated with the Italian Football Association (FIGC), and its €2,000 registration fee was raised by crowdfunding. St Ambroeus FC's co-founder is Gian Marco Duina. He tells me that St Ambroeus FC was formed out of the need to provide migrants who played football in the city of Milan with a more appropriate structure to practise sport in a more professional and stimulating way, and within a stable organisation that allows them to participate in official championships. St Ambroeus FC plays organised football in the FIGC's 'third category', which helps the club to share its message with a wider audience than it would simply playing spontaneous matches, Duina explains. 'When the team was born the players were all migrants, but now they have also been joined by Italian guys who see in this project an alternative to modern football,' Duina says. 'The founding members all came from backgrounds that used football as a tool for social inclusion and as a vehicle for messages such as anti-racism, anti-fascism, anti-sexism outside and inside the world of sport.'

St Ambroeus has even attracted its own ultra group, the *Armata Pirata 161*, to add atmosphere on match days. 'Football is a mirror of our society: everything that happens in society also happens in stadiums and on football pitches. [Not just] in the Premier League stadiums but also in the lower categories,' Duina continues. 'We know this, and we have always known it, and that is why we decided to join the official federation from the lowest rung and not to remain within the more amateur dynamics and environments closer to our own. Racism is present in society, both in parliament and in the neighbourhoods, and consequently also on the football pitches we walk on. With this in mind, we decided to take to the field with a team of migrants, refugees and asylum seekers to break down certain prejudices about racism, xenophobia and the rejection of migrants. Instead, we bring clear and unambiguous positions: "refugees welcome", "anti-fascism" and more. Doing this through football makes it more understandable and receptive, even for those who are not close to our world or are new to it. Italian politics might have moved to the right lately, but it doesn't change our perspective: to be the change it's important to start from the bottom, through education, in the neighbourhood and doing it daily with passion and dedication.'

Duina believes that football is a universal language, and that it is capable of communicating across linguistic, cultural or religious barriers. 'Football brings people together and St Ambroeus is a small demonstration of this,' he adds. 'Currently, St Ambroeus has two teams with almost 50 players from all over the world, including sub-Saharan Africa, Maghreb, Central and South America and Europe. We speak Italian because it is the language that unites us in Italy, but we also speak the language of football, and this is the most beautiful thing. The response has been negative in some cases, such as when we have been the target of racist insults, but on the other hand we have received a lot of support for the project and we have found brotherhood and support on and off the field even beyond the 90th minute; this has been the most beautiful victory.'

In the south, in the Neapolitan suburb of Quarto, the Associazione Sportiva Dilettantistica (ASD – Amateur Sports Association) Quartograd was established in June 2012 by a group of young communist and anti-capitalist football fans, together with some older Napoli ultras who had left the *curve* of the San Paolo Stadium because they were tired of modern football. They started organising anti-fascist and anti-racist eight-a-side football tournaments, and then, picking the best players of the participating clubs, they decided to create a team to enter the official Italian football league. The name 'Quartograd' is a tribute to the Soviet defence of Stalingrad (1942/43), a key turning point in World War II. 'The idea behind the project is to spread an alternative way of living one's passion for football, bringing it back to the old values based on collective management. In popular football, the fans and the players themselves are the owners of the team,' one Quartograd member tells me. 'Quartograd makes not only anti-fascism, but also an attachment to one's own territory, one of its fundamental characteristics. It is in the suburbs like ours that there is a need for spaces for socialising and meeting, and we think that sport can and should offer an alternative to the degradation that too often surrounds us. This is why Quartograd wants to be part of that larger movement that struggles to change the existing state of affairs. Our commitment, in fact, does not end on the football field, but continues every day in our city. One of the slogans that most represents us is: "Another football is possible, another world is necessary."'

Attendance at Quartograd matches can reach several hundred people depending on the tournament and the opposition. The club's fans have carried out a number of community initiatives, such as organising football tournaments for children and after-school activities for young people and migrants. The club has also created a women's five-a-side football team, which a member described to me as 'a concrete way of trying to fight the sexism that is still prevalent in the world of sport as well as in our society'. One former club president has even become a city councillor. Being a left-wing club in Italy, Quartograd fans have also experienced resentment from some right-wing ultras. In a match in Ischia in 2018, a brawl began between home fans and visitors, which led to several arrests. Quartograd fans claim they were victims of an attack by Ischia fans, which included members of the neo-fascist CasaPound movement.[52] Unsurprisingly, Quartograd finds affinity with clubs that share its values, such as neighbouring Pianura and its supporters. The club also has friendships with many Italian anti-fascist football clubs and some further away, including Clapton CFC in London and Ménilmontant Football Club 1871 in Paris. 'The fans have also established ties of knowledge and respect with some ultra anti-fascist groups at an international level, thanks also to their participation in the Rebel Ultras network,' Quartograd's members explain. 'These include Standard Ultras Inferno from Liège (Belgium), Omonoia Nicosia Gate 9 (Cyprus) – who have now also created their own popular football team – some Werder Bremen fans and also some St Pauli fans from Hamburg.'

Further south, fans of the Calabrian club Cosenza on Italy's 'toe' have gained a reputation for their progressive anti-fascist politics. And they live by example, having provided shelter for immigrants and opened a food bank for the poor. Like Livorno in the north, Cosenza and its people have a history of rebellious, anti-establishment politics. When writing his book on Italy's ultras, Tobias Jones travelled with the Cosenza *tifosi* to share their experience around Italy. I asked him whether ultra groups have much impact outside their respective *curve* to spread a wider message. 'I think organised antifa ultras have a huge impact,' Jones affirms. 'It's not newsworthy, but groups in Cosenza have been like an emergency support organisation during the Covid crisis. For them, delivering food parcels is an integral part of supporting the team of the city. The resonance there is huge, not so much on social media – where arguments and needling occur with regularity between different groups – but by word of mouth and street intelligence. Some very concrete things have happened far beyond stadium slogans: play-parks for disabled kids are created, hundreds of homeless people are housed, education programmes are begun, radio stations launched, boxing gyms founded.'

Early Italian football was shaped by Mussolini, from its tournaments – the *Serie A* nationwide league system and the revamped *Coppa Italia* knockout competition – to much of its infrastructure. A century on from Mussolini's takeover of power, Italian football is still political, featuring activity from both extremes. Tobias Jones notes that some far-right ultra groups have either a bust or portrait of Mussolini in their headquarters.

So why is *Il Duce* still admired by some in Italy when the same sentiment towards his contemporaries, such as Hitler in Germany, would cause outrage? 'He's popular because there are still millions who think he is the greatest Italian since Garibaldi!' Jones says. 'Italy likes a strong man, or so the stereotype goes, and Italian democracy has been so unpopular at times that technocrats are more popular than democratic politicians. That derision for democracy makes people nostalgic for a leader who, the cliché goes, was a good man until it went slightly ugly towards the end. It's largely down to ignorance. People don't know their history, but it's not always easily accessible and it's hard to find honesty in TV studio discussions about Mussolini's dictatorship because there are still so many politicians who gain votes by lauding and eulogising him. And so it goes round in circles.' Jones adds that in some parts of Italy, it is perceived as 'cooler' or 'tougher' to be a fascist – two things that ultras long to be.

For Tobias Jones, the FIGC needs to understand ultra mentality if it wants to develop an effective strategy for combatting racism on Italy's terraces. 'If there's a minute's silence for drowned refugees, of course, far-right groups which are live on television will get instant notoriety by turning their backs, raising right arms and singing the national anthem. It's an open goal,' he laments. The rise of the far right in and around Italy's stadiums is something the authorities continue to struggle with. John Foot says that there have been numerous attempts to deal with racism, including the closure of whole stadia in the past, none of which have really worked. 'It's a reflection of society. It's a reflection of politics. The *curve* are very fertile recruiting grounds for the far right. Some clubs have a long tradition of far right, near-fascist, ultra activity, while others have more recently gone over to that world. Others have seen a contestation within the *curva* between two types of fans, some who don't want politics at all and some who do,' he explains. 'Fascism and anti-fascism is a huge issue in Italian society. You've got fascist mainstream parties and they have been in government. So, these things have deep historical roots and football is one arena where it's played out.'

1 Foot, John, *Calcio: A History of Italian Football* (London: HarperPerennial, 2007, p33)

2 *Evesham Standard & West Midland Observer*, 25 August 1928, p3

3 Martin, Simon, *Football and Fascism: The National Game Under Mussolini* (Oxford: Berg, 2004, p153)

4 https://giocopulito.it/bruno-neri-il-calciatore-partigiano/ (retrieved 13/09/21)

5 https://www.minutosettantotto.it/antifascisti-in-rossonero-lucchese-1936-37/ (retrieved 18/06/21)

6 Bliss, Dominic, *Erbstein: The Triumph and Tragedy of Football's Forgotten Pioneer* (Sunderland: Blizzard Books, 2014, loc.2391/5887)

7 https://www.playingpasts.co.uk/articles/football/and-then-we-were-boycotted-new-discoveries-about-the-birth-of-womens-football-in-italy-1933/ (retrieved 15/05/21)

8 https://talksport.com/football/124282/world-cup-1934-did-italy-fix-world-cup-qualifier-14030482049/ (retrieved 27/05/21)

9 Martin, Simon, *Football and Fascism: The National Game Under Mussolini* (Oxford: Berg, 2004, p195)

10 Martin, Simon, *Football and Fascism: The National Game Under Mussolini* (Oxford: Berg, 2004, p184)

11 Glanville, Brian, *The Story of the World Cup* (London, Faber & Faber, 2018, p25)

12 Martin, Simon, *Football and Fascism: The National Game Under Mussolini* (Oxford: Berg, 2004, p196)

13 *Birmingham Daily Gazette*, 22 March 1937 (p3)

14 *Bradford Observer*, 23 March 1937 (p1)

15 *Northern Whig*, 9 April 1937 (p11)

16 *Nottingham Journal*, 9 April 1937 (p1)

17 *Belfast Telegraph*, 5 July 1937 (p6)

18 *Ibid*

19 *Daily Mirror*, 12 July 1937 (p5)

20 Martin, Simon, *Football and Fascism: The National Game Under Mussolini* (Oxford: Berg, 2004, p182)

21 Martin, Simon, *Football and Fascism: The National Game Under Mussolini* (Oxford: Berg, 2004, p181)

22 https://www.theguardian.com/football/blog/2014/apr/01/world-cup-moments-1938-italy-benito-mussolini (retrieved 10/11/21)

23 *Le Petit Journal*, 13 June 1938 (p8)

24 *Le Miroir des Sports*, 21 June 1938 (p5)

25 *Daily Herald*, 13 May 1939 (p11)

26 *Falkirk Herald*, 17 May 1939 (p2)

27 *Daily Herald*, 15 May 1939 (p7)

28 Mills, Richard, *The Politics of Football in Yugoslavia: Sport, Nationalism and the State* (London: I.B. Tauris, 2018, loc.688/8977)

29 https://www.tuttobolognaweb.it/quella-volta-che/il-1943-e-la-statua-del-duce/ (retrieved 25/09/21)

30 Villalobos Salas, Cristóbal, *Fútbol y Fascismo* (Madrid: Altamerea, 2020 p56/174)

31 Molinelli, Edoardo, *Cuori Partigiani: La Storia Dei Calciatori Professionisti Nella Resistenza Italiana* (Rome, Red Star Press, 2019, p89)

32 https://quattrotretre.it/calcio-fascismo-e-resistenza-tre-storie-per-la-liberazione/ (retrieved 20/05/21)

33 *Ibid* (retrieved 20/05/21)

34 https://changingthechants.eu/wp-content/uploads/2021/05/compendium5-8.pdf (retrieved 22/07/21)

35 https://www.acspezia.com/it/lo-scudetto-del-1944.12081.html (retrieved 01/05/21)

36 Molinelli, Edoardo, *Cuori Partigiani: La Storia Dei Calciatori Professionisti Nella Resistenza Italiana* (Rome: Red Star Press, 2019, p48)

37 *Ibid*

38 https://www.warhistoryonline.com/world-war-ii/the-death-of-mussolini-april-28-1945-m-2.html (retrieved 01/01/22)

39 Jones, Tobias, *Ultra: The Underworld of Italian Football* (London: Head of Zeus, 2019)

40 https://gentlemanultra.com/2018/05/01/a-culture-of-violence-how-political-and-social-turmoil-gave-rise-to-romes-ultras/ (retrieved 07/09/21)

41 https://www.gentlemanultra.com/2018/09/22/cristiano-lucarelli-and-livorno-a-bond-forged-in-red/ (retrieved 15/10/21)
42 https://www.theguardian.com/football/2000/feb/02/newsstory.sport5 (retrieved 24/10/21)
43 https://www.thesun.co.uk/sport/football/4769740/lazio-fans-nazi-fascists-anne-frank-juventus/ (retrieved 18/06/21)
44 *Irish Independent*, 13 December 2005 (p19)
45 https://www.mirror.co.uk/sport/football/news/paolo-di-canio-sacked-sky-8835073 (retrieved 01/01/22)
46 https://www.corriere.it/cronache/17_gennaio_02/paolo-canio-non-sono-razzista-tatuaggi-mostrano-miei-errori-3a6eef40-d131-11e6-bd06-82890b12aab1.shtml (retrieved 18/06/21)
47 Molinelli, Edoardo, *Cuori Partigiani: La Storia Dei Calciatori Professionisti Nella Resistenza Italiana* (Rome: Red Star Press, 2019, p131)
48 https://cslebowski.it/storia/ (retrieved 24/09/21)
49 https://www.cslebowski.it/wp-content/uploads/2018/11/STATUTE.pdf (retrieved 24/09/21)
50 https://www.fourfourtwo.com/features/anti-fascist-anti-racist-and-anti-hellas-meet-virtus-veronas-proud-third-club (retrieved 03/05/21)
51 https://www.bbc.co.uk/sport/football/50281847 (retrieved 03/05/21)
52 https://www.napolitoday.it/cronaca/arresti-scontri-tifosi-quartograd-ischia.html (retrieved 06/10/21)

Chapter 2

Iberia

IN APRIL 2019, an intriguing match took place in the northern suburbs of Barcelona. Club Esportiu Júpiter of Spain's fifth tier welcomed non-league east London side Clapton Community Football Club to its Camp Municipal de la Verneda stadium. The visitors wore their away kit – a red, yellow and purple outfit with yellow tridents dotted throughout. The kit was inspired by the colours of the flag of Spain's Second Republic (1931–39) and the International Brigades, overseas volunteers who travelled to Spain to fight for the Republic against the fascist *coup d'etat* led by General Francisco Franco. The shirt was designed to commemorate the 80th anniversary of the end of the Spanish Civil War (17 July 1936–1 April 1939) and proved an instant hit with fans. The Catalan side won 5-0 to the chants of *'¡No pasarán!'* (They shall not pass), a famous Republican battlecry. The match was part of Barcelona's *Primavera Republicana* (Republican Spring) celebrations, and entry was free. To understand the rise of fascism in Spain that led to the outbreak of civil war in 1936 and nearly four decades of dictatorship up to Franco's death on 20 November 1975, we have to go back centuries. It is also important to note that horrific atrocities were committed by both Nationalist and Republican sides during the Spanish Civil War.

The Spanish empire had grown across the Americas since its emergence in 1492, when Christopher Columbus, sponsored by the Spanish crown, landed in what is now called the Americas. Yet by the 19th century Spanish power was in retreat, with independence movements successfully overthrowing Spanish rule across the American continent. The sight of the Spanish Navy limping back into his home port of El Ferrol in Galicia at the end of the Spanish-American War in 1898 is said to have left a lasting impression on Franco as a child. He had been destined to enter the navy, but Spain's American empire was over and its navy in tatters, so Franco pursued a career in the army instead. Franco's rise up the ranks of the Spanish army coincided with a period of internal instability and violent power struggles between the traditional elites – the landowners and the church – and the people. Franco would come to play a key role in defining the political landscape of Spain for much of the 20th century, including its football. In turn, his political opponents also used football to respond to his regime.

Yet anti-autocratic activity in Spanish football pre-dates even Franco's rule by a decade and a half, starting in Barcelona. Founded in the working-class *barrio* of Poblenou by Scots textile staff on 12 May 1909, Club Esportiu Júpiter's early years coincided with rising *Catalisme* – a Catalan national awakening. The club found itself on the frontline throughout periods of political upheaval in Spain. As was common in Barcelona at the start of the 20th century, many of CE Júpiter's playing staff and fans were linked to anarchist trade unions. The club was founded just two months before the *Tragic Week* of late July 1909, when army reservists clashed with anarchists and socialists in the streets of Barcelona, leaving more than 100 dead. CE Júpiter's crest features *La Senyera* – the red and gold stripes of Catalonia – along with a blue star. This resembles the modern *La Senyera Estelada* – the starred Senyera – which includes a blue triangle and a white star at one end. It is the flag of the Catalan independence movement and was inspired by the flags of Cuba and Puerto Rico, two countries that had already gained freedom from Spanish rule. Like Italy, Catalonia had its own 'years of lead' from 1919 to 1923. The *Conferación Nacional del Trabajo* (CNT – The National Confederation of Work) called for strikes pushing for an eight-hour shift and better pay and conditions. The Spanish government of King Alfonso XIII – who, due to his personal enthusiasm for football, had bestowed the name *Real* (Royal) on many clubs – had no answer. The situation deteriorated into violent chaos on both sides, and *pistolerismo* (gun violence) erupted throughout Spain. An estimated 424 people died in Barcelona alone.[1] Those Club Esportiu Júpiter players who had links to anarchist trade unions used the club's facilities to store and smuggle weapons, even hiding guns in leather balls.[2] The years of violence were brought to an end by a *coup d'etat* led by Captain General Miguel Primo de Rivera in 1923, resulting in a period of military dictatorship. Primo de Rivera outlawed the CNT and set about the suppression of Catalan separatism.

On 30 April 1924, Judge Cristóbal Fernández, the civil governor of the province, denounced CE Júpiter's crest as a 'clear dissimulation for the Catalan separatist flag'[3] – now banned by the Primo de Rivera dictatorship, along with the speaking of Catalan in public – and the club was forced to change it. A crown representing the city of Barcelona replaced the star.[4] The following year CE Júpiter, champions of the Catalan Second Division, visited Catalan First Division champions FC Barcelona at Barça's Les Corts ground. The friendly was a benefit match for Catalan choral society *Orfeó Català*. A British Royal Navy band had been invited to provide crowd entertainment at half time. Unaware of the internal tensions within Spain, the band struck up *La Marcha Real* (Royal March), the Spanish national anthem. Cue mayhem. The 14,000-strong crowd hurled down a derisory chorus of whistles until the bemused band stopped playing after just five bars. In its stead, the visiting musicians started playing *God Save the King*, which was received with rapturous applause.[5] The de Rivera government shut FC Barcelona down for six months as punishment for its fans' jeering of *La Marcha Real*, and the club's founder and president Joan Gamper was forced to resign.[6]

At the end of the decade, Barcelona had a modern Metro system and hosted its International Exposition in 1929. By now, Primo de Rivera's grip on power was slipping. He lost the support of King Alfonso XIII, who himself was deposed in 1931 with the coming of the democratically elected Second Republic. The new government was good news for Catalonia as it conferred autonomy upon the region, and CE Júpiter was able to revert to its original crest. In 1931, Barcelona was also a contender to host the 1936 Olympic Games. The International Olympic Committee opted instead for Berlin, which was then the capital of the Weimar Republic. A lot changed in Germany in the five years between 1931 and 1936. Hitler's ascent to power in 1933 ushered in a severe lurch to the far right for Germany, resulting in organised, state-fuelled antisemitism and violence against left-wing activists and parties. In response, the 'People's Olympiad' was organised to be held in Barcelona between 22 and 26 July, the month before the official games in Berlin. Thousands of sportsmen and women – including many Jewish athletes – travelled to the Catalan capital to take part. The French delegation alone was 1,500 strong. 'Hundreds of workmen are toiling night and day in feverish preparations for the great People's Sport Olympiad – a counter blast to the Nazi Olympic Games,' one British observer wrote. 'Every playing field, football ground and swimming bath in and around Barcelona has been put at the disposal of the organisers of the sports.'[7] One of those host football grounds was CE Júpiter's Poblenou base. However, the People's Olympiad never happened. On 17 July 1936, Franco's *coup d'etat* kicked off hostilities, and instead CE Júpiter became the meeting place for many local militants looking to organise the defence of Barcelona against the fascist coup. As in the years of *pistolerismo*, CE Júpiter's home held a small arsenal.[8]

Within weeks, the Civil War claimed Spanish football's first high-profile victim. The president of FC Barcelona at the start of hostilities was the lawyer Josep Suñol (sometimes spelled the Catalan way 'Sunyol'). Despite his well-to-do background, Suñol was prominent in a left-wing group called *Esquerra Republicana de Catalunya* (ERC – The Republican Left of Catalonia) and established the left-leaning newspaper *La Rambla* towards the end of Primo de Rivera's rule. Through his writing, Suñol helped build the vision of football as a political vehicle for Catalonia. Indeed, the publication had the subtitle 'sport and citizenship'.[9] Suñol had acted as president of the Catalan Football Federation during the 1929/30 season and was elected president of FC Barcelona in 1935. On 6 August 1936, Suñol had travelled to Madrid to visit the Republican front line with three other people. However, somewhere in the Sierra de Guadarrama north of the city, his car entered territory already taken by Nationalist forces. Suñol was spotted, arrested and shot there and then by rebel troops, along with his companions. Suñol's shooting was probably not a result of his being FC Barcelona president, but more to do with his being a Republican caught on the wrong side of the fast-changing frontline of fighting. A Republican voluntary group of athletes – the *Batallón Deportivo* (Sports Battalion) – was named after Suñol and a friendly was arranged between the *Batallón Deportivo* and Athletic de Madrid (now Atlético de Madrid). The combined athletes won 2-0 with goals from Trichant of Ferroviaria and Pablito of Nacional.[10] In 1996, a group of journalists and academics got together to create *Els Amics de Josep Sunyol* (The Friends of Josep Suñol), a group aimed at rekindling the memory of the former Barça president. Suñol's body was located and exhumed, and a plaque marking the centenary of his birth was put up in Barcelona's Rambla in 1998.[11]

The founder of the ERC in March 1931 was Lluís Companys i Jover. Companys was president of Catalonia's *Generalitat* (government) in 1936. Companys fled to France in January 1939 to run the *Generalitat* in exile. Just 18 months later, when France had fallen to the Nazis, Companys was arrested by the Gestapo and deported back to Spain. He was executed by firing squad in Montjuïc, Barcelona. In 2001, Barcelona's Olympic stadium in Montjuïc – at the time home to RCD Espanyol – was renamed Estadi Olímpic Lluís Companys.

Football continues in Republican Spain

In a 2008 interview with *GQ* magazine, Manchester United manager Sir Alex Ferguson – frustrated at Real Madrid's overtures to sign Portuguese star Cristiano Ronaldo – referred to the Spanish giants as 'General Franco's club'.[12] The Spanish press latched on to the comments. Madrid-based sports paper *Marca* reminded readers that Ferguson was a Labour Party supporter.[13] The tag of being perceived as 'Franco's club' is something Real Madrid still lives with, even though the dictator died in 1975. How accurate is the tag? Before the Civil War – and during it – Madrid Football Club's leadership and fan base was, if anything, *anti*-fascist. Madrid Football Club was founded in 1902 by well-connected soccer enthusiasts in the Spanish capital. Within three years, it had its first silverware and by the time King Alfonso XIII bestowed the *Real* title on the club in 1920, it was well established among the big three sides in Spain, along with arch-rivals FC Barcelona and Athletic Club de Bilbao. When the Second Republic was installed in 1931, the King fled the country and the *Real* title was dropped. By the time war broke out in July 1936, the city of Madrid and its leading football club were on the frontline of the conflict. Madrid FC had only won its seventh domestic cup against Barça at Valencia's Mestalla stadium the month before. The Nationalist ground assault of Madrid started on 7 November 1936, with Franco's side confident of a swift victory. Madrid held on until 28 March 1939. Many of Madrid FC's players headed home as soon as hostilities commenced, including its overseas stars. Basque brothers Pedro and Luis Regueiro would spend their war raising money for the Republican cause in benefit matches.

A key figure at the outbreak of the war was Madrid FC's president Rafael Sánchez-Guerra. The left-wing politician defeated former club striker Santiago Bernabéu to become club president in 1935. In his time, Sánchez-Guerra managed to prevent the extension of major Madrid thoroughfare, Paseo de la Castellana, which would have led to the demolition of Madrid FC's then home, Estadio Chamartín. Bernabéu's time would come, but for now it was the socialist Sánchez-Guerra – who had announced the Second Republic in April 1931 at the imposing *Casa de Correos* (Post Office) in Madrid – who took the helm at the Estadio Chamartín. Sánchez-Guerra oversaw several big signings, reduced ticket prices to a single peseta and gave all members a vote. He also had designs on moving the club to a larger stadium, but then war broke out. When it was clear that it was not safe to remain in Madrid, Sánchez-Guerra could have moved to Valencia with the rest of the Spanish government, but chose instead to stay.[14] However, he did resign the club presidency after just one year and left it in the hands of fellow Republicans Juan José Vallejo and Antonio Ortega. Ortega was a staunch communist and active colonel in the defence of Madrid. Much of Madrid FC's Estadio Chamartín was dismantled and used as barricades in the defence of the city from the Nationalist siege. Sánchez-Guerra was captured by Franco's forces when Madrid fell in March 1939. He spent a year in prison before securing a release and escaping to France, where he joined the Spanish

Republican government in exile. Ortega was not so fortunate. After his capture by the Nationalists, he was tried and executed by garrotte in July 1939. Madrid FC added a purple stripe to its crest in 1931 as a sign of its Castilian roots, which was also the same colour as the purple in the flag of the Spanish Republic. The purple stripe was retained when the club returned to being Real Madrid after the war and was still on the crest until a rebrand in 2001.

Former Real Madrid player Álvaro Peláez Antón, who had played alongside Santiago Bernabéu in the 1920s, had joined the Communist Party and worked in the Post Office during the Second Republic. In 1939, he fled to French Algeria and later to the USSR. He later settled in Warsaw and worked as a translator, including when Spanish sports teams visited Poland. After more than three decades in exile from the country, it appears Bernabéu himself wrote a favourable letter of support for Peláez Antón to return to Spain, which he did in 1971.[15]

None of Madrid FC's 1935/36 season team was killed during the Civil War, but veteran goalkeeper Ricardo Zamora – hero of the 1936 cup final – came close. Zamora had apparent right-leaning sympathies and had even written articles for a conservative newspaper, *Ya*.[16] At least twice, Zamora's celebrity saved him. Once, when held at knifepoint, his would-be assailant – a Madrid fan – recognised him and instead hugged him. Secondly, when inaccurate news reports surfaced that Republicans had executed him, left-wing militia, knowing where to find Zamora in Madrid, arrested him and took him to Modelo prison. Here, his guards enjoyed the stories of his long career. Zamora had been playing for two decades at this point, including being part of Spain's first-ever national team squad in 1920 and its first World Cup squad in 1934. The guards also enjoyed kick-abouts with him in the yard just so they could say they had played football with him.[17] Zamora was eventually released and ended up playing for OGC

Nice in France alongside former club and international team-mate Josep Samitier. Once the tide of war was clearly in favour of a Francoist win, Zamora returned to take part in a fund-raising match between Spain and Real Sociedad in San Sebastián to raise money for Nationalist soldiers. Zamora's loyalty was rewarded by Franco in the 1950s with the presentation of the Great Cross of the Order of Cisneros.[18] The medal was established by Franco in 1944 to reward those who had supported his cause during the war and after.

Across town, Athletic de Madrid did not escape the war unscathed. It lost eight players during the war, and its Metropolitano stadium was in ruins. At the end of the conflict, Athletic merged with Aviación Nacional, the Zaragoza-based sporting arm of the Spanish Air Force, to become Athletic Aviación de Madrid. In the north, Real Oviedo was permitted extra time to rebuild its devastated infrastructure, so a play-off was contested between Athletic Aviación and Osasuna at Valencia's repaired Mestalla ground to see who would take Oviedo's place in the top flight. Athletic Aviación came from behind to win 3-1. In the 1939/40 season, with football rebooted, Athletic Aviación won its first *La Liga* title. The club's title-winning coach was none other than Ricardo Zamora. The club retained the title in the 1940/41 season. That year, it was forced to rebrand as Atlético Aviación de Madrid because Franco, now in full control of the country, followed the example of Mussolini in Italy before him by banning foreign names. In 1947, the organisation finally settled on Club Atlético de Madrid.

While Madrid resisted assaults from land and air at the start of the conflict, the Spanish government had set up a new base in Valencia as early as November 1936. The east coast of Spain was mostly in Republican hands and was the last place to fall to Franco. Valencia CF's Estadio Mestalla had been used for political rallies by both sides before the conflict. In August 1936,

Republican Dolores Ibárruri, also known as *La Pasionaria* (The Passionflower) – who is credited with coining the republican call *¡No Pasarán!* – delivered a famous speech at Mestalla. The 1936/37 La Liga season was cancelled as football on a national level was now impossible. Regional football continued in Republican areas with the *Campeonato de Cataluña* (Catalonian Championship) and the *Campeonato Superregional* (Championship of Levante), which included sides from the Valencia Community and Murcia region. In 1937, Republicans established the *Liga Mediterránea de Fútbol* (Mediterranean Football League) and *La Copa España Libre* (Free Spain Cup). Six teams from both the Catalan and Levante championships were due to form a 12-team league, but teams from the southern end of the coast – Hércules FC from Alicante, Cartagena and Murcia – withdrew as their cities were being bombed and were therefore unsafe.

Instead, an eight-team league was established featuring Catalonia's top four sides – FC Barcelona, Girona FC, Esport Club Granollers and Espanyol – and four Levante sides – Valencia CF, Levante, Gimnástico and Athletic Club de Castellón. The league season ran from January to May 1937. Madrid FC and Athlétic Club de Madrid applied to join the league but were blocked by some of the eastern clubs. FC Barcelona won the tournament, losing just one match *en route* to the title – 2-0 away to Girona. Barça was coached by Irishman Patrick O'Connell, who had led Real Betis of Seville to an unlikely first title in 1935. After the tournament, O'Connell accepted an offer from a Catalan businessman now based in Mexico, Manuel Mas Soriano, to tour the country. O'Connell took a 16-man squad to play matches in the US and Mexico, making $12,500 profit in the process. The money was stashed in a Parisian bank account to make it inaccessible to hostile forces. At the end of the tour, just four players returned with O'Connell.[19] The top four teams of the Mediterranean Football League were due to play in the Free

Spain Cup, but with champions FC Barcelona away in Mexico, fifth-placed Levante was admitted instead. Over June and July 1937, the competition was held in a mini-league format, with teams playing each other twice and the top two teams qualifying for the final. Levante finished top ahead of cross-town rivals Valencia CF to qualify for the Free Spain Cup Final at Espanyol's Estadio de Sarriá in Barcelona.

The match took place on 18 July 1937, the anniversary of the outbreak of hostilities. A single goal from Levante forward Nieto separated the two sides and, against all odds, the team that should never have even been in the contest emerged victorious. The *Copa España Libre* remains the only silverware that Levante UD, as the club is now known following a merger with Gimnástico, has ever won. Yet, the club's solitary trophy is not recognised by Spanish football's governing body, the *Real Federación Española de Fútbol* (RFEF – Royal Spanish Football Federation). In 2013, a delegation of the Levante board of directors along with the president of the Valencian Football Federation, Vicente Muñoz, travelled to Las Rozas, north of Madrid, to present the RFEF with a replica of the *Copa España Libre*, where it is now on display in Spain's football museum. Levante also resurrected its blue-and-white striped shirt design worn by the victorious 1937 team as its change strip for the 2019/20 season.[20] Likewise, FC Barcelona is seeking official recognition for its Mediterranean Football League victory to add to its already huge pile of honours.

While Cartagena and Murcia could not join the league as both cities were under fire from Nationalists, the two *Segunda División* rivals embarked on a series of fund-raising friendlies for hospitals and the Cartagena militia forces before they headed north to fight. Two matches took place in August 1936, the first of which was attended by a huge crowd, including 400 militias in Cartagena. The game was kicked off by a militiawoman called Antonia Bueno and a trophy was at stake! The home side won 5-1 with a hat-trick from Nieto. Incredibly, in the return leg a week later, Murcia overturned the deficit and won 5-0![21]

The Basque experience

The Basque Country immediately found itself on the front line in the Spanish Civil War. Bilbao was a critical port and many Basques had seen the Second Republic as a chance to enjoy greater autonomy. The region's premier club, Athletic Club de Bilbao, was among the most successful sides in Spain in the period leading up to the Civil War. Under Englishman Fred Pentland, the club won the second edition of *La Liga* in 1930, retaining the championship the following season. The club were defending champions at the outbreak of war before the 1936/37 season was cancelled. On 5 October 1936, the statute of autonomy under the Spanish Republic led to the first self-determining Basque Government, led by the *Partido Nacionalista Vasco* (PNV – Basque Nationalist Party). The party's president was José Antonio Aguirre, who had played for Athletic Club in the previous decade, winning the *Copa del Rey* in 1923. The 1930s was a period of national awakening in the Basque Country. Even Real Sociedad de Foot-ball de San Sebastián localised its name to Donostia Club de Fútbol after the Basque name for the coastal city.

By the spring of 1937, Nationalist forces were closing in on the Basque Country. On 31 March, the town of Durango was bombed on market day, and on 26 April Guernica succumbed to five waves of German and Italian bombers. Basque market towns had become the testbed for fascist aerial assaults in future conflicts. The following month, thousands of Basque children were evacuated to countries in Europe and to Mexico. Nearly 4,000 Basque children arrived on the *SS Habana* into Southampton. Fittingly, it was this English port city whose football club's colours – red and white stripes with black shorts

– had been adopted by Athletic Club back in the 1900s. It was a close escape as on 19 June, Bilbao fell to Franco. The children had been dispersed to homes and camps around Britain and football was to play a big role in some of their lives. Derby County's England international winger Sammy Crooks donated a ball to the 49 Basque children staying at nearby Burnaston House. When the children learned of the fall of Bilbao, football helped distract them from their anguish. '[The children] were upset, but Capt. A. Houldsworth, the superintendent, said the ball from Sammy Crooks arrived at the psychological moment, and the boys went off to play football,' the *Nottingham Journal* reported.[22] Six of the Basque children would go on to enjoy professional careers in Britain. Emilio Aldecoa was the first Spanish-born player to ply his trade in England, signing for Wolverhampton Wanderers before playing for Athletic Club on his return to Iberia. José Bilbao played for Coventry City, while Southampton took Sabino Barinaga and Raimundo Lezama. Lezama would also return to play for Athletic Club after the war, while Barinaga turned out for Real Madrid. Finally, brothers Antonio and José Gallego enjoyed spells at Norwich City and Brentford respectively, among others.[23]

Football was also used to raise funds for the Basque government, counteract negative Francoist propaganda and generate sympathy for the Basque and Republican cause abroad. Charity matches were held in the Basque Country between two nationalist parties – Aguirre's PNV and *Acción Nacionalista Vasco* (ANV – Basque Nationalist Action). The two regions of Bizkaia and Gipuzkoa also faced each other. Following these friendlies and at Aguirre's request, a Basque national football team was put together to travel the world as the region's ambassador. By the time Bilbao fell to Franco, the Basque Country's best players had already spent two months touring Europe. On 26 April 1937, the same day that Guernica was bombed, they beat

French champions Racing Club 3-0 at the Parc des Princes in Paris before moving on play matches across the continent, from France to Czechoslovakia and Poland. The Basques – dressed in the green, white and red of the Basque flag, the *Ikurriña* – played nine matches in the Soviet Union at the invitation of the *Politburo* in June, losing just one. Here, the tour took on great symbolic importance as the players were introduced to Basque children who had been given refuge in the USSR due to the war. While they were in the Soviet Union, the Basque players learned that Bilbao had fallen to Franco's troops. The team completed its European tour by sweeping aside three more teams in Scandinavia.

Beñat Gutierrez is a football writer and podcaster based in the Basque Country. He tells me that the tour's effort to raise sympathy for the Basque cause was successful. 'Wherever they played, they were received with honours and expressions of affection,' Gutierrez says. 'In addition, the Basque team's results gained a lot of praise for their play.' The only exception to a successful European tour came in Poland, where the Basques were branded as 'communists', with some Poles apparently failing to understand that the Basques were a fellow Catholic people. Back home, the Basque population learned about the 1937 tour through the local press, such as the *Eguna* or *La Tarde* newspapers, who referred to the team as the *Embajadora Deportiva* (Sporting Embassy), Gutierrez explains. 'The team was viewed as an extension of the attempts being made by the Basque government to receive international aid,' he adds. 'However, it must be borne in mind that when the tour started, the situation was already very complicated. This made it difficult for the news to reach Basque citizens. When the expedition was in Moscow, Bilbao fell. That put an end to local Basque media, thus preventing any information from reaching the Basque Country beyond that which was done in secret.'

Rather than head home to an occupied Basque Country, most of the team decided to leave for Latin America. By November 1937, the Basques were in Mexico. Here, they helped add credibility to the Basque government in exile and became a beacon for the Basque diaspora, especially in the Americas. The Mexican FA allowed the Basques to take part in the top flight of Mexican football, which was still amateur at the time. The Basques competed as *Club Deportivo Euskadi* (Basque Country Sporting Club) in the 1938/39 season, and also played in the Mexico City district league, as well as continuing to tour Latin America. 'The way in which the Basque players fought against fascism was by joining the tour,' Gutierrez tells me. 'It must be considered that they made a great personal effort, in many cases giving up the best years of their careers. They had the opportunity to have signed for teams in the countries they visited and chose to remain loyal to the cause.'

Only two players left the tour, including Guillermo Gorostiza, the Athletic Club forward who had represented Spain at the 1934 FIFA World Cup. He missed the Latin American tour and returned to Bilbao, winning the *Campeonato Regional de Vizcaya* (Biscay Regional Championship) with Athletic Club. He then moved to Valencia, where he won *La Liga* twice and the *Copa del Generalíssimo*. Many of Gorostiza's former team-mates from the 'Sporting Embassy' never returned to the Basque Country.

Footballers and the Spanish Civil War

The Basque Country is neighboured by Navarra. Now one of Spain's wealthiest autonomous communities, Navarra is closely connected culturally and linguistically to the Basque Country. The region's capital Pamplona (*Iruña* in Basque) is home to the region's biggest football club, Club Atlético Osasuna. Osasuna, the Basque word for 'health', was founded on 24 October 1920 in the city's Café Kutz. The club had just reached promotion to the First Division, *La Liga*, for the 1935/36 season. At home, Osasuna played well, winning many games by handsome margins, and finishing the season as the fifth highest-scoring team. However, the team was relegated in last place without gaining a single point away from home. The team also reached the *Copa del Presidente de la República* semi-finals two years in a row. Just a month before the coup of 19 July, Osasuna beat Barcelona 4-2 in a first-leg tie in the presence of General Mola, one of Franco's close associates, along with many of those who would later be assassinated by 'reds' in Pamplona.

Osasuna found itself on the frontline of the new war as Pamplona became its early epicentre. Several people connected to Osasuna were among 300 shot for opposing Franco's coup of July 1936. Among the victims were the founders of Osasuna, Fortunato Aguirre and Eladio Zilbeti. Aguirre was a member of the Basque branch of the PNV in Navarra and Zilbeti was a member of ANV. Other victims included the president of the club, Natalio Cayuela, who was also director of the *Izquierda Republicana* (Republican Left) party; Osasuna directors Ramón Bengaray and Alberto Lorenzo, and the goalkeeper Filomeno Urdiroz. The list also included councillors Florencio Alfaro and Victorino García Enciso, who had been directors; the lawyer Enrique Astiz; the president of *Socorro Rojos Internacional* (International Red Aid), Leandro Villafranca and his son Jose Javier, who died in the Modelo prison in Barcelona. Many others were arrested, imprisoned, or fled and went into exile. The fascists who broke into a player's house even took several Osasuna jerseys and burned them because they were red, the colour of communism.[24]

Mikel Huarte is an Osasuna fan based in Pamplona and wrote a book about the experience of Osasuna players and staff during the Civil War, entitled *Rojos: Fútbol, Política y Represión en Osasuna* (*Reds: Football, Politics and Repression at Osasuna*). He tells me the story of Andrés Jaso Garde from Navarra, who joined Osasuna in 1930, when he was 18 years old. Jaso Garde went on to play for Zaragoza, Sabadell and Levante, but failed to break into Valencia CF in the First Division. He signed for Second Division side Sporting de Gijón in 1935. Jaso Garde was famous for his fearsome left-foot shot and scored eight goals in 12 games in his first season with the club, despite missing much of the start of the campaign due to a fracture. Jaso Garde lost two brothers in the first months of the war. His 19-year-old brother José was executed by Franco's forces in October 1936 along with 225 other Navarrese. The following month, his older brother Aurelio, the local secretary of the *Unión General de Trabajadores* (UGT – General Union of Workers), was killed in Madrid's first line of defence on the city's university campus. Jaso Garde himself enlisted in Gijón and was in Battalion 219, the *Batallón Galicia*. Reportedly, Jaso was killed in an air raid in Cangas de Onís, Asturias in 1937 while travelling on a bus chartered by Sporting. Jaso's body, like those of countless thousands of people on both sides of the conflict, has never been recovered. In recent years, a campaign has been launched to find his body.[25] Huarte tells me that he became interested in Osasuna's experience in the Civil War when he was researching stories for the club's centenary. 'The more I investigated, the more stories began to unfold, and I was soon writing an article every week for the local press,' he says. 'The regional government of Navarra has been very supportive of our project, but the key is to take the message to Madrid and get the Spanish football public in general to talk about what happened during the Civil War.'

In the Valencian Community, Santa Pola CF's stadium is named after Manolo Maciá. Maciá, a tough defender with a strong tackle, turned out for the club before joining his elder brother in 1930 at Hércules CF in Alicante. At the outbreak of war, Maciá joined the defence of the Republican-held Valencian Community, before leaving the country and playing for OGC Nice alongside Josep Samitier and Ricardo Zamora. When Maciá returned to Spain in 1940, a false allegation about burning down a church in Santa Pola during the war led to a six-month jail sentence. Upon release, Maciá turned down approaches from both Real Madrid and FC Barcelona.[26] Meanwhile, Levante's Salvador Artigas signed up as a pilot for the Republic before heading to France in 1938, where he played for Girondins de Bordeaux and Rennes before returning to Spain with Real Sociedad in 1949.[27] At Bordeaux, Artigas played under the Basque coach Benito Diaz. Diaz had made his name at Real Sociedad and coached Spain at the 1928 Amsterdam Olympics. He had crossed the Pyrenees to escape the war and had been interned at the Gurs refugee camp near Pau in France. Here, Diaz had posted an advertisement regarding his skills and keenness to coach a French team. Girondins came calling and, thanks in part to a handful of Spanish players, Diaz set about building a side that went on to win Girondins' first major trophy, *Le Coupe de France*, in 1941.[28] Diaz returned to San Sebastian in 1942. Another player to arrive at Girondins via Gurs was Valencia CF's Francisco Mateo, who played in France for a decade in Bordeaux and Strasbourg before switching to management. Other Spanish players made their way to France, including FC Barcelona's Josep Raich Garriga, who signed for FC Sète in 1936.

In Galicia, in Spain's north-west, Racing Santander goalkeeper Francisco 'Paco' Trigo García was lucky to avoid being shot by Falangists while he was in La Coruña. After being accused of being a communist involved in a local resistance movement known as *Los Niños de la Lejía* (The Bleach Boys), Trigo was about to be taken off to be shot near Deportivo de La Coruña's Riazor stadium. While *en route*, he was noticed by former Depor footballer Hilario Marrero, then of Real Madrid, who recognised him as the Racing Santander goalkeeper.[29]

Marrero's fame and awareness had saved a fellow professional, but it was a close shave.

Joining the Republicans were members of the International Brigades. Two and a half thousand men and women joined from Britain and Ireland alone to support the cause and travelled to Spain. Some 526 died in action. Among those was John McEwan from Dundee, a former junior footballer who was killed at Jarama in February 1937, aged 25. 'If I don't go and fight fascism, I'll have to wait and fight it here,' he is reported to have told his family before heading to Spain.[30] Football would become an essential pastime for Republican fighters. In March 1937, a British mission took a stock of 36 footballs to the Spanish border to 'divert the minds of the warring factions to more peaceful pursuits'.[31]

For some Spanish footballers fighting for the Republic, the war did not end in 1939. Midfielder Saturnino Navazo had played semi-professional football for Madrid club Deportivo Nacional, where he appeared in the second and third tiers of the Spanish league. He was about to sign for Real Betis – champions in 1934/35 – when the Spanish Civil War broke out. Navazo fought in a Republican brigade. At the end of the Spanish Civil War, he fled across the Pyrenees and was held at a refugee camp in France. In France, he joined a resistance group to fight the invading Germans and was captured. Nazi Germany asked their fellow fascists in the new Francoist government whether they would like their Spanish prisoners back and Spain refused, leaving the Spanish prisoners of war outside Spain effectively stateless. Navazo was sent to the infamous Mauthausen concentration camp in Austria. On arrival on 17 January 1941, he was given the number #5656. It was a particularly brutal camp where two-thirds of Spanish male prisoners died in their first 18 months there.[32] To raise spirits, the prisoners at Mauthausen, who came from all over occupied Europe, organised camp football matches.

Kevin E. Simpson is the author of *Soccer Under the Swastika: Defiance and Survival in the Nazi Camps and Ghettos*. He tells me that in a place like Mauthausen, where many Spanish Republicans ended up, prisoners would need protection from camp guards and *kapos* to survive. 'Mauthausen was the worst of all the labour camps. If you were sent there, your life would be measured in days and weeks rather than months, so you needed protection, you needed the food that was provided,' Simpson explains. 'Saturnino Navazo helped organise the league at Mauthausen.' Navazo was joined by Antonio Pérez Galindo, from Málaga club Vélez CF, who gained a reputation as a prolific goalscorer. By being successful players, the Spanish players enjoyed rare privileges and extra provisions from the prison commandants. Navazo was made responsible for the 200 Spanish prisoners held there. American troops liberated Mauthausen on 5 May 1945. While Galindo did not survive Mauthausen, Navazo did and went on to adopt a Jewish boy from the camp.[33]

Football under Franco

You can tell the tumultuous story of Spain's 20th century through the name of its cup competitions. Just as the *Copa del Rey* (King's Cup) gave way to become the *Copa del Presidente de la República* (The Cup of the President of the Republic) at the coming of the Second Republic, so the *Copa España Libre* was shelved and a national cup competition was reinstated in Franco's name – *La Copa del Generalíssimo*. After Franco's death in 1975, King Juan Carlos returned to reclaim the Spanish throne and the *Copa del Rey* was back. During the Franco dictatorship, football, like many other areas of Spanish life, was taken over and directed by his new fascist regime. Despite having met Adolf Hitler at Hendaye on the Spanish-French border on 23 October 1940, Franco resisted committing Spain to join in World War II. Franco installed Falangist General José

Moscardó to run sports, with a view to emulating German and Italian success in national physical improvement. And, as in Germany and Italy, players were made to raise their right arm in salute pre-match and sing the Falangist anthem, *Cara al Sol* (Face to the Sun).

As early as the winter of 1937, 16 months into the Civil War, Franco felt ready to field a team representative of the regions of Spain that he occupied. Spain would play Portugal, its Iberian neighbour, which was also under a right-wing dictatorship. The team representing Spain wore all-blue, the colour of the *Falange*, rather than the traditional *Roja* (red), a colour the Francoists associated with communists. Spain would continue to wear blue and hold the fascist salute until after the fall of the Axis powers, as it sought to build bridges with the international community. On 28 November 1937, the team representing Franco-occupied Spain and Portugal – who also broke from tradition and wore white shirts and blue shorts, to avoid wearing red – took to the field at Estadio de Balaídos in Vigo, Galicia. Spanish football had been interrupted for more than a year, and selectors only had players from Francoist-occupied areas to hand. Portugal won 2-1, its first victory over Spain, but the match was not officially recognised, neither was the return match held in Lisbon on 30 January 1938.[34] At the Lisbon match, some of the Portugal team defied orders to perform the pre-match fascist salute. Belenenses forward Artur Quaresma held his hands by his side, while his club team-mate, midfielder Mariano Amaro, clenched his fist, as did goalkeeper João Azevedo from Sporting. Photos and mentions of the incident were left out of press reports, and the defiant players were detained and interviewed by the Portuguese state police, PIDE.[35] Spain's other internationals during World War II were restricted to fascist-occupied European states, such as Italy, Vichy France and Germany, where 100,000 spectators attended the Olympiastadion in Berlin.

According to Alejandro Quiroga, a reader in Spanish history at the University of Newcastle, when *La Liga* resumed in 1939 Spain was in ruins with roughly a million Spaniards estimated to be in concentration camps or prisons. 'It was very difficult for players with Republican sympathies to reintegrate to football after the war,' Quiroga tells me. Members of Franco's far-right Falange party were installed in the boardrooms of football clubs across Spain, including at FC Barcelona and Athletic Club de Bilbao. Both were forced to change their English-sounding names to Castilian ones. FC Barcelona became Club de Fútbol Barcelona and was made to withdraw the Catalan flag from its badge, while Athletic Club became Atlético Bilbao. During the 1950s, some members at Athletic Club used their privileged position to present a combined Spanish and Basque identity, Quiroga tells me, even raising old myths about the Basque Country being the original 'Spain' and therefore Athletic Club as the 'real Spaniards'. This became especially acute in the 1950s when Real Madrid fielded so many foreign players, such as the Argentine Alfredo di Stéfano, Hungarian Ferenc Puskás and Frenchman Raymond Kopa. The Basque club was staying true to its unwritten *Cantera* policy that had stood since 1912 of only fielding players with a direct Basque connection. 'The Franco dictatorship was very happy with the idea of the *Cantera*,' Quiroga adds. 'It was never threatened. In a way it proved what they wanted; this was the only club to play Spanish-only players.'

During Franco's 36 years in power, his regime evolved from one being closer to that of Hitler's Germany or Mussolini's Italy in the 1940s to one that – while still far right – was less extreme to court US investment. By the 1960s and '70s, Spain was seeking to modernise. The use of local languages also changed during this time. While Catalan was not used in FC Barcelona's club communications during the 1940s and 1950s, by the late 1950s articles started appearing in Catalan, and by 1974 match tickets were printed in Catalan, Quiroga explains. 'In the last decade, we have reached a much more nuanced understanding of the question of identity and the role of FC Barcelona and Athletic Club de Bilbao,' he tells me. Athletic Club did not use Basque, probably because most of the people in Bilbao used Castilian as their first language, while elsewhere in the Basque Country, in places such as San Sebastian, Basque was used in the publications of that city's club, Real Sociedad.

Back in the capital, Santiago Bernabéu, Real Madrid's president from 1943 until his death in June 1978, had fought with Nationalist forces during the Civil War. He was pivotal in rebuilding from scratch a club in ruins. Franco's close association with Real Madrid did not start until the mid-1950s, when the club started to win the European Cup; it won the first five competitions and added a sixth a few years later. 'Franco used Real Madrid, and Real Madrid used Franco,' Quiroga affirms. 'It was a mutual, convenient relationship for both. Members of Real Madrid from the '50s and '60s told me that they were fully aware that they were being used by the dictatorship in terms of propaganda, but on the other hand they were quite happy with that idea – not because they were Francoists but because they thought they would get money, concessions and support when they went abroad to play finals of the European Cup.' Real Madrid is a club that adapts to the political climate. It was close to Alfonso XIII when he bestowed upon them the 'Royal' title, but it also pivoted to being a Republican club during the Second Spanish Republic. The club became closely associated with the Franco regime, but then after the transition to democracy the club became very democratic. Rumours will always persist over Franco's involvement in, for example, the signing of Alfredo di Stefano, or Falange pressure that reportedly led to FC Barcelona capitulating to a record 11-1 defeat to Real Madrid in a 1943 *Copa del Generalíssimo* tie.[36]

The Spanish national side's success also offered Franco some reflected glory. At the time of an international dispute with Britain over Gibraltar, England played Spain in Rio de Janeiro at the 1950 World Cup. Spain's 1-0 victory courtesy of a Telmo Zarra goal knocked England out and saw Spain progress at the expense of 'perfidious Albion'.[37] In June 1964, Spain beat the Soviet Union 2-1 in Madrid to win the UEFA European Championship, four years after Franco had refused to allow Spain to play the communist USSR in the first tournament and been disqualified as a result. But now, at home, on the 25th anniversary of the end of the Civil War against a team from the most prominent communist country at the height of the Cold War, it was propaganda gold for Franco. 'The football victory was linked as a continuation of the Civil War, which was presented as a victory against communist forces in Spain and the Soviet Union had helped communist forces in Spain,' says Quiroga. 'It came at a time when the regime was modernising, so was also presented as evidence that the country was progressing.' Meanwhile, in Moscow, Quiroga recounts the story of a number of exiled Spanish communists who had been invited to watch the final on television. The Soviets had hoped that the Spanish exiles would support the USSR as a sign of their belief in international communism. However, to their hosts' surprise, the Spaniards were elated when the second Spanish goal went in.

Football provided something for exiled or ex-patriot Spaniards to feel proud of at a time when Spain was isolated internationally, despite Franco's attempts to 'de-fascisticise' after the defeat of his allies, Hitler and Mussolini, in 1945. In 1949, at a friendly match against France at Stade de Colombes in Paris, a group of Spanish fans waved the red, yellow and purple flag of the Spanish Republic to cheer on their homeland. And in the '50s and '60s, Real Madrid's successes in European competition drew large numbers of the Spanish diaspora wherever they played. Like the Basque Country's team of exiles in the 1930s, Real Madrid had become something of a 'sporting embassy'.

Despite the challenges fans faced in displaying opposition to the Franco regime, some did manage to make a stand. In January 1947, ahead of a *Día de los Reyes* (Epiphany – 6 January) match held at San Mamés, home of Athletic Club, a daring night-time sabotage took place. The friendly match had been arranged by the Spanish government between Athletic Club and Buenos Aires club San Lorenzo de Almagro to celebrate treaties signed between Franco and Argentine president Juan Perón. Days before the match, painted *Ikurriñas* – the outlawed Basque flag – and anti-match slogans appeared on walls around Bilbao. On the night of 3/4 January, a group led by Ramón de Galarza, who had been a captain in the Basque army during the Civil War, broke into the San Mamés ground. Their intention was to destroy the pitch, or at least make it unplayable, and to saw the goalposts. 'They managed to damage the grass but were discovered on their way to the goal, which forced them to flee,' Beñat Gutierrez explains. 'Although the match day chronicles do not make any reference to the state of the pitch, the images show its poor condition and how sand had been used to cover up the damage that this anti-fascist group had managed to cause to the San Mamés grass.'

One of the most iconic images of sport against the Franco regime came in 1970 at the Anoeta sports complex in San Sebastian (Donostia). It was the opening ceremony of the World Pelota Championship, chaired by General Franco. Joseba Elosegi, a Basque Civil War veteran and Nationalist, set fire to himself and threw himself towards the dictator, shouting '*Gore Euskadi Askatuta!*' (Long live a free Basque Country!). Elosegi said he wanted to bring the fire that destroyed Guernica into the sight of the man who caused it. By the early 1970s, the Franco regime was in its death throes. In December 1973, Franco's appointed successor, Prime Minister Luis Carrero Blanco, was assassinated on his way home from mass by a car bomb planted by Basque separatist group, *Euskadi Ta Askatasuna* (ETA – Basque Homeland and Liberty). In September 1975, just weeks before Franco himself died, the Council of Ministers confirmed the death penalty for the last of those on the regime's execution list. The list included five Basques, among them members of ETA and the *Frente Revolutionario Antifacista y Patriota* (FRAP – Revolutionary Antifascist Patriotic Front). Despite international opposition, the executions went ahead. Many Basques responded to a call for a three-day general strike, unprecedented in the Franco era, and football was not exempt. 'Athletic Club wore black armbands in memory of the deceased during their visit to Los Cármenes to face Granada,' Gutierrez says. 'It was captain José Ángel Iribar who encouraged his team-mates to carry out this action, which the *rojiblanco* (red and white) club had to justify by saying that it was a tribute to the late former Athletic player Luis Albert. Everyone knew that was not the reason. For this reason, the 11 that entered the Los Cármenes pitch deserves as much recognition as those who have filled Ibaigane's [Athletic Club's headquarters] trophy room. Iribar, Astrain, Goikoetxea, Lasa, Villar, Irureta, Escalza, Dani, Rojo II, Txetxu Rojo and Amorrortu were the protagonists of that demanding day.'

According to Gutierrez, the Athletic Club players were not alone. The day after the executions, Cantabrian club Racing de Santander faced Elche at their home ground, *El Sardinero*. Racing's Basque player Aitor Aguirre and Valencian Sergio Manzanera wore black ribbons around their wrists without telling anyone beforehand. Once spotted, murmurs spread around the ground, and the government delegation quizzed Racing's president, who was unaware of the situation. At half-time, a large police deployment entered Racing's changing room and demanded that Aguirre and Manzanera remove their ribbons or face arrest. Under pressure, the two removed their ribbons and were fined 100,000 pesetas each the next day. In the following days, both received death threats from far-right groups. Aguirre went on to sign for Athletic Club in 1977 and retired in 1984. 'From that afternoon in *El Sardinero*, Aguirre's name was forever associated with a small gesture full of symbolism and courage, proof that football can stand up to fascism,' Gutierrez concludes. The execution of the five political prisoners had international implications, too. Protests in Rome against the Franco regime's actions led Lazio to refuse to play FC Barcelona in their UEFA Cup match in Rome scheduled for 22 October. Lazio president Umberto Lenzini said the executions 'have had repercussions throughout Europe and the risk of anti-Spanish demonstrations is too great for us to take responsibility for staging the match.'[38] FC Barcelona was awarded a 3-0 walkover first-leg win.

Football in the post-Franco era

General Francisco Franco died on 20 November 1975 and was succeeded as head of state by King Juan Carlos, the grandson of King Alfonso XIII. Monarchy returned to Spain under a new constitution for the first time since 1931 and Spain was finally able to take steps towards becoming a modern democracy. However, unlike South Africa, where the Truth and Reconciliation Commission helped expose the wrongs of apartheid with the intention of healing divisions and bringing the country together, no such undertaking occurred in post-Franco Spain. Quite the opposite happened. An amnesty in 1977 meant members of the dictatorship and other Francoist followers could not be tried and an unwritten *Pacto del Olvido* (Pact of Forgetting) entered the lexicon. Only in 2007 would Spain pass a law that honoured Franco's victims.[39] In the period immediately after Franco's death, many legacy laws remained in place, including the banning of nationalist symbols such as the flag of the Basque Country, the

Ikurriña, which had been created in 1894. In May 1976, the Spanish government had authorised the use of regional flags across Spain with the exception of the Basque *Ikurriña*, viewing it as a separatist flag rather than a regional one. But for Basques, the legalisation of the *Ikurriña* was an urgent demand.

Ahead of the Basque Country derby between Real Sociedad of San Sebastian and Athletic Club de Bilbao on 5 December 1976, the captains of both clubs risked arrest by walking on to the pitch together holding the *Ikurriña*, with the unanimous consent of their team-mates. The idea to make the defiant gesture and display the still-banned *Ikurriña* in public had been that of Real Sociedad midfielder José Antonio de la Hoz Uranga, who had convinced his sister to sew the flag. De la Hoz managed to get the flag through a police checkpoint and into the ground. 'You have to get closer to the context to understand the magnitude of what that gesture meant,' Beñat Gutierrez tells me. 'Franco had died little more than a year before, and the transition to democracy was advancing on a very fragile balance. They were years of great instability and of great political uncertainty.'

Real Sociedad captain Inaxio Kortabarria and Athletic Club skipper José Ángel Iribar emerged into the Atotxa stadium with the *Ikurriña* in hand, placing it in the centre circle. The police did not react, so this match has been viewed as a significant moment in the legitimisation of the *Ikurriña*.[40] 'These three players [de la Hoz Uranga, Kortabarria and Iribar] took a risk to show that they were with the majority sentiment of Basque society. They showed that the Basque people were not afraid and that they were willing to organise so that their rights were recognised,' Gutierrez says. Kortabarria earned four Spanish caps but gave up playing for Spain for political reasons, the only Basque player to do so. Both captains went on to establish careers in politics after hanging up their boots, while de la Hoz Uranga entered law, mainly in cases related to *Abertzale* (left-wing Basque nationalists). In

1994, he was sentenced to eight years in prison for collaborating with an armed gang. He only spent six months in jail and was pardoned in 2009.[41] 'The story of these three footballers is that of a generation of Basques who at a very difficult time decided to fight for the rights of their people. That is why they continue to be remembered every time Athletic and *La Real* [Real Sociedad] meet,' Gutierrez concludes.

The Vallecas story

As in Italy, ultra groups emerged on Spanish terraces in the 1970s and '80s. In the *Fondo Sur* (South Stand) at the Estadio Bernabéu, a potent right-wing fan group emerged in the 1980s, the *Ultras Sur*. When I was a student in Madrid in the mid-90s, I remember seeing various fascist insignia in the *Fondo Sur*, such as a Celtic cross, and fans were known to display the flag of Franco-era Spain with its black eagle. The group has been banned from the Bernabéu by the club, and across Spain other clubs have struggled with far-right supporters, with both FC Barcelona and Espanyol having banned far-right groups.[42]

However, within Madrid, there is another strong ultra movement, very much aligned with anti-fascism. In the southeast of Madrid is the famously working-class *barrio* of Vallecas. Before Madrid's post-Civil War urban sprawl absorbed it, Vallecas was a small *pueblo* on the road to Valencia. Spain's history has helped shape Vallecas into one of Madrid's most characterful *barrios*. Vallecas became an affordable option for new migrants into Madrid as it expanded outwards. Fans of Spanish director Pedro Almodóvar's work will have seen Penelope Cruz walk the streets of Vallecas past its famous single-story *casas bajas* in his 2006 film, *Volver*. In recent decades, in particular, football has played a key role in raising the international profile of Vallecas and as a platform to express the character and politics of the neighbourhood. On 29 May 1924, a group of young men formed a football club – *El Rayo* (The Lightning) – with the support of the wealthy Huerta family. The club's first president was Julián Huerta Priego, a member of Spain's *Guardia Civil* police force. Huerta could not combine his police ambitions with the role of Rayo president and, in 1926, the role was filled by local businessman José Montoya Arribas. In the 1931/32 season, the club took part in the new *Federación Obrera de Fútbol* (Workers' Football Federation) until the outbreak of war in 1936.[43] Robbie Dunne is the author of *Working Class Heroes: The Story of Rayo Vallecano, Madrid's Forgotten Team*. 'I don't think clubs were left or right wing in the way we think of ultra groups now, but the areas the clubs started from might have been left or right and through a form of osmosis, the clubs adopted the political leanings of its members,' Dunne tells me. 'Rayo started as a community club in the house of Doña Prudencia and the involvement of her family. In the sense that it was a community-based club that has always been about the grassroots, then it has always been to the left.'

During the summer of 1936, Rayo's Estadio de Vallecas ground was used to stage fundraising matches. Being situated on the critical route between Madrid and the Republican capital in Valencia, the area was bombed heavily during the Civil War, with the damage still visible today. Once Francoist troops secured Madrid at the end of March 1939, they commandeered the Estadio de Vallecas and used it as a concentration camp for a few weeks until May. Falangists from the 25th San Quintín regiment held several hundred captured Republican prisoners, many of whom were from Vallecas itself, out in the open playing field exposed to the elements all day and night.[44] Dunne explains that in Vallecas, as in much of Madrid, there were safe houses that harboured communists and anti-fascists who were on the run. He adds that there has been a very clear demarcation in Spain since the Civil War and many areas in Madrid, as in Spain at large, have kept their political leanings. 'I know people talk about Rayo and they should because they're a great little club, but Rayo are an avatar for the way Spain was split and remains divided to this day,' Dunne explains. 'This is the crux of Rayo's importance and what made for the conditions for Rayo to grow as they have, as one of the last bastions of left-wing fan groups.'

Rayo's ultras are called the *Bukaneros* (Buccaneers). The group was founded in 1992 and describes Rayo Vallecano as a 'symbol and pride of the working class that goes each Sunday to the Nuevo Estadio de Vallekas', and the group is against racism and repression.[45] By 1996/97, the season I first attended a Rayo match, the *Bukaneros* had grown and introduced banners, drums and its own fanzine. In 1997, in collaboration with various political groups in Madrid, the *Bukaneros* took part in the *Día contra el Racismo en los Estadios de Fútbol* (Day Against Racism in Football Stadiums). It is now a regular occurrence, and the group invites migrants to come to a match. The group also takes part in anti-racist football tournaments.[46] 'English fan culture has a lot to do with Rayo developing into a politically conscious club,' Dunne explains. 'They have *peñas* (supporters' groups) in Spain, of course, but it wasn't until the '80s and '90s when fans in Spain saw English fan groups collectivising and developing attitudes towards things other than just what was happening on the field. That made Rayo and the *Bukaneros* into a club with a conscience. Before that, Rayo were Rayo: a club from the *barrio* with no collective voice.'

With Real Madrid perceived as the team of the governing institution, whomever that happens to be, and Atlético de Madrid with its complex history, Rayo sits in stark contrast to the two Madrid giants. 'With Madrid, it is a class issue,' Dunne continues. 'Real Madrid are seen as being the *pijos* – the posh ones – and are viewed as a Spanish institution. Being anti-establishment, Rayo fans will naturally entrench themselves opposite to whatever Madrid want and think. They are also seen as being very conservative while Rayo and Vallecas in general is more radical in every aspect from politics to religion. With Atlético, it's more about Atlético's links with the military many years ago, and that link remains today.' Dunne emphasises that Atlético has a very working-class base, and so many Rayo and *Atléti* fans have the same political leanings. 'But there's a militaristic, nationalistic undercurrent with some Atlético fans, which is also the exact opposite of Rayo's fanbase,' he adds. 'Rayo stand alone as the working class, left-wing team in Madrid.'

The *Bukaneros* even hold players to account for their alleged political views.[47] In 2019, officials had to call off a match between Rayo and Albacete at half time after one of its players received 'grave insults and threats' from home fans due to his alleged political views.[48] In 2021, when Rayo's owner hosted two leaders of the far-right Vox party at a match against Albacete, Rayo fans dressed in biohazard gear descended on the ground and 'cleaned' it with disinfectant. They also unveiled a banner which read that Vallecas was 'not a place for fascists or useful idiots'.[49] Inviting Vox into the press box 'was a spit in the face of everything the club stands for,' Robbie Dunne tells me. 'Even if you don't support everything the *Bukaneros* do or say, that was a nasty and petty thing to do to a fan group that remains proud of its working-class, multicultural neighbourhood.'

Dunne concludes that it is an interesting time to observe Spanish politics as the country has seen a political awakening in recent years, for better and worse. 'I think it manifests itself in Spain more strongly than any other country that I've been in because there was a clear divide back at the start of the last century. You were either a fascist or an anti-fascist – but being an anti-fascist meant many things such as a communist, socialist, anarchist, and that itself proved divisive,' he tells me. 'The Spanish Civil war has been referred to as the opening flashes of World War II, and we haven't seen anything like the fight for democracy and what those volunteers did back then since.*

That is why, as I tried to explain in my own book but didn't fully understand at the time, politics is inherent in everything here in Spain, and that divide remains to this day. You're either a fascist or anti-fascist and those words get thrown around daily. And I'm not sure that it's going anywhere, so Rayo's fans, the ultras in particular, will continue to protest against inequality at games and at rallies that take place in and around Madrid.'

This interview took place long before Russia's invasion of Ukraine in February 2022, which also saw volunteers sign up to fight for democracy.

In 2018, a new kid arrived on the Vallecas block. Club Deportivo Independiente de Vallecas was founded by local residents with a new vision for football in the neighbourhood and currently plays in the eighth tier of Spanish football. The four founders and many of its followers are Rayo Vallecano fans. Joaquín Maidagan Goldenzweig is Independiente de Vallecas' vice-president and founding member No.2. 'The main objective is to pay tribute to the neighbourhood through a popular football model – by and for its fans and partners – that moves away from the commercial approach so common today,' he explains. 'We are clear that, above all, today we are a football club. But we want to go a little further and use football – and, in the future, we are open to other sports – as a social tool to fight racism, xenophobia, machismo, classism, individualism or social exclusion. All without losing sight of the fact that we are a football club. And being clear that our principles are not incompatible with sporting ambition. We don't want to win at all costs or at any price or grow unnaturally, but that doesn't mean we don't want to be ambitious. We always say that we are not a political organisation that also plays soccer, but rather that we are a soccer club that also engages in social issues as far as possible.'

I asked Maidagan Goldenzweig whether a recent lurch to the right in Spanish politics has meant that the time is right for a club like Independiente de Vallecas. 'There has always been the extreme right in Spain, but now it is normalising and whitewashing its speech in a very dangerous way. Openly racist, xenophobic, classist or sexist speeches that should not have a place in politics or public opinion since they are not simple opinions,' he continues. 'Furthermore, a fascist cannot be equated with an anti-fascist, and that happens continuously in Spain. And to top it all, those who have the opportunity to counteract that ultra-right-wing discourse – so easily dismantled – from those major media, rarely succeed, either through collusion or inability.' Regardless of which way Spain's national political discourse takes, this corner of Madrid will continue to make itself heard on the terraces.

Football in a changing Spain

Back in Barcelona, CE Júpiter looks set to benefit from fans who are disillusioned with elite football. Natxo Parra is a Barcelona-based academic and author. He tells me that as FC Barcelona increasingly looks to expand internationally into new markets, so some fans have drifted away from Barça's Camp Nou to smaller *barrio* clubs for a more authentic football experience. 'There are people who are leaving following Barça to go to other stadiums, similar to what happened to FC St. Pauli in Germany in the 1980s,' Parra explains. 'They are going to the terraces at CE Júpiter, CE Europa and Sant Andreu – much smaller clubs than Barça. These are places with much closer connection with the local people. This is where people find the atmosphere they want – a connection with their political values, connection with the anti-fascist movement, enjoyment of football and sharing terraces with their comrades.'

In 2007, Spain passed the *Ley de Memoria Histórica* (Historical Memory Law), which recognises the victims of the Civil War and subsequent Franco dictatorship, decades after both events. Tom Wardle is a doctoral researcher at the University of

Southampton in England. 'On the one hand, the law attempted to remove the traces of Francoism, such as street names and monuments,' Wardle explains. 'On the other, it was intended to be a victims' law, recognising the suffering of those who had been murdered, exiled, tortured and repressed by the Francoist regime.' In the very south of Spain, in Cádiz, Andalusia, the city council announced a vote would be held in the summer of 2021 to rename the local football stadium. The Estadio Ramón de Carranza had been named after a former mayor of Cádiz during the time of the Primo de Rivera dictatorship. He had been forced out when the Second Republic was elected, but returned as mayor after Franco's 1936 *coup d'état*. Although Ramón de Carranza died in 1937, the stadium was named after him at its inauguration in 1955. Following the Historical Memory Law, Cádiz city council had already removed de Carranza's name from a street, now known as the *Avenida Del 4 de Diciembre* (Fourth of December Avenue). Now, the name 'Ramón de Carranza' would also be retired from the city's football arena and replaced with a new title from a shortlist of eight candidates based on fans' suggestions. The selection would not include the names of people from history. Although the voting process had complications, the title 'Nuevo Mirandilla' topped the poll with 25.8 per cent of the vote. The original 'Mirandilla' had been Cádiz CF's first ground back in the 1930s.

The move to rename the Estadio Ramón de Carranza was not without its critics. Some fans even protested by suggesting the name of Francisco Franco and Santiago Abascal, leader of the right-wing Vox party.[50] So why is the law so controversial? 'According to its critics, mainly from the right wing, the Historical Memory Law is a divisive, unnecessary re-opening of old wounds and airing of dirty laundry,' Wardle continues. 'This, they argue, goes against the ostensibly harmonious spirit of the transition to democracy following Franco's death. At the other end of the spectrum, the fact that a new Memory Law is being brought forwards is proof of the failure of the previous law from 2007. Many of the policies of the legislation have simply been ignored and many memory activists have argued that it never went far enough. They make the point that Spain is put to shame by other post-fascist countries, namely Germany, Italy and Argentina, who have done much more to reconcile their dictatorships' legacies.' Cádiz CF also has an anti-fascist ultra group. *Brigadas Amarillas* (Yellow Brigades) was founded in 1982 at a time when Spanish ultra culture was starting to emerge. Spanish ultra groups took inspiration from what they saw in Italy and England, and the *Brigadas Amarillas* took their place in the Carranza's *Fondo Sur* (South Stand). Like Livorno's ultras, *Brigadas Amarillas* display the iconic image of Argentinian *guerrillero* Ernesto 'Che' Guevara. The Brigadas Amarillas have *gemellaggi* with like-minded ultras across Spain, including the *Bukaneros* at Rayo Vallecano, various Basque clubs, and *Riazor Blues* from Galicia's Deportivo La Coruña.

As in many other parts of Europe, football clubs are being established in Spain with social transformation as a key objective. Known as *fútbol popular* (popular football), this movement includes clubs formed as a response to disillusion with the growing commercialism at the top echelons of the sport, with the fans often either running the club collectively or at least having a significant say in decisions. Club de Accionariado Popular (CAP) Ciudad de Murcia was founded in 2010 by fans of the city's original club, CF Ciudad de Murcia – dissolved in 2006 – and was among the first such clubs in Spain. Independiente de Vallecas in Madrid is another example, but there are plenty of others. In the southern Navarrese town of Tudela, Unión Tutera was established to develop a fairer, more respectful and inclusive society through the transformative power of sport. The club promotes gender equality and respect, cultural integration, and also promotes learning of the Basque language in an area where it has been in retreat.[51] Meanwhile, in Tarragona, Catalonia, FC Tarraca was founded in November 2012 as a social force for good and was the first such popular shareholding football club in the region. The club fields both men's and women's teams in the local Catalan leagues.[52] Although many of Spain's emerging *fútbol popular* clubs may not have an explicit political agenda, more often than not their ethos is community-focused and aims to use football for the betterment of society.

When football kicked against Europe's longest-running dictatorship

In neighbouring Portugal, a right-wing authoritarian system thrived for nearly half a century. Following a military coup in May 1926, António de Oliveira Salazar rose quickly through the ranks of government to become prime minister in July 1932. Salazar set about creating his *Estado Novo* (New State), which was based on nationalism and Catholicism. Despite being politically close to neighbouring Spain, Salazar did not share Franco's vision for using football as a political tool. And, while Salazar was inspired by Mussolini, he did not promote sport for the nationalist cause in the same way *Il Duce* did. The *Estado Novo* prohibited professionalism in sport and limited its ability to grow. This is why Portugal's club sides and the national team only really started to make an impact on the international stage as late as the 1960s. As a result, we do not see any teams alleged to be close to the ruling regime in Portugal, as had occurred next door in Spain with Real Madrid. While football was a largely urban sport in Portugal, Salazar was a rural man with a deeply conservative mindset. He also held a long-standing grudge against the British for the 'British Ultimatum' of 1890, relating to both countries' colonial ambitions in Africa, so football -– as a British importation – was a particularly sensitive issue for Salazar.

All Portugal's 'big three' clubs – Benfica and Sporting from the capital, Lisbon, and FC Porto from the north – enjoyed fairly good relations with the regime. Benfica, however, was singled out on occasions. The regime asked Benfica to change its anthem *Avante pelo Benfica* (Onwards, Benfica) because the word *avante* (forward or onwards) was the same name as the Communist Party's underground newspaper. Similarly, Benfica was known as 'the Reds' (*Vermelhos*), a colour synonymous with communism, so the regime encouraged the use of the word *Encarnados* – 'the Scarlets'. In the 1960s, just as Portugal's clubs and national team were enjoying international success, the country became embroiled in various wars in its African colonies, Angola, Guinea and Mozambique. In 1961, Benfica won the European Cup under the guidance of Hungarian coach, Béla Guttmann – himself a holocaust survivor – and retained it the following season with the help of the great Mozambique-born attacker, Eusébio da Silva Ferreira. Portuguese clubs had been bringing footballing talent across from the country's African colonies since the late 1940s to support the notion of integration within a country that was still the head of an empire, according to Portuguese football journalist Miguel Pereira. 'Nevertheless, as with all things with Salazar, there was never truly an intention to support football clubs economically or use football as a propaganda weapon,' Pereira tells me. 'They simply took advantage of events, and that great Benfica generation and the national team forged with their attacking line-up for the 1966 World Cup was one of those opportunities.'

While the regime surfed the wave of popularity that Benfica created, the *Encarnados* did not enjoy any favouritism. For example, days after winning the 1961 European Cup, Benfica was made to play a *Taça de Portugal* (Portuguese Cup) tie against Vitoria Setúbal that the club had asked to delay. Benfica lost the match. Portuguese clubs were also forbidden from selling their best players abroad, as the regime considered them the property of the state. It was also around this period that the *Estado Novo* started elevating the role of football, including it in the 'Three Fs' to promote the image of Portugal abroad – *Fado* (folk music), *Futebol* (football) and *Fátima*, the Catholic pilgrimage site.

Portugal finished third in the 1966 World Cup in England, but discontent with the colonial wars at home was growing, with protesters even taking to the streets. Among the key sources of public dissent were the universities, none more so than the country's most prestigious university and one of the world's oldest, Coimbra. The wars against African colonial uprising began in 1962, and students who failed at universities often found themselves drafted into the army to go to Africa to fight the rebels. This stoked anti-government strikes and protests. Salazar charged his protégé Marcello Caetano to deal with them. When Salazar suffered a stroke in 1968, his role as prime minister was assumed by Caetano. Caetano and his ministers and military personnel visited Coimbra to open a new building at the university in 1969, but were confronted by a student protest led by Alberto Martins, who would himself go on to serve as a government minister in the 1990s. The student protest could be heard over the live radio broadcast for the first time, and the event led to a stand-off with students barricading themselves into campus. The siege went on for weeks, but a compromise was struck so that students could resume class in exchange for an end to the practice of sending learners who failed away to fight in Africa.

Coimbra's local side is Académica de Coimbra. Students could play for the club at that point, right up until it went professional in the 1980s. 'Académica at that time was a very political club,' Miguel Pereira explains. 'A lot of players who wanted to get a degree went to Académica while they were studying before signing for bigger teams. Players like Toni,

Artur Jorge and Manuel António. A lot of the players were also students that came from the African colonies, and most of them had connections with the military resistance groups.' Indeed, on a club tour to Angola during the 1960s, four African Académica de Coimbra players slipped away to join pro-independence resistance movements. With incredible timing, in the summer of 1969, Académica de Coimbra made it to its fourth *Taça de Portugal* final. The showpiece season finale is held at Lisbon's historic Estádio Nacional do Jamor and is a huge occasion in Portugal. With students continuing their protests and emboldened by the worldwide youth protests of 1968, the final presented Académica's players with a significant platform. Earlier in the tournament, Académica's players had demonstrated their solidarity for students by observing 30 seconds of silence ahead of a game against Vitoria Guimarães. In the two-legged semi-final against Sporting, a club often associated with Portugal's elite, Académica players switched from their traditional all-black kit to white with a black armband to symbolise mourning.[53]

Ricardo Martins is the writer and director of a 2009 film about Académica's 1969 cup run, *Futebol de Causas (Football with a Cause)*. He spent months delving through the national film and TV archives, and interviewing former players. 'Académica players were privileged compared to other students because they weren't sent to war, but they did share houses with friends that did, so they decided to make a stand,' Martins tells me. 'They believed it wasn't fair that young people didn't have a say in society, so – in solidarity – every player set out to spread the word.' On the day of the final against Benfica, more than 30,000 students from Coimbra and Lisbon descended on the capital's streets to support the Coimbra side. They held banners, and as a result the cup final was not broadcast on TV, although radio listeners could hear the students chanting throughout the match. Students also handed out flyers to the Benfica fans in the Jamor who had no idea what was going on at Coimbra. Neither the President of the Republic, Américo Thomáz – a Belenenses supporter – nor Caetano or any other high-ranking official attended. The police were ordered not to intervene to avoid a potential massacre. Académica de Coimbra's players took to the field in black students' gowns to drive home their support, and walked on to the pitch slowly, as if they were pallbearers. Benfica midfielder Toni had played for Académica four years previously and briefed his *Encarnados* teammates about the situation. They also walked slowly on to the pitch and agreed to celebrate with Académica, should the Coimbra side win. When the match kicked off, Académica took a first-minute lead in the final through an António goal. The plan was that if they won, the Académica players would take the *Taça de Portugal* trophy into the stands to share their victory with the students.

The Coimbra side hung on until five minutes from time when Simões levelled for Benfica. Eusébio netted the winner in extra time for Benfica, but – true to their word – the Benfica players swapped shirts and collected the trophy dressed in the black Académica shirt as a sign of respect for the students. Académica had lost the match but certainly gained a lot of respect and attention for the students' cause. 'It would have been a tremendous moment if Académica had won and done that lap of honour,' Martins adds. 'Most Académica players told me they had to make a stand for their conscience. They had sacrificed their football careers for the cause, and I felt I had to tell their story.' Despite being one of the leading clubs in Portugal in the 1960s, none of the Académica team was selected for the national side. Instead, they went on to become brilliant doctors, lawyers, politicians, teachers, and some were even leaders of the 1974 Carnation Revolution. The incapacitated Salazar died in 1970, and the entire authoritarian regime fell on 25 April 1974. Former president Thomáz was exiled to Brazil. 'No one talks about what caused the 1974 revolution – it started in 1969,' Martins concludes. 'I find young people do not know the Académica story, but older people who remember it were grateful that the story was once again in the spotlight.'

Cândido de Oliveira: National hero turned anti-fascist spy

Lisbon's early football scene was very much dominated by the social elites. It was not until the creation of the Casa Pia Atlético Clube in 1920 by former students of the Casa Pia orphanage in Lisbon that football was opened up to the working classes. One of Casa Pia Atlético Clube's founders was former Benfica player Cândido de Oliveira, who had grown up in the orphanage. The new club won the Lisbon Championship unbeaten in its first season, posing a serious threat to the established sides. Cândido de Oliveira went on to coach Portugal's football team at the 1928 Olympic Games in Amsterdam, reaching the quarter-finals. He then spent some time coaching in London with Arsenal FC, the leading English club of the early 1930s under the legendary manager, Herbert Chapman. His grip of both English and Portuguese, along with his personal connections, made Cândido de Oliveira the perfect spy for British intelligence during World War II. Despite the war being fought by ideologically aligned fascist powers in Nazi Germany and Mussolini's Italy, Portugal remained neutral. Lisbon, however, was the hub of espionage, with leaders of resistance movements hosting clandestine meetings in the capital, as well as being the departure point for many refugees heading for the safety of a new life in the Americas. Even Ian Fleming, the creator of James Bond, was inspired by his time near Lisbon at the Palácio Estoril Hotel in 1941, basing many of his characters on people he met during his time there.

Cândido de Oliveira's opposition to the Salazar regime was known, and he was recruited by the British to pass intel to its network in the Portuguese capital, where he had been working in the postal service. He was arrested by the Portuguese authorities and detained in the notorious Tarrafal camp in the Cape Verde archipelago. The camp had been set up in 1933 and used to house resistance leaders from Portugal's African colonies and other domestic political opponents, such as communists. Because Portugal had banned the death penalty in the 1860s, the camp was known as a place where prisoners could expect a 'slow death' due to sickness. Cândido de Oliveira held out, and when the tide of war turned against the Nazis, Salazar reluctantly released him in 1944 when the British government inquired about his whereabouts. He was cleared of all charges and was left alone by the *Estado Novo* while he continued his coaching and journalism career until his death in 1958.

Far-right dictatorships lasted longer in Iberia than other parts of Europe and football was a key instrument of their propaganda. Aside from the actions of Cândido de Oliveira and Académica de Coimbra's brave stance in the 1960s, Portugal has not seen a great deal of political activity in its football, according to the journalists I spoke to. Portugal is a politically conservative country at heart, although some local clubs in the working-class areas of southern Lisbon have had left-wing roots.

1 https://www.elnacional.cat/es/cultura/los-anos-de-plomo-del-pistolerismo_367558_102.html (retrieved 07/03/21)

2 Usall, Ramon, *Futbolítica: Històries de Clubs Políticament Singulars* (Barcelona: Ara Llibres, 2017, p130)

3 *Ibid* (p131)

4 http://www.cejupiter.cat/club/1909 (retrieved 07/03/21)

5 Ball, Phil, *Morbo: The Story of Spanish Football* (London: WSC Books, 2001, p109)

6 https://www.fcbarcelona.com/en/news/645478/joan-gamp=er-1908-1909-1910-1913-1917-1919-1921-1923-1924-1925 (retrieved 28/11/21)

7 *Daily Herald*, 18 July 1936 (p11)

8 Usall, Ramon, *Futbolítica: Històries de Clubs Políticament Singulars* (Barcelona: Ara Llibres, 2017, p133)

9 https://www.fcbarcelona.com/en/card/645396/josep-sunol-1935-1936 (retrieved 07/03/21)

10 https://as.com/futbol/2016/08/29/mas_futbol/1472453502_992514.html (retrieved 30/08/21)

11 https://www.amicsdelarambla.cat/cat/turisme/placa-en-memoria-de-josep-sunyol (retrieved 15/10/21)

12 https://www.goal.com/en/news/8/main/2008/10/30/939580/calderón-and-marca-hit-back-at-senile-fergie (retrieved 07/03/21)

13 http://archivo.marca.com/edicion/marca/futbol/1a_division/real_madrid/es/desarrollo/1179080.html (retrieved 07/03/21)

14 https://www.marca.com/futbol/real-madrid/2019/04/14/5cb0612ae5f dea38418b4606.html (retrieved 07/03/21)

15 https://www.cyltv.es/Noticia/949A77FB-FF5E-0CFF-FBF4E48FC759B9F6/24092016/santiago/bernabeu/avalo/franquismo/republicano/expatriado/vuelta/espa%C3%B1a (retrieved 09/12/21)

16 https://thesefootballtimes.co/2019/02/13/how-ricardo-zamora-became-spanish-footballs-first-idol-and-blazed-a-path-for-future-goalkeeping-greats/ (retrieved 07/03/21)

17 Ball, Phil, *Morbo: The Story of Spanish Football* (London, WSC Books, 2001, p113)

18 https://thesefootballtimes.co/2019/02/13/how-ricardo-zamora-became-spanish-footballs-first-idol-and-blazed-a-path-for-future-goalkeeping-greats/ (retrieved 15/10/21)

19 https://www.worldsoccer.com/blogs/spanish-civil-war-334468 (retrieved 07/03/21)

20 https://museo.levanteud.com/2020/06/29/contexto-historico/ (retrieved 07/03/21)

21 https://www.laverdad.es/murcia/cartagena/201503/28/gran-derbi-principio-guerra-20150328010009-v.html (retrieved 23/06/21)

22 *Nottingham Journal*, 23 June 1937 (p7)

23 https://www.wlv.ac.uk/research/institutes-and-centres/centre-for-historical-research/football-and-war-network/football-and-war-blog/2019/football-and-the-spanish-civil-war-beyond-el-clasico/ (retrieved 23/06/21)

24 https://osasunarenmemoria.wordpress.com/2020/04/01/murillo-el-cuende-donde-los-golpistas-quemaban-camisetas-de-osasuna/ (retrieved 08/07/21)

25 https://outsidewrite.co.uk/the-mystery-of-andres-jaso-garde-sporting-de-gijons-fearsome-striker-and-missing-victim-of-fascism/ (retrieved 07/03/21)

26 https://ganninaway.wordpress.com/2011/10/10/santa-pola-cf/ (retrieved 07/03/21)

27 https://www.sevillafc.es/actualidad/noticias/salvador-artigas-entrenador-rennes-sevilla (retrieved 02/07/21)

28 https://www.girondinsretro.fr/DIAZ_Benito.tO.htm (retrieved 06/12/21)

29 https://footballcitizens.com/hilario-marrero-un-heroe-en-el-real-madrid/ (retrieved 08/07/21)

30 *Dundee Courier*, 20 August 1937 (p7)

31 *Lancashire Evening Post*, 5 March 1937 (p6)

32 https://www.aljazeera.com/program/football-rebels/2021/4/8/saturnino-navazo-spanish-survivor-of-a-nazi-concentration-camp (retrieved 30/04/21)

33 Simpson, Kevin. E.; *Soccer Under the Swastika: Defiance and Survival in the Nazi Camps and Ghettos* (London: Rowman & Littlefield, 2020, revised edition, loc1450/5410)

34 https://ionline.sapo.pt/artigo/615807/portugal-espanha-franco-franco-franco-salazar-salazar-salazar-?seccao=Desporto (retrieved 07/03/21)

35 Villalobos Salas, Cristóbal, *Fútbol y Fascismo* (Madrid: Altamerea, 2020, p79/174)

36 https://www.goal.com/en-gb/news/general-franco-real-madrid-king-history-behind-clubs-link/fcoqldp8h2bb1841o2rspmuhe (retrieved 23/06/21)

37 https://www.newsweek.com/la-roja-jimmy-burns-roots-soccers-spanish-fury-65559 (retrieved 23/06/21)

38 *Daily Mirror*, 11 October 1975 (p28)

39 https://www.theguardian.com/commentisfree/2007/nov/03/comment.spain (retrieved 06/04/21)

40 https://thesefootballtimes.co/2016/02/19/how-a-basque-derby-brought-about-the-legalisation-of-the-basque-flag/ (retrieved 04/06/21)

41 https://www.marca.com/futbol/2016/01/31/56ae8aaf268e3e5e188b462a.html (retrieved 24/10/21)

42 https://english.elpais.com/elpais/2014/12/12/inenglish/1418379310_978569.html (retrieved 23/06/21)

43 http://www.rayovallecano.es/club/historia (retrieved 07/03/21)

44 https://as.com/futbol/2020/05/29/reportajes/1590714407_781526.html (retrieved 07/03/21)

45 https://bukaneros.org/acerca-de/ (retrieved 09/06/21)

46 https://bukaneros.org/historia/ (retrieved 09/06/21)

47 Dunne, Robbie, *Working Class Heroes: The Story of Rayo Vallecano, Madrid's Forgotten Team* (Worthing: Pitch Publishing, 2017, loc.1936/3113)

48 https://www.theguardian.com/football/2019/dec/15/spanish-football-nazi-chants-roman-zozulya-rayo-vallecano-albacete-valencia-real-madrid (retrieved 11/06/21)

49 https://twitter.com/carrusel/status/1387095312259497990?s=20 (retrieved 30/04/21)

50 https://www.marca.com/en/football/spanish-football/2020/09/15/5f60fce6e2704eba148b460f.html (retrieved 01/09/21)

51 https://www.noticiasdenavarra.com/navarra/tudela-y-ribera/2021/07/04/union-tutera-equipo-diferente/1161688.html (retrieved 31/10/21)

52 http://www.elfutbolpopular.com/2020/10/tarraco-fc-el-futbol-de-verdad.html?m=1 (retrieved 31/10/21)

53 http://www.academica-oaf.pt/home/2018-07-18-15-13-58/historia/# (retrieved 07/03/21)

Chapter 3

Central and Western Europe

FOLLOWING GERMANY'S defeat in the Great War (1914–18), the victors – France, Great Britain and the United States – imposed strict economic and military conditions on the country, which led to widespread hardship and internal division in the following years. Many Germans turned to parties from both extremes of the political spectrum in communism on one side and national socialism on the other. This division was accelerated further by the economic blow of the Wall Street Crash in 1929. Adolf Hitler's *Nationalsozialistische Deutsche Arbeiterpartie* (NSDAP – National Socialist German Workers' Party) saw its share of the vote grow from a tiny 2.6 per cent in 1928 to 18 per cent in September 1930. By January 1933, and despite a fall in support for the NSDAP, German president Hindenburg offered Hitler the position of chancellor to stave off what he saw as a communist threat. Hitler exploited his new position – and the Reichstag fire, which he blamed on communist agitators – to secure his power base and wipe away democratic freedoms via the Enabling Bill in March 1933. All opposition parties were banned by the new Nazi leadership. Activity was stepped up against opposition parties, minority groups – most notably Germany's sizeable Jewish population – and those within the political and military system not deemed loyal to Hitler.

In sport, the Nazis looked to Mussolini's successful model, but, in football at least, failed to reach the same levels of success. The Nazi sports ministry, the *Deutscher Reichsbund für Leibesübungen* (DRL – German Reich Commission for Physical Exercise), was headed by the aristocrat Hans von Tschammer und Osten. Germany's national knockout football cup tournament – now called the *DFB-Pokal* – was named the *Tschammer-Pokal* between 1935 and 1943 and was open to all 14,000-plus clubs in Germany to enter. Significant changes were enforced across the board for enemies of the new leadership and football was no exception. Kevin E. Simpson is the author of *Soccer Under the Swastika*. 'The oppression begins pretty much from day one, once the Nazis are in control,' Simpson tells me. 'You see the enemies of the Third Reich rounded up, you see the near-total control of the society, including the press and sporting organisations. Clubs are directed to purge their leadership and rosters of Jewish players. The clubs often didn't need much cajoling or intimidating; they often moved ahead of the edicts.'

Football was an early victim of new anti-Jewish laws. The *Deutscher Fußball-Bund* (DFB), Germany's national football association, had informed its members that Jews and Marxists were no longer permitted to lead football clubs and organisations two months before excluding Jews from sporting clubs became official Nazi policy in June 1933.[1] The announcement was made in *kicker* magazine, Germany's premier football publication. Ironically, *kicker* had been founded in 1920 by Walter Bensemann, a Jewish football pioneer who had also formed clubs and arranged international matches in the 1890s and 1900s. Bensemann had also been influential in the founding of the DFB in 1900. Bensemann fled to Montreux, Switzerland, in March 1933 and died the following year.[2] One of the football clubs Bensemann had founded was Karlsruhe FV (KFV). The club's youth team coach in the spring of 1933 was former Germany international and Great War veteran Julius Hirsch. He had been only the second Jew to represent Germany at international level, and won the German championship with KFV in 1910, but in April 1933 he resigned from the club. In his resignation letter, he highlighted that he had been a loyal club member since 1902 and mentioned his family's war record serving Germany.[3] Hirsch was not permitted to enter Karlsruhe FV's stadium for home matches, but a former player managed to sneak him in.[4] For its part, KFV's correspondence with Hirsch appears to show the club didn't want to lose him.

At a match away at Nancy in France in December 1933, KFV had apparently been asked not to perform the Nazi salute pre-match, as was by now obligatory for German sides, for fear that the display could cause disorder in the crowd. The club agreed, concerned that it would not receive its share of the gate receipts, and its players did not perform the 'German greeting'. Once the Nazi sports ministry heard about the incident, it banned KFV from playing friendlies abroad for a year.[5] Hirsch died at the Auschwitz concentration camp in 1945. Hirsch's memory has been rekindled in recent decades; the DFB's anti-discrimination award carries his name, and he has a street named after him near Karlsruher FV's former ground. Hirsch's contemporary, Gottfried Fuchs, was the first Jewish player to pull on a German national shirt. He scored ten goals in Germany's 16-0 rout of Russia at the 1912 Olympics and was a decorated war veteran but fled Germany in 1937, eventually settling in Canada.

Meanwhile, in the south, FC Bayern München (Munich) has been the most successful club in Germany since the 1970s. However, the club had to wait a while for its success. Founded in 1900, FC Bayern did not win its first national championship until 1932 under Jewish coach Richard Kohn. It was the reigning German champion at the start of Nazi control over the country. The club's president for the decade leading up to

FC Bayern's first title was Kurt Landauer, who had played for the club as a youth at the turn of the century. He had set up the club's youth development programme and raised the profile of the Bavarian club. However, Landauer hailed from a Jewish family, so the Nazis now considered FC Bayern a 'Jewish club'.[6] Landauer stepped down as president in March 1933 and also lost his publishing job soon after. Briefly interned by the Nazis at the Dachau concentration camp, Landauer moved to neutral Switzerland in March 1939. In 1943, Bayern players appearing in a friendly match in Zurich had risked the wrath of the Nazi top brass by assembling to wave to Landauer, who was sat in the stands.[7] Landauer returned after the war to take on the FC Bayern presidency once more in 1947.

Another so-called 'Jewish club' in the eyes of the Nazi authorities was Eintracht Frankfurt. The club's Jewish treasurer, Hugo Reiss, was let go in April 1933. Six years later, he sailed to Chile and never returned to Germany.[8] Barred from so-called 'Aryan' associations, many Jews formed their own football clubs. Several of these were called '*Hakoah*', meaning 'Strength' in Hebrew, or '*Makkabi*', named after the Jewish Maccabee warriors of ancient Judea. They played in local Jewish leagues, such as Berlin's *Jüdische Stadtliga* (Jewish City League).

It wasn't just Jewish-associated clubs that were subject to state oppression. In 1933, left-leaning Munich club SpVgg Unterhaching was dissolved due to 'political unreliability' and was not reinstated until the fall of Nazi Germany in 1945.[9] In the industrial Ruhr, Borussia Dortmund (BVB) was living in the shadow of the most successful club of the 1930s and '40s, FC Schalke 04 of nearby Gelsenkirchen. BVB's Catholic chairman Egon Pentrup was replaced in 1934, as he was apparently unsympathetic to the new regime.[10] During the National Socialist era, other BVB members produced anti-Nazi literature, including former player Heinrich Czerkus, who had been active in the German Communist Party (KPD). Czerkus was arrested and murdered by the Gestapo in the last weeks of World War, II and his name lives on in the name of a BVB fan club. The Nazis also targeted trade unions. In Britain, the National Workers' Sports Association, affiliated with the Trades Union Congress (TUC), had planned to tour Germany to play the German Workers' Sports Association at football over the Easter of 1933. However, the trip was cancelled when the German government banned the matches on grounds that 'public safety would be endangered if they took place'.[11] The German workers' football scene had been fairly strong in the decade before the NSDAP seized power, complete with its own association, the *Arbeiter Turn und Sportbund* (ATSB – Workers' Gymnastics and Sports Association), as something of a rival to the DFB. The ATSB even sent a team to the second Workers' Olympiad in Vienna in 1931. Here, Erwin Seeler – father of future West Germany international Uwe Seeler – scored in a 3-2 defeat to Austria. Communist clubs later split away to form their own competitions, but in 1933 all workers' football associations were banned. One of the leading football clubs of Berlin's pre-Nazi era was Sparta Lichtenberg. One of its former players was the communist Olympic wrestler Werner Seelenbinder. At the German Championships in 1933, Seelenbinder refused to display the Nazi salute and received an 18-month ban for his defiance. Seelenbinder was selected for the 1936 Olympics in Berlin, where he wanted to repeat his refusal to display the salute, but – hampered by injury – failed to make the podium. Seelenbinder was active in the communist resistance during World War II before his arrest in 1942. He was imprisoned for two years in various labour camps, subjected to torture and was executed on 24 October 1944.[12]

By June 1933, the activities of the new Nazi Party in Germany were causing consternation across the border in Austria. The

Austrian government banned the Nazi Party in the country. After a prolonged debate, the Austrian Football Association decided to cancel an upcoming match with Germany.[13] A friendly match with Poland also became embroiled in politics in December 1933. While the Germans beat the Poles 1-0 in Berlin, a counter-match took place in Warsaw between a Polish workers team and a Jewish side, with the gate receipts going to a fund for German refugees in Poland. The Nazi hierarchy understood the propaganda value of football, and there was one country that was held in such esteem at the time – even though it did not enter the initial World Cups and had been at war with Germany less than two decades before – that an invitation to play there was impossible to resist. The Germans were heading to England.

A controversial night at White Hart Lane

In early September 1935, the Football Association (FA) had invited Germany to play a friendly match in England. 'A greater distinction for German football cannot be imagined,' the newspaper *Berliner Tageblatt* enthused.[14] To play England in England, the home of football, was a great honour indeed, in German eyes. The match was set for Wednesday, 4 December. However, just a week after the invitation was made, the Nazis imposed the Nuremberg race laws. These laws prevented Jews from marrying 'Aryan' Germans and also denied Jews from holding German citizenship, among other cynical moves against the Jewish population. Suddenly, England versus Germany became problematic for the FA and the British government.

England international matches were not held at Wembley in this period and often moved around London grounds. Highbury had been the scene of England's infamous match against the world champions Italy the previous year, for example. On 8 October, the FA announced that the friendly with Germany was to be held at White Hart Lane, Tottenham – right on the doorstep of north

London's sizeable Jewish community. The Jewish population of London had swelled significantly at the end of the 19th century as Russian pogroms drove many Jews from their homes in modern-day Poland, Ukraine and Russia to London's cosmopolitan East End. Many Jews had opted to support Tottenham Hotspur over east London clubs such as Leyton Orient and West Ham. White Hart Lane was a controversial venue for a fixture against Nazi Germany; arguably, there could not have been a more problematic venue in London to host this international. Pressure from Jewish groups and anti-Nazi organisations led to discussions with the FA as early as October about the game being moved to another venue, potentially one outside London. Anti-fascist groups contacted clubs asking them to boycott the match and not make their players available for selection. A mid-match mass walkout was planned for a Spurs home match at White Hart Lane for 19 October but averted after Jewish and anti-Nazi organisations met Tottenham Hotspur club secretary Arthur Turner, who promised to pass on their concerns to the FA.[15]

However, FA secretary Stanley Rous was keen the game was 'not upset by side issues'.[16] Over in Germany, the Nazi newspaper *Volkischer Beobachter* wrote that the 'Jews of London' would 'probably mobilise all criminals in order to make the match impossible'.[17] Opposition to the England versus Germany fixture grew as match day approached. The TUC and supportive associations of the British Labour Party fiercely opposed the staging of the fixture, seen by many as propaganda building up to the Berlin Olympics, which were set to be held in the German capital in August of the following year. The TUC met the Home Secretary Sir John Simon in the days before the game to protest over the political nature of the German visit and the political capital the Nazi administration aimed to make out of it. For his part, Simon reiterated his belief that the fixture did not have any political implications, despite TUC concerns that the match could be perceived as a sympathy gesture for Nazi actions against Jews. In the week leading up to the match, the press questioned whether it would indeed go ahead.

On 2 December, the German national team, led by Otto Nerz, landed at Croydon Airport, south of London, to take on England. The team was met by Sir Frederick Wall, former secretary of the Football Association, and the German Ambassador in London, Herr von Hoersch. German officials also warned the estimated 10,000 Germans travelling over land and sea to the match to downplay their patriotism by not wearing swastikas or singing patriotic songs. Many of the fans were travelling with *Kraft durch Freude* (KdF – Strength Through Joy), the Nazi party's own holiday organisation. On the arrival of one of many steamers, the *Columbus*, into dock in Southampton, the Albion Silver Band, which played before Southampton FC's home matches, gave a rendition of the German national anthem to welcome visitors. The new arrivals 'stood erect and silent, giving the Nazi salute,' according to local reports.[18] To avoid any anti-fascist demonstrations, bus drivers taking German fans on sight-seeing tours of London were only briefed on their route via sealed orders once they had left their bases. Some Germans even laid a wreath at the Cenotaph to honour the dead from the Great War. Meanwhile, at White Hart Lane, security was in place to avoid any sabotage of the pitch. On the day before the big match, the German team enjoyed sight-seeing in London, even witnessing the state opening of Parliament, apparently 'oblivious of the excitement they have created in the TUC and Jewish circles,' one paper reported.[19] The Germans became the first visiting football team to require a police bodyguard.

On the day, 54,164 fans attended the match – then a record for White Hart Lane. There were just 14 arrests pre-match at Victoria Station and around the Spurs ground. Police seized posters reading, 'Stop the Nazi Match', and anti-Nazi graffiti around the ground was blacked out by the authorities. One protester managed to scale the stadium roof and cut the guy-rope hoisting the German swastika, but the flag was quickly restored before many in the ground even noticed. The German team and its travelling thousands raised the fascist salute during the anthem, but the match itself was something of a mismatch as England swept aside the German amateurs – none of whom were over six feet tall – 3-0. At the post-match dinner hosted by the FA, the organisation's president Sir Charles Clegg apologised to the visiting German party for the TUC activity. 'The Trades Union Council have thought fit to interfere in a matter that was absolutely outside their business,' he said. Clegg added that he hoped the TUC had learned a lesson and would not interfere in football again.[20] The *Daily Mirror* reported that Dr Erbach, head of the German delegation, then toasted Adolf Hitler, while Clegg proposed a toast to King George V. German captain Fritz Szepan wrapped up the evening by leading a singsong, using his cigar to conduct his choir of team-mates.[21]

As for the protesters, 34-year-old Ernest Wooley from Shoreditch, east London, was charged with causing damage by cutting the rope that held the German flag above the East Stand at White Hart Lane, claiming he just meant to unfurl it. Wooley pleaded not guilty to doing damage worth 3s 6d to the rope belonging to Spurs. The case was dismissed. Barnet Becow, a 25-year-old cabinet maker from Whitechapel in east London, was also in the dock for allegedly obstructing an officer. Becow had been concealing a poster that read, 'Fair play – release Thaelmann', referring to Ernst Thälmann, the leader of the Communist Party of Germany (KPD), who had been under arrest since 1933 and would go on to die in the Buchenwald concentration camp in 1944. Becow is quoted as saying he went to White Hart Lane to express his disapproval of '10,000 fascist murderers' coming to London to 'start their fascist propaganda'.[22]

Shop assistant Harry Marks, 31, also of East London, was fined ten shillings for refusing to give up a poster to a police officer. The poster bore a swastika with the words 'Nazi emblem of murder' written on it. Meanwhile, in the House of Commons, Conservative MP Hall Cain asked Sir John Simon if he had a list of bodies that had protested about the match and if there was a list of countries that would not raise similar objections playing in Britain. Simon responded that the match had been held in the best spirit and without serious incident. He did not think it necessary to provide the requested list.[23]

In October the following year, a few months after the controversial Berlin Olympics, there was opposition in Britain again when Germany visited Glasgow to play Scotland at Ibrox Park. In response, the Glasgow Trades and Labour Council wrote to the Scottish Football Association (SFA). By inviting Nazi Germany to play in Glasgow, the SFA had 'offered a gross insult to all who desire freedom and preservation of democratic thought and action in Britain,' according to the letter.[24] Citing the Nazis' continued oppression of Jews and trade unionists, the letter questioned Germany's worthiness to participate in Britain's national sport. In the end, around 400 Germans made the trip and sat in the 60,000-strong crowd. The German players performed the Nazi salute pre-match and the swastika fluttered above Ibrox Park. A sizeable police presence deterred any potential for trouble, although two men were detained for hanging up a banner around half time. On the banner, in white writing on a red background, they asked, 'Who murdered Jewish footballers?'[25]

By the time a German police force team from Wupperthal visited Brighton in August 1938 to take on the Sussex police football team in a friendly, the atmosphere had deteriorated considerably. On their arrival at Hove station, the Germans were greeted with boos, jeers and the singing of communist anthem

The Internationale. The singing of the German national anthem was also drowned out by protesters. Due to the protests, the organisers had to cancel the team's planned day trip to Hastings the following day.[26]

Football at the 1936 Olympics

In the summer of 1936, Berlin hosted the Olympic Games. The German capital had been awarded the right to host the Games before the NSDAP seized power. While the 1936 Games were the first to be broadcast on television and introduced the concept of the torch relay, they will always be remembered for Hitler's attempts to use the Games for propaganda reasons and Jesse Owens' four gold medals. As a heavily politicised Games taking place just as fascism and democracy were embroiled in battle in Spain, the tournament proved controversial – before it had even started. Despite calls for a universal boycott of the Games, only the Soviet Union followed through and did not send a team. A number of Jewish athletes also withdrew.

Athletes, including footballers, immediately became caught up in a debate that would continue to rage in the three years running up to the outbreak of war in September 1939 – should non-Germans display the Nazi salute? Steve Menary is the author of *GB United?: British Olympic Football and the End of the Amateur Dream.* Menary tells me that the German organisers of the Berlin Games wanted visiting players to give the Nazi salute, but the last surviving member of the GB Olympic football team, Daniel Pettit, told him in an interview that the players all refused. Instead, they opted for the 'eyes right' military acknowledgement. The Olympic players all met leading Nazis like Joseph Goebbels and Joachim von Ribbentrop at a British embassy function and, at some point, went to meet Hitler at his Bavarian retreat in Berchtesgaden. 'I think how the Games were viewed by the players changed the further away they were and with a bit of historical context,' Menary explains. 'But the Nazis wanted a British rather than a purely English side – as had taken part in previous Olympics – and wrote to the FA asking for exactly this as they knew this all helped their big PR drive.' The GB team in 1936 featured amateurs from Corinthian FC, its sister club Casuals FC, among other English sides, Queen's Park from Scotland, and Cliftonville and Belfast Celtic from Northern Ireland. The Royal Navy provided two Welsh players to complete the 'Home Nations' contingent.

The standout match from the 1936 Olympic football tournament is probably the quarter-final between the hosts Germany and Norway on 7 August. The game was held at Poststadion in central Berlin, famous for its impressive Art Deco grandstand. Germany came into the match buoyed by a 9-0 win over Luxembourg, while Norway had swept past Turkey 4-0 in its first match. Famously, this is the first and only football match that Adolf Hitler is thought to have attended. Expecting nothing short of a German victory, Hitler took his seat at Poststadion alongside his propaganda minister Joseph Goebbels, *Luftwaffe* commander Hermann Göring and party deputy Rudolf Hess. After just six minutes, Norway took the lead through Magnar Isaksen. The Norwegians then appear to have parked the bus for the rest of the match under intense pressure from the Germans before Isaksen again scored a breakaway goal minutes from full time, prompting Hitler to leave the ground.[27]

The Norwegian side that went on to take the bronze medal was coached by Asbjørn Halvorsen, a veteran of Norway's 1920 Olympic campaign, where it surprisingly upset an amateur Great Britain side. Halvorsen had also won the German championship twice with Hamburger SV in 1923 and 1928. Halvorsen was general secretary of the *Norges Fotballforbund* (NFF – Norwegian Football Federation) when Nazi Germany occupied Norway in 1940. Here, he encouraged Norwegian players to refuse to play in the new Nazi-run football set-up in the country and, as a result, was arrested and detained. Firstly, he was held in a camp near Oslo before being moved to France and later Germany.[28]

It would be the Italian amateur side that ultimately took the gold medal at the 1936 Olympics. Italy beat an Austrian side that was reinstated following a controversial defeat to Peru after their quarter-final was marred by a pitch invasion and a replay arranged. Peru, who had led 4-2 in extra time, withdrew in protest. Germany's national team coach Otto Nerz's influence waned as his replacement Sepp Herberger took the reins. The German national team players were all made honorary members of the NSDAP. However, some – including star striker Fritz Szepan of the potent Schalke 04 club – joined voluntarily.[29]

On 1 May 1937, Germany visited Zurich to take on the Swiss national side. German fans were treated to a hostile reception from the Swiss, who pelted the visitors with rotten fruit and attempted to seize their swastikas.[30] Switzerland benefitted from a neutral stance, but its neighbour in Austria was consistently undermined by the NSDAP. As early as 1934, Austrian-born Hitler had encouraged Nazis in Austria to create difficulties for the government there, which resulted in the assassination of Chancellor Engelbert Dollfuss on 25 July that year. Austria's position was compromised further by the sealing of Hitler and Mussolini's Rome-Berlin axis in 1936, based on their shared involvement in Spain. Austria's new chancellor Kurt Schuschnigg was stuck in a tough position between the two fascist leaders, especially with Hitler's openly stated aim of absorbing Austria into Germany. On 9 March 1938, Schuschnigg announced his intention to hold a referendum for the Austrians to decide if they wanted to become part of Germany. At the time, both the British and French parliaments were divided over how to approach Hitler, and he took advantage of the inertia by ordering his troops to march into Austria on Saturday, 12 March 1938.

The Anschluss

One of Europe's most exciting teams in the first half of the 1930s had been Austria's *Wunderteam* (Wonder team). The team was built around exciting forward Matthias Sindelar of FK Austria Wien. Nicknamed *'Der Papierene'* (The Paper Man) for his slender poise, Sindelar relied on his intelligence over his physical presence. His skill on the ball was supported perfectly by Austria's veteran coach Hugo Meisl. In 1931, Austria became the first continental side to beat Scotland in a 5-0 rout. Austria pushed England to the limit at Stamford Bridge in London the following year, losing 4-3. At the start of the 1930s, the *Wunderteam* was by far the best national side in Central Europe, demolishing Germany 6-0 in Berlin and 5-0 at home, and netting eight goals against both Switzerland and Hungary. If Austria had travelled to the 1930 World Cup in Uruguay, it would have had an excellent chance of being the first world champions.

However, by the time its World Cup debut came around in 1934 in Italy, the team had already peaked, and was without midfielder Johann Horvath for the crucial semi-final with the hosts in Milan. Meisl was not confident going into the match, and Sindelar himself struggled to shake off his man-marker Luis Monti. Austria lost the match, as well as the third-place play-off to Germany. Meisl's team won silver at the Berlin Olympics of 1936, but by the 1938 World Cup in France there was no Austrian national side because the country had been annexed by Germany. Many Austrians had already lurched to the right when German troops marched into Austrian territory in March 1938, and the country now found itself subject to the same laws as its new twin. The Austrian Football Association (ÖFB – *Österreichischer Fußball-Bund*) was wound down and its place at FIFA withdrawn.[31] As in Germany, Jewish clubs in particular were targeted. The burgeoning women's football scene, which had been tolerated by the ÖFB, if not supported, was also outlawed by the Nazis. As part of the Nazi's annexation celebrations, a football match – now known as the *Anschlusspiel* (Anschluss match) – was scheduled for 3 April 1938 at the Prater Stadium in Vienna. It would bring the curtain down on a 12-year international career for Sindelar, who refused to turn out for a new combined German international side. Footballers were not alone; two of Austria's best tennis players chose not to join the wider German Davis Cup team, electing to represent their countries of birth instead.

Sindelar, now 35 years old, was still Austria's most popular player. The Austrian team that day was not referred to as *Österreich* (Austria) to emphasise the point that Austria was now part of the expanded German Reich, but did appear in its change strip of red and white. This kit was worn so as not to clash with Germany, who also wore white shirts and black shorts, but the post-*Anschlusspiel* narrative often follows that the choice of red and white – the colours of the Austrian flag – was down to Sindelar's insistence.[32] During the match itself, many reports imply that the Austrians were obliged to draw the match and missed a lot of chances in the first half, despite their clear superiority. Sindelar knocked in a rebound off the post on the 62nd minute and reputedly danced in celebration in front of the Nazi officials. The second goal from Sindelar's FK Austria Wien team-mate Karl Sesta sealed a 2-0 win. The *Wunderteam* finished a decade of success with a final victory over Austria's new overlords to the chants of '*Österreich! Österreich!*' from the Viennese crowd. While Sindelar refused to play for Sepp Herberger's German side, Sesta was one of more than 20 Austrian-born footballers who played for the German national side between 1938 and 1942.[33] On 10 April, a plebiscite returned nearly 100 per cent backing for Austria to be absorbed into the German Reich. Just a few months later, Sindelar was dead. His death was put down to carbon monoxide poisoning, potentially caused by a blocked chimney.

Austrian sides now competed alongside German ones by entering the next *Tschammer-Pokal*. In the league, Austrian clubs competed in the newly renamed *Gauliga Ostmar*k, with the top sides taking part in the German Championship, which by 1939/40 included clubs from Poland and Czechoslovakia. One early sign of the Austrian's football dominance came when Rapid Wien (Vienna) won the first post-Anschluss *Tschammer-Pokal*, beating FSV Frankfurt 3-1 in Berlin in atrocious winter weather. After the *Anschluss* match, there were no real political acts of defiance from Austria's football community. The majority of players went along with the new system. When incidents did occur in matches between Austrian and German clubs, such as riots in matches between Rapid Wien and SpVgg Greuther Fürth in October 1940 or Admira versus FC Schalke 04 the following month, they were more anti-German in motivation than anti-Nazi. On 22 June 1941, Rapid Wien became the first and only Austrian champion of the German Reich, beating Schalke 4-3 in Berlin in the final. On the very same day, Germany initiated its attack on the Soviet Union.

A combined German and Austrian team went to the third FIFA World Cup finals held in France in the summer of 1938. Herberger's side headed to France with four Austrians lining up in Germany's first match of the 15-team tournament against Switzerland. According to Aidan Williams, the addition of Austrians in the German squad should have strengthened the side. Instead, it had the opposite effect as teamwork and harmony went out the window. 'The two factions were essentially two teams within a team; they ate separately, they socialised separately and, at times, they more or less played separately – the Austrians passed to the Austrians, and the Germans passed to the Germans,' he says. Williams describes Germany's first match in Paris against the Swiss as taking place in front of a very hostile anti-fascist crowd. 'Bottles were hurled from the stands at the players, and the noise was very much against the Germans and in Switzerland's favour,' Williams adds. The game ended 1-1 and required a replay. Germany led the second match 2-0, but the Swiss came back to win 4-2 to eliminate Germany. Herberger blamed the defeat on the Austrian contingent. 'The political situation destroyed both Austria and Germany's hopes of World Cup success,' Williams argues. 'Just a final point to add to the political intrigue, the Swiss were coached by Karl Rappan, who was Austrian. The political symbolism of a Swiss side coached by an Austrian knocking out a German side featuring Austrians who didn't want to play for Germany is hugely significant, I think.' As in Germany, Austrian football has looked into the Nazi era. In a 2009 report, Rapid Wien found that around half its officials had been members of the Nazi Party but found that none of its players had.[34] The club's first secretary, Wilhelm Goldschmidt, who had proposed that the club change its name from Wiener Arbeiter Fußball Club (Vienna Workers Football Club) to Rapid Wien, was deported to Poland in 1942, where he died in a concentration camp.

Infamous matches in Berlin

Just weeks after the *Anschluss*, the front page of the *Volkischer Beobachter* newspaper on 15 May 1938 was propaganda gold for the Nazi party. It carried a photo of the English national side displaying the Nazi salute before its 6-3 victory over Germany at Berlin's Olympiastadion the previous day. The match had been highly anticipated for months, with half a million applications for the 100,000 available tickets. Sixty-three special trains had been laid on to bring fans to the match. No Austrian players appeared in the German team and Adolf Hitler was not among the crowd, but several of his top brass – including Joseph Goebbels, Herman

Göring and Rudolf Hess – were. The issue of whether or not to perform the salute had been a topic of discussion within the Football Association in the run-up to the game. The England national side had become embroiled in the politics of appeasement at a time when British prime minister Neville Chamberlain (1937–40) was desperately trying to avoid conflict with Nazi Germany. This climate of appeasement led to the discussions between British diplomats and the FA as to whether the England team should join the German team in performing the salute before the game. The players initially refused but were eventually persuaded by the Football Association.[35] England players joined the Germans in holding their arms aloft for the entirety of both the German national anthem of the time – *Deutschland über Alles* (Germany Over Everyone) – and the Nazi anthem, the *Horst Wessel* song. One England squad player who refused to go along with the request to display the salute was Wolves defender Stan Cullis. 'Count me out,' Cullis is reported to have said.[36] Cullis was not selected in the team for the Berlin match, apparently due to lack of fitness, but featured in the rest of the tour matches in Switzerland and France.

Professor Peter J. Beck of Kingston University in London is the author of *Scoring For Britain: International Football and International Politics, 1900–1939*, which explores the relationship between British politics and sport. Beck explains that in 1938 there was not a lot of opposition to, or criticism of, the salute given by the England team in the media, especially as the football authorities warned the British media in advance that it was going to happen, so the salute itself was not a surprise. Indeed, it was carried by several news outlets that England might perform it. Beck adds that the main critiques of the performance of the salute appear in player memoirs after living through a long war.[37] As we see in Chapter Six, many English footballers went on to play active roles in the war effort against Nazi Germany.

Unlike the gentlemen amateurs of the Great Britain team at the Berlin Olympics two years previously, the 1938 England football team in Berlin were all professionals. 'I suspect it was easier for the Olympians to refuse as they came from the same background as the gentlemen amateurs who held sway in the FA, and also the two managers of the football party in Berlin, Stanley Rous and Charles Wreford Brown,' Steve Menary tells me. 'Two years later, the political situation was more fraught, and the players then were also professionals. It's easy to forget the role of class at that time.' The day after the England national team had displayed the Nazi salute, Aston Villa played an exhibition match at the Olympiastadion against a combined German-Austrian XI. The Villa squad had been present at the England match the day before and had seen the salute performed. It appears that protocol was not relayed to the Villa players, as they performed the salute as instructed before the game but did not take part in the post-match salute. Instead, they walked off to the changing rooms at the final whistle as they would in any game back home. This prompted whistles from a crowd that had already apparently been incensed by Villa's rough play in its 3-2 win. The feeling within the Villa camp seems to be that the incident had been blown up by the British press and not been mentioned in a single newspaper in Germany.[38]

In a long editorial in the popular UK Sunday paper *Reynolds's Newspaper*, sports editor Paul Irwin wrote that the FA had 'blundered badly' over the German tour by ordering England players to 'give the Nazi glad-hand'. Irwin poses the question of whether England or Villa's soccer tour 'could stop Germany making one less bombing plane, one less gun, one less bayonet? Of course not.'[39] A strongly worded editorial in the *Daily Mirror* a few days later highlighted how unhappy several of the England players were with being asked to perform the Nazi salute and that, as the sign of a political party, it should not have been performed.[40] Villa moved on to a second match in Düsseldorf, losing 2-1 to a combined German-Austrian XI and performed the salute before and after the game, as the team did in their final match in Stuttgart. Eventually, the FA did not hold the inquiry that had been threatened following Villa's first match, but the heightened sensitivity around whether or not to salute shows how careful the British establishment was not to create a diplomatic furore with Germany in what turned out to be the last year of peace before war broke out.

The situation around saluting in the Irish Free State (now the Republic of Ireland) was also complicated. Because the British home nations of England, Scotland, Wales and Northern Ireland refused to play football against the Irish Free State, the new nation had to look further afield for opponents of a similar level. As a result, the Irish Free State played Nazi Germany both home and away in the 1930s, and even played against a Rhineland XI after Hitler had breached international treaties and re-militarised the area. Irish football historian Gerard Farrell tells me, 'Given that Germany was seeking a certain level of sporting credibility and seems to be adept at using sport as propaganda, it doesn't seem surprising that they played each other so often, and there does seem to have been a good relationship on a personal level between the two associations.' Farrell explains that the Germans had helped arm the Irish revolutionaries who were now in power in the 1930s, and that some of the foremost scholars on Irish folklore and the Irish language were German, while Dublin especially had a small but important German community. The Irish beat Germany 5-2 at Dalymount Park, Dublin in October 1936, but the Nazis scored a small propaganda victory when their photographer encouraged some members of the crowd behind one goal to raise their arms and sent the picture home to Germany.[41] At the same venue, Bohemian FC had played a team of crew members from the visiting German battleship, the

Schleswig-Holstein, which would later fire the first shots of World War II. There was a keen sense that European politics should be left out of sport in Ireland. In May 1939, just four months before Nazi Germany's invasion of Poland, the Irish Free State held the Germans to a 1-1 draw in Bremen. Here, the Irish team conducted the Nazi salute pre-match, although Farrell explains that there was some resistance and discomfort among the Irish players, if not the officials. The Irish team included Manchester United's Johnny Carey, who went on to volunteer to fight with the British Army in World War II. Other Irish players to fight against Nazi Germany in World War II included Peter Doherty and Alex Stevenson in the Royal Air Force.

Meanwhile, back in Germany, in late 1938 the last of the Jewish football clubs were outlawed as anti-Jewish activity within Germany turned increasingly violent leading up to the outbreak of war. Football continued in Germany throughout the war to distract populations from their ever-worsening conditions. A match was even played in Hamburg the day before Adolf Hitler took his own life in April 1945.[42] The German international side played regularly until 1942 against its allies in Central Europe, its neutral neighbour Switzerland, the Scandinavian countries and even hosted Spain in Berlin in April 1942.

Football in the Nazi death camps

For the vibrant Jewish football culture that had existed in the countries now taken over by the Nazis, things would never be the same again. Before the outbreak of World War II in September 1939, Central European football had been abundant with Jewish-founded football clubs. In the capitals of Budapest, Prague and Vienna, in particular, Jewish clubs and players had thrived. In Budapest, Magyar Testgyakorlók Köre Budapest Futball Club – MTK – a club formed from a gymnasium by mostly middle-class Jews, had won the Hungarian title 15 times before 1939. In Prague, Deutscher Fußball-Club Prag (DFC Prag) had been founded in 1896 by Jewish students from Charles University in the Bohemian capital. It went on to become a founder member of the *Deutscher Fußball Bund* (DFB – German Football Association) in 1900 and contested the first German championship in Hamburg in 1903, losing to VfL Leipzig in the final. German troops marched into Czechoslovakia in October 1938 following the annexation of Sudetenland in the west of the country. While the British and French thought this policy of appeasing Hitler would keep the peace, everything changed for the Jewish population. DFC Prag was denounced as a *Judenklub* when club members declined invitations to join the right-wing Sudeten German Party and the club was dissolved.[43] Many of the club's Jewish players left the country while others were eventually rounded up by the Nazis and sent to camps, including at Terezin/Theresienstadt, an 18th century fortress complex and camp just under 50 kms north of Prague. Terezin was often used as a holding camp by the Nazis before they transported their victims on to other death camps, including Auschwitz. Former DFC Prag player Pavel Mahrer, who had Jewish heritage, was among those sent to Terezin, and he would survive the war, as would Czech striker Honza Burka.[44]

In Vienna, multi-sports club Hakoah Wien had won the newly professional Austrian Championship in the 1924/25 season. Sporting blue-and-white halves with a Star of David on the crest, Hakoah was a successful, globetrotting side. Its star was undoubtedly Hungarian Béla Guttmann, who had left the growing antisemitism of Budapest in the early 1920s for Vienna, the other major centre of the 'Danubian School' of football. Hakoah Wien had been the first continental European club to beat a senior English club in England when it trounced West Ham 5-0 in London in September 1923. When Hakoah played an exhibition match in New York in 1926, it attracted a then-record US soccer crowd of 46,000, which stood until the 1970s. The team's visit inspired the creation of New York Hakoah, which would also feature Béla Guttmann. Following the *Anschluss* of March 1938, Jewish clubs such as Hakoah Wien were forced to close as the Nazis moved quickly to exclude Austrian Jewish sportsmen and women, as they already had in Germany. One Hakoah player – Karl Ehrlich – even ended up in England playing for non-league Redhill. FK Austria Wien, another organisation viewed as a *Judenklub* by Austria's new Nazi overlords, was forced to change its name to SC Ostmark. The club of Matthias Sindelar, twice winners of the Mitropa Cup – a forerunner of the European Cup – in the 1930s, lost some of its best players and was a weakened force in the *Gauliga Ostmark*, the new Austrian top flight. FK Austria Wien player Walter Nausch, who had captained the *Wunderteam*, was not Jewish himself, but his wife was, so he took his family to Switzerland for their safety. He would return to coach Austria to third place in the 1954 World Cup. In all, an estimated 300 Jewish footballers disappeared or died at the hands of the Nazis.[45]

Footballers from all across fascist-occupied Europe were transported to Nazi labour camps across Central and Eastern Europe, whether due to their political leanings, their defiance, or their Jewish origins. In the camps, football became a form of entertainment for the guards and a vital means of survival for the players themselves. As young men, footballers would provide valuable muscle in the labour camps, where prisoners were worked to death – either through exhaustion, hunger or illness. Any advantage they could seek to give themselves a marginal chance of survival was vital, and football was often their salvation.

Kevin E. Simpson has written extensively about the role of football in Nazi camps. 'In these camps, there's a lot of downtime, so this is a way for those who had protected status to occupy themselves, and oftentimes the Nazi guards and *kapos* would be betting on the games, so they would help organise them and make resources available, such as balls and nets,' he tells me. 'Soccer was an inspiration and a means by which to survive. If you were in one of these places and you had access to protected work details or extra food, then soccer often meant survival.' Prisoners could gain privileged positions in the kitchen, for example, or less harsh work details if they impressed a particular *kapo*. So, for many – such as Spanish player Saturnino Navazo, who survived the Mauthausen camp in Austria – football became a matter of life or death.

According to Simpson, one of the most famous prison leagues was at Terezin. There was a promotion and relegation set-up, teams were often sorted by nationality and sometimes wore kits, and there was even a transfer market of sorts when players were deported. Well-known players would often be recruited into a team as soon as they arrived. Professionals could be wildly popular. Sometimes, several thousand prisoners and guards would gather to watch a game in the camps. 'In some way, it seems perverse to talk about whether or not there was quality football in these camps, but I think it's important to note because, initially, when the testimonies were collected of the survivors that played in these camps and ghettos, they were somewhat dismissed or ignored because they weren't seen as essential, but the more we learn about sport and the cultural activity in the camps, we realise they were life-sustaining, inspiring, and very, very crucial,' Simpson affirms.

At Terezin, the league had been established by athlete Fredy Hirsch. The initial 12 teams in 1942 were named according to the jobs the players were involved in within the camp. The first title was won by the 'Children's Care Department'.[46] 'There are a number of accounts of prisoners who would be watching these matches being OK with extra rations being given to the footballers, who would sometimes have practices as well,' Simpson tells me. 'These young men represented Jewish strength, they represented resistance to the Nazi madness, so they provided to the other prisoners a sense of what was before the war and what maybe could be if they could just find a way to hang on and survive.' Football at Terezin even features in a 1944 propaganda film that the Nazis had forced German Jewish actor and director Kurt Gerron to create. The film was intended to portray the camp in a positive light to the neutral countries, and the Nazis promised to spare Gerron's life. However, after delivering the film, Gerron and his wife were transported to Auschwitz, where they were murdered on 28 October 1944.[47]

In one remarkable story recounted in the British press in 1941, a prisoner corps escaped imprisonment by forming a works football team and arranging a match with a team across the border in Switzerland. They left for the match in their gear, but the game never took place, and the 11 men did not return to Germany.[48] For the most part, football provided a brief respite for prisoners during World War II. Simpson concludes, 'For me, the most important form of resistance is survival, because the Nazi ideology is meant to destroy, and so many survivors in their memoirs talk about simply surviving as the ultimate sign of resistance.'

Footballing resistance to the Nazis in Hungary

Hungary had sided with the Axis powers of Nazi Germany and Italy in November 1940 after its right-wing government had tried to stay neutral. The country had lost a lot of land in the Treaty of Trianon in 1920 after the Great War. Hungary had already benefitted from its close relationship with Nazi Germany by having land it claimed awarded to it from neighbouring Czechoslovakia and Romania. In return, its troops assisted the Germans in their campaigns in the Balkans and the Soviet

Union. When the war appeared to be turning against the Axis – especially after Hungarian troops supporting Nazi advances into the USSR were heavily defeated by the Soviets in early 1943 – Hungarian prime minister Miklós Kállay engaged in secret negotiations with the Allies. In response, Hitler ordered his troops to occupy Hungary to secure its assets and install a loyal government. Persecution against the Jewish community was stepped up, and mass deportations to death camps began, first in the countryside and then in the capital, Budapest. More than 400,000 people were transported to Poland, sometimes at the rate of 12,000 a day.[49] In October 1944, Ferenc Szálasi, leader of the Hungarian fascist group Arrow Cross, was installed as a puppet leader. His henchmen scoured the streets, seeking out Jewish families and left-wingers for deportation.

Football in Hungary continued during the war, with Ferencváros and Csepel both winning two titles. Nagyvárad, birthplace of future Torino manager Ernö Egri Erbstein and a town now in modern-day Romania, also won the 1943/44 title. Erbstein had been coaching in Italy before antisemitic laws there forced him to look abroad. He had eventually returned to Budapest with his family, but in 1944 was forced to report to a Hungarian-run labour camp. His tasks included laying railway tracks and, by chance, his team *kapo* was someone with whom Erbstein had served in World War I two and a half decades before. In December 1944, with the Red Army approaching Budapest and prisoner transportation ramping up, Erbstein and four other prisoners managed to slip away and split up. The group of escapees included the former Hakoah Wien star, Béla Guttmann, who had been in Budapest coaching Újpest, where he had won the Hungarian championship and the Mitropa Cup. Erbstein was eventually reunited with his family and returned to Italy after the war to build *Il Grande Torino* – the great Torino FC – which won four titles between 1945/46 and 1948/49, and made up the majority of the Italian national side. On 4 May 1949, Erbstein and his Torino side were returning from a friendly testimonial match against Benfica in Lisbon when their plane crashed into the Basilica di Superga, a church above Turin, in poor weather. There were no survivors. As the Italian national team coach, Vittorio Pozzo was called on to confirm the identity of the victims. Guttmann also returned to coaching straight after the war, winning the title on his return to Újpest in 1946/47. Guttmann's pinnacle came in Lisbon, where he signed 18-year-old rising star Eusébio for Benfica after hearing a tip-off on a trip to the barbershop. Guttmann led the *Encarnados* to two domestic titles and two European Cup wins, breaking Real Madrid's five-year hold on the continent's top honour. Guttmann left Benfica after his request for a pay rise was turned down by the Benfica board. The Hungarian is reported to have said, 'Not in a hundred years from now will Benfica ever be European champion.'[50] Benfica have appeared in five European Cup/Champions League finals since and have lost them all, leading many to believe in 'the curse of Guttmann'.

Along with Erbstein and Guttmann, Géza Kertész had been one of a number of Hungarian coaches who had gained a lot of respect in Italy. Kertész had managed several clubs, including Atalanta of Bergamo and Lazio in Rome, and had not long been installed as coach at AS Roma before he was recalled to Hungary in September 1943 to take up military service as a trainer. He was able to resume coaching as head of the competitive Újpest side. Kertész teamed up with former Ferencváros player and Hungary international István Tóth-Potya to run an underground operation with the support of American military officers. The 'Dallam' group collected intelligence on the defences around Budapest.[51] Kertész and Tóth also helped many Jews escape deportation by finding places for them to shelter – including private houses and religious institutions. Kertész even donned a Nazi officer's uniform at one point as part of his deception.[52] The two were denounced to the Gestapo and executed at dawn on 6 February 1945 at Budapest Castle. Their bodies were later exhumed and the pair buried as national heroes in the Kerepesi Cemetery in Budapest. Kértesz has a sports complex in Bergamo named in his honour, along with a street in Catania, another Italian city where he worked. The Nazi era destroyed a strong Jewish football culture in Hungary. Former MTK and Hungarian international winger József 'Csibi' Braun, who appeared at the 1924 Olympics, was taken to dig trenches as part of forced labour for the Hungarian army on the Eastern front and died in Ukraine in 1943. Former Olympian and Ferencváros star Sándor Bródy perished in April 1944 in the first few weeks of the Nazi takeover. One month later, former Hungarian international and seven-time league champion with MTK, Henrik Nádler, died in a labour camp. Fellow MTK stars Ferenc Weisz, Antal Vágó and Imre Taussig also died at the hands of the Nazis.[53]

The Czech experience

In Czechoslovakia, the Nazis had banned sports meetings across the Czech region of Bohemia as early as June 1939 after a football match in Prague became the scene of anti-German sentiment. A visiting team from Berlin were subjected to abuse from the crowd, beer was thrown from the stands and – with the encouragement of the home crowd – the Prague side appeared to play dirty, and a Berlin player had to be stretchered off. Scuffles broke out between Czech and German supporters, including soldiers. The ban impacted Slavia's Mitropa Cup match with Beogradski of Yugoslavia, which Slavia eventually lost 4-2 on aggregate. In the early days of the war, 11 protesters, including nine youths and two women, were shot dead by Nazi executioners at Slavia Praha's stadium.[54] Domestic football continued during the war. Spearheaded by prolific striker Josef Bican, Slavia Praha won five Bohemia-Moravia league titles during the years of Nazi occupation, bookended by two titles for arch-rival Sparta. Just to the west of Prague, SK Kladno plays at the Stadion Františka Kloze. The ground is named after František Kloz, who is not only SK Kladno's all-time top goalscorer and a former Czechoslovakian international; he also managed the side in the 1942/43 season. Kloz volunteered to join the anti-fascist resistance in the final days of the war. On 7 May 1945, Kloz was shot in the leg during an assault on an ammunition depot at Hříškov, west of Kladno. Surgeons recommended he have the leg amputated but Kloz refused, and he died from his wounds on 13 June.[55] Kloz's former SK Kladno team-mate Josef Kusala was also killed fighting Nazis during the Prague Uprising on 8 May 1945. The very next day, Prague was liberated.

In 2015, 76 years after being forced to close by Nazi occupiers, DFC Prag was reformed by Germans living in the Czech capital. It was for a recreation of the first German championship in May 1903, which the original DFC Prag lost to VfB Leipzig. The following June, eight enthusiasts formally relaunched the club at the Hybernia Theatre in Prague and the organisation now fields youth teams. Meanwhile, across Prague in Vršovice, Bohemians Praha 1905 is home to the Czech Republic's standout left-wing fanbase, something of an outlier in the country's football scene. The club was saved from going bust with support from fans and it enjoys a fierce rivalry with the country's oldest football club, Slavia Praha, whose stadium is just 1km away.

Footballers and the French Resistance

France fell to invading Nazi forces on 25 June 1940. The country remained occupied until 25 August 1944, when it was finally liberated by the Allies. During the German invasion – known as the Battle of France – several footballers had been mobilised to resist the Nazis' advance. Georges Hatz, a goalkeeper who would win the French league and cup double with Lille in 1946, was injured by shrapnel in May 1940. Jacques Mairesse, a defender who had spells at Red Star (Paris) and AS Strasbourg, among others, had represented France at the 1934 World Cup and had been the first president of the professional players' union. He was shot by German forces at Véron on 15 June 1940. Former US Tourcoing winger Victor Farvacques, who had one French cap to his name, died in the Nazi advance at Gravelines in northern France. Another former UC Tourcoing player, Noël Lietaer, was captured and died a year later as a prisoner of war at Rostock in Germany.

During the four years of Nazi occupation, France was split into two areas, one of which was under German control in the north and west coast, and the other a collaborative government based in Vichy under Marshal Philippe Pétain contained to the south and east. The Vichy government is believed to have deported more than 75,000 Jews and other French nationals to Nazi concentration camps during its time in power.[56] French domestic football continued during the years of occupation. In Alsace, which Germany annexed in July 1940, the Nazi SS seized control of Red Star Strasbourg and made it *Sportgemeinschaft der SS* (SS Sports Community). Across town, arch-rivals Racing Club was renamed *Rasensportclub Straßburg* (Lawn Sports Club Strasbourg) and appeared in the highest regional amateur league, the *Gauliga Elsaß*. Several Racing Club Strasbourg players fled or asked their team-mates to inflict injuries on them to avoid joining the *Sportsgemeinschaft der SS*. They were also threatened with conscription into the German army, including star and French international Oscar Heisserer, who had fought in the defence of France in 1940. Heisserer fled to neutral Switzerland.[57] Some Racing Club de Strasbourg players managed to re-establish the club in Périgueux, south-west France and continued to compete in French competition. Back in Strasbourg, Racing Club/

Rasensportclub players who did cross over to the new SS team were roundly heckled by the watching Alsatian public when playing against their former club. Racing Club's colours were blue shirts and white shorts. In one infamous match between the club and an SS representative XI, the Racing Club players donned red socks to make up the French red, white and blue *tricolore*, which proved popular with the watching public. Heisserer returned to Strasbourg with the Allied forces in 1945 and went back to Racing Club.

Elsewhere, a strong resistance network emerged throughout France, which included footballers. Several either played for – or had previously turned out for – the club now known as Red Star Football Club in Paris. Red Star was founded in 1897 by Jules Rimet, who went on to create the FIFA World Cup. Red Star FC is based in Saint-Ouen, traditionally a working-class district of northern Paris. Rather like Rayo Vallecano in Madrid, Saint-Ouen's politics have been reflected on the terraces of its football club. In recent decades, Red Star FC has become something of a magnet for left-wing and anti-fascist football fans. While the origins of the name 'Red Star' were inspired by the name of the shipping line linking France and Britain and not communism, the club can count socialist former president François Hollande as a fan.[58] The pacy, right-footed winger Rino Della Negra only played five matches for Red Star Olympique, as the club was known during World War II. He was also a member of the FTP-MOI (*Francs-Tireurs et Partisans – Main-d'Oeuvre Immigrée* – French Shooters and Partisans – Immigrant Division) resistance group that consisted mostly of communists led by the Armenian poet Missak Manouchian. Della Negra's parents had left their native Italy due to the rise of Mussolini and headed to Argenteuil in the north of Paris. He continued to play football while partaking in clandestine anti-Nazi action.[59] Della Negra was arrested on 12 November 1943, tried by a German military court and shot by firing squad on 21 February 1944. He wrote to his brother before he died to say, 'hello and goodbye to all at Red Star'.[60] All 23 members of the Manouchian Group were caught and tried by the Nazis. The names and faces of ten of them appeared on the infamous *L'Affiche Rouge* (Red Poster), a propaganda poster issued by the Vichy and Nazi authorities in spring 1944. The Red Poster contained the names of the ten listed combatants, highlighting their Jewish or communist origins and details of their actions. It was intended to serve as both a warning and to discredit resistance activity. Each February, to mark the anniversary of Della Negra's death, Red Star FC fans pay tribute to him at Le Stade Bauer.

Many other Red Star players defied the Nazis. Maurice Thédié, who had won the French Cup in 1922 with Red Star, was arrested by the Gestapo on 19 May 1944 and died on a train bound for the Dachau concentration camp. His name lives on in that of a street and a stadium in his hometown of Amiens. Former Red Star and Racing Club de France forward Emilien Devic joined the resistance and was shot dead in August 1944. Henri Joncourt, a *Coupe de France* winner with Red Star Olympique in 1942, fought for the *Francs-Tireurs et Partisans Français* (FTPF) in the Breton town of Concarneau. He survived the war but died in Algeria in 1957. Another member of the 1942 *Coupe de France* winning team was Roger Vandevelde. He had joined the resistance in 1941 and was arrested in 1943 and deported to Germany but survived until liberation. He was a pilot, parachutist and reached the rank of colonel. He was awarded the *Croix de Guerre* and the *Légion d'Honneur*, two of the highest honours available in France. Former Red Star striker Eugène Maës – who once scored five goals for France in a match against Luxembourg in 1913 – was denounced for his anti-German comments and was deported to the Mittelbau-Dora concentration camp, where he died on 30 March 1945, a few weeks away from liberation.

Across Paris, 21-year-old Racing Club player Georges Delrieu managed to get to England in 1940 to join the Free French Forces. He saw action in north Africa for the Allied Forces, including the second battle of El Alamein, one of the turning points of World War II, before being posted to Italy. He was killed in action at Tivoli near Rome on 5 June 1944. In the south, OGC Nice star Léon Rossi helped transport weapons to supply Maquis resistance fighters.[61] Former FC Sochaux and French international Étienne Mattler also moved supplies for the resistance, helping to recover arms that had been dropped in by Allied planes. He was denounced to the Gestapo in early 1944 and endured three months of interrogation, during which time he wore his French team tracksuit. Mattler fled to Switzerland before returning to help liberate his region and eventually going back to FC Sochaux as player-coach after the war.[62] Mattler won two *Croix de Guerre* medals, the first for his actions in defending his homeland in the Battle of France (1940) and for his resistance activity (1945). He died in 1986, aged 80.[63] One of the leading lights of the women's game in France was Carmen Pomiès. During her playing career, she turned out for Parisian side Fémina Sport and the French national side. She also toured North America and later with pioneering English women's team, Dick, Kerr Ladies. During the war, Pomiès was active in the French resistance, helping people secure passports to flee the country.

Neighbouring Luxembourg had also fallen to Nazi Germany in May 1940. Nicolas Birtz, a player with Stade Dudelange, saw his club absorbed into the new German *Gauliga Moselland* championship in 1941 and its name germanified to FV Stadt Düdelingen. The club won the debut edition of the league. Birtz was also a member of a local resistance group. He was arrested in 1942 and detained for the rest of the war, but survived and went on to represent his country at the 1948 Olympic Games in London, where he won his only cap.

After France was liberated, the national league structure was re-established with Lille Olympique Sporting Club, formed in late 1944 out of a merger of two clubs within the northern city, emerging as league and cup double winners in the 1945/46 season. Following the liberation of France, reprisals began against those who had collaborated with the Nazis during their occupation. One of those to face the justice of the firing squad on 26 December 1944 was Alex Villaplane. The former Nîmes and Racing Club hero had led the French national side out on its World Cup debut against Mexico at the Estadio Pocitos in Montevideo 14 years earlier. Villaplane had already been involved in various sporting scandals during the 1930s before becoming a chauffeur for a high-ranking member of the *Carlingue*, the French Gestapo, during the Nazi occupation. Villaplane became involved in racketeering and was also capable of terrible cruelty. On one occasion, Villaplane forced an old woman whom he had accused of harbouring a Jew to watch two of her neighbours being tortured to gain a confession, setting fire to them before shooting them.[64] Villaplane, who had once made history as the first north African to play for France and captain the team at a World Cup finals, was hunted down, arrested and shot at the Fort de Montrouge in Paris with other prominent members of the *Carlingue*.

In modern French football, across town from Red Star FC in Saint-Ouen is Ménilmontant Football Club 1871. The amateur side was inspired by the Paris Commune of 1871, a breakaway community that refused to recognise the new French Third Republic. The working-class *Communards* seized control briefly and instigated an egalitarian way of living before being crushed by the French military in *la semaine sanglante* (bloody week), which is thought to have cost the lives of 20,000 rebels. Thousands more were deported. In 2014, Ménilmontant Football Club 1871 was founded with an ethos based on equality and rejects prejudice. The club is openly against racism, homophobia and police violence, and encourages people to 'love football, hate fascism'.[65] In the south-east of France, in multicultural Marseille, the Commandos Ultra '84 group of Olympique de Marseille (OM) is the oldest ultra group in France and has long been associated with the political left.

Football resistance in the Netherlands

While Europe fell into conflict around them, the Dutch sought to stay neutral, much as they had during World War I. These efforts proved fruitless, and on 10 May 1940 Nazi troops invaded the Netherlands. The Dutch resisted for five days in the face of heavy aerial bombardment before surrendering to the German invaders. The Royal family fled into exile in England along with the Dutch government. Two lucky escapees were former England international Billy Marsden and his wife. Marsden had spent almost a decade coaching in the Netherlands when the Nazis started landing on the beach near his bungalow. Evading bullets, the Marsdens managed to gather a few possessions – including Marsden's international caps and medals won at Sheffield Wednesday – and boarded a train and boat back to England. Ten years previously, Marsden had featured in England's first match against pre-Nazi Germany in Berlin, and his life had been saved by German doctors after a career-ending neck injury sustained in that game.[66]

Back in the Netherlands, all political parties were banned, with the exception of the Nazi-supporting *Nationaal-Socialistische Beweging* (NSB – National Socialist Movement in the Netherlands). Anti-Jewish laws came into effect, mirroring those in other parts of occupied Europe. Jews were forced to wear the Star of David, take on dangerous work in factories and to build defences. They were exposed not only to the oppression of their Nazi overlords but also Allied bombing raids. In reaction to the anti-Jewish laws and pogroms, the Dutch went on a two-day strike in February 1941. It was quickly suppressed. In 1940, an estimated 140,000 Jews lived in the Netherlands, yet by the time the war ended in 1945, more than three-quarters of Dutch Jews had died in the Holocaust.[67] Some Dutch people even tried to sail the 160km to safety in Britain, including several footballers. These so-called *Engelandvaarders* (England sailors) often ended up drowning, or being arrested or shot, with just a few making it safely across the Channel, where they were interrogated in case they were spies.

Despite the initial shock of the Nazi invasion, Dutch football continued throughout the war, disrupted only in the final year, when the 1944/45 season was cancelled due to the conflict. Participation in football actually rose as the Dutch looked to sport and other entertainment as a distraction from the war. Yet, as in other parts of Nazi-occupied Europe, clubs and associations were pressured to exclude Jewish members, players and officials. This presented a problem as many of the Netherlands referees were Jews. Signs appeared at grounds announcing that Jews were not permitted entry, and Jewish players and coaches faced an uncertain fate. Many ended up at the Westerbork transit camp in the Netherlands before being sent to labour camps around Europe. Hungarian coach Árpad Weisz had already been forced to leave Italy due to antisemitic laws, despite being the youngest coach to win the *Scudetto* with Ambrosiana (Internazionale) and twice with Bologna in the 1930s. Weisz took a position at FC Dordrecht in 1940. A year later, he was banished from the club and in August 1942 he and his family received the dreaded knock on the door in the middle of the night from the Gestapo. Weisz died at the Birkenau camp on 31 January 1944. Similarly, former footballer and radio commentator Hartog 'Han' Hollander, who had been key in popularising the game in the Netherlands during the 1930s, had his contract terminated and, along with his wife, was deported to the Sobibor extermination camp in 1943.

As in France, resistance movements were established straight away, often acting in small groups risking capture and death to disrupt Nazi logistics. Strong sea defences and radar technology made it hard for the Dutch resistance to maintain contact with Britain, which was supplying other resistance movements. As such, Dutch resistance to Nazism mostly took the form of strikes, intelligence gathering and sheltering Jews or Allied airmen who had been shot down over the Netherlands. One former player involved in the passing of intelligence messages was former Sparta Rotterdam outside-right Rein Boomsma. Boomsma had played in the Netherlands' first official internationals in 1905, captaining his country in the second match. He had risen to colonel in the Dutch military and had useful cryptography skills but was arrested by the Gestapo while receiving coded British messages from a Dutch airman. He died at the Neuengamme camp near Hamburg on 27 May 1943, aged 63.

Dutch football historian Jurryt van de Vooren runs the *VoetbalMonument.nl* (Football Monument) website and has collected data on more than 2,600 people involved in Dutch football who fell victim to the Nazis during the five-year occupation of the Netherlands, including 400 players. According to van de Vooren's research, at least 140 footballers were among the estimated 2,300 Dutchmen killed during the Nazi invasion of May 1940. During the early weeks of the war, both the Catholic league clubs – who played in their own division – and the Dutch FA, the KNVB, posted updates on members who had died in the conflict. 'As far as I know, there was no club at all that resisted the demands to ban Jewish members. It was impossible to do so, but there are many stories of bravery from footballers in the Dutch resistance,' van de Vooren tells me. While it was impossible for Dutch clubs to refuse the laws against Jewish members, some clubs did make a stand in other ways. In 1941, at Unitas, one of the Netherlands' oldest clubs based in Gorinchem, members refused to take an NSB figure, former player Arie de Jong, back on to the board as treasurer. Members put up a rival candidate, Teunis Walraven, to board elections, with Walraven defeating de Jong by 61 votes to nine. The NSB pressured the club to install de Jong and ban another member who had supported Walraven's bid. Rather than submit, the club's members chose to close down the organisation altogether in 1942. When a local sporting club made a field available to former Unitas players, the NSB forbade it. On the club's 75th anniversary in 1973, Unitas was awarded the Honorary Medal of Merit in recognition of its wartime resistance.[68]

Hercules from Almelo won the 1940/41 national championship, which was followed by back-to-back titles for ADO Den Haag (The Hague). While many clubs had NSB connections, ADO somehow gained a reputation during the war as an 'NSB club'. This was in part due to the similarity of its triangular crest at the time to the NSB's, and also because one of the club's strikers, Gerrit Vreken, was openly an NSB member.[69] Vreken joined the NSB as a teen and travelled to matches in his uniform and boots, which was an unpopular move even among his team-mates. Opposing fans would attend ADO Den Haag matches featuring Vreken just to jeer them.[70] Fans of Amsterdam-Noord club De Volewijckers even travelled with their team to The Hague just to get into fights with ADO fans. In contrast to ADO Den Haag, De Volewijckers gained a reputation as a club of the resistance. As early as 1935, the board – led by club secretary Karel Corstens and chairman Douwe Wagenaar – lobbied the KNVB and Royal Dutch Athletics Federation (KNAU) to boycott the Berlin Olympics. De Volewijckers had even been invited to the anti-Nazi alternative People's Olympiad in Barcelona scheduled for July 1936, which was cancelled due to the outbreak of the Spanish Civil War. De Volewijckers lost its Mosveld ground to a bombing raid, so decamped to Ajax's De Meer Stadium for much of the war. On 3 August 1943, De Volewijckers swapped its traditional green and white for orange shirts, the Dutch national colour, for a match against VUC from The Hague. Douwe Wagenaar was arrested straight after the match and held for three days.[71] In the 1943/44 season, De Volewijckers dethroned ADO Den Haag as *Landskampioen* (national champion) under the capable coaching of Jaap van der Leck.

Elsewhere, Jewish referee Leo Horn adopted the pseudonym Doctor Van Dongen and joined a resistance group in the south of Amsterdam. The group included Kuki Krol, whose son Ruud (born 1949) would later make his name for Ajax and the Dutch national side, the *Oranje*.[72] Horn was involved in finding safe houses for people and distributing the outlawed publication *Het Parool* (*The Watchword*). Horn also took part in a daring assault on a German ammunition depot, which secured valuable guns, ammunition and grenades for the resistance. He survived the war and even became a camp guard, watching over those he had been fighting against for four years.[73] In 1953, Horn was invited to Wembley to referee England versus Hungary, an encounter that would go down in history as 'The Match of the Century', in which Hungary's 'Mighty Magyars' beat England 6-3.

Outside elite football, the sport remained a vital diversion from the day-to-day of life under Nazi occupation. This was equally the case for people in hiding, some of whom managed to play football in secret despite the very likely threat of arrest, deportation and death if they were caught. In the southern Dutch village of Tungelroy, not far from the Belgian border, the local population had been swelled by around 40 people in hiding by 1943, according to a local resident's diary. Together with those in hiding, the locals played football in a remote wooded area where the Germans would not go. The formation of new football clubs was outlawed at this time, but the club adopted the name *Olympia*, reviving the name of a former club in the village that had been formed in the 1920s. After the liberation in 1945, Olympia changed its name to Crescentia and joined the KNVB.[74] At the time of writing, the club plays in the fifth tier of Dutch football.

During the war, one of the Netherlands' 'Big Three', Ajax, was based in De Meer, an area of Amsterdam that was famous for its Jewish population. For many visiting fans walking through the area to watch their team play Ajax, this was their first exposure to Jewish culture. The club lost one former player during the Holocaust. Eddy Hamel, the former Ajax star who had been born in New York to Dutch Jewish parents, was arrested in a Nazi round-up in 1942. He died at Auschwitz on 30 April 1943. One rising star at Ajax was Jan Wijnbergen from the club's Under-23 side. He was training three times a week but decided to give up football to devote his time to his resistance work, which involved smuggling Jewish children out of Amsterdam across the country to safe houses.[75] Much like Tottenham Hotspur in England, Ajax fans would foster an identity that has existed since before the war as a 'Jewish club' in the face of opposition taunts due to the historic demographic of its original neighbourhood. Ajax fans often refer to *Superjoden* ('Super Jews') in their songs. And, like Tottenham, you will see flags with the Star of David fluttering at stalls near the ground on match days. Rival fans have been known to sing antisemitic songs and make hissing noises to imitate the sound of the gas chambers aimed at Ajax fans. In response, in the mid-1970s, Ajax fan groups began to adopt Jewish symbols as part of their club's identity, much as at Spurs. In recent years, fans of Feyenoord and AZ Alkmaar have been caught on film singing antisemitic songs that refer to Palestinian group Hamas or the SS. Meanwhile, some ADO Den Haag fans daubed a green swastika on a trip to Amsterdam and vandalised the statue of *De Dokwerker* (The Dockworker), which was erected to commemorate the general strike of February 1941 against anti-Jewish laws imposed by the Nazis. ADO Den Haag distanced itself from those fans involved and, in a statement, condemned the vandalism.[76] ADO has taken great steps to detect and counter discriminatory behaviour inside its stadium, including facial recognition and identity checks. Feyenoord and FC Utrecht have also initiated education programmes for fans around racism and antisemitism.[77]

Modern Germany's progressive football culture

One of the most famous anti-fascist football clubs in the world is based in Hamburg's dockland district of St Pauli. The area is world renowned for its party street, the Reeperbahn – the scene of early Beatles gigs and many a stag weekend. It is just a few hundred metres south of the Millerntorstadion, home of FC St Pauli. Here, at the Millerntor, you will see rainbow flags, anti-fascist symbols and FC St Pauli's famous *Totenkopf*, the skull and crossbones like you would find on a pirate's flag. In 2019, the *Totenkopf* was even added to a UK Home Office counter-terror watchlist designed to help police and other officials recognise and identify political symbols, a decision that surprised many.[78] While the club has something of a cult status as a left-wing political club, this is a relatively new identity. The football club was founded in 1910 by members of St Pauli's upper classes and has flitted around the divisions below the German top flight for most of its history. Meanwhile, across the city, Hamburger SV has enjoyed European success and was the longest-running club never to have been relegated from the German Bundesliga until it sank into the second division, 2.Bundesliga, in 2018.

FC St Pauli did not gain the anti-fascist identity that the club and its fans are known across the world for until the late 1970s and '80s, when the fanbase within the stadium began reflecting the society of the surrounding area. Indeed, during the Nazi era in the 1930s and '40s, some players and directors had even been members of the NSDAP. FC St Pauli's ground had for many years been named after one its former presidents and NSDAP member Wilhelm Koch.[79] The stadium was renamed Millerntor in 1998 after one of the historical gates of Hamburg.

Hamburg was almost entirely destroyed by Allied bombers during the summer of 1943. The city was rebuilt but by the late 1970s a long period of economic decline led to many buildings in the St Pauli district being occupied by squatters. During the 1980s, disputes broke out between the squatters and the police. At the same time, the Millerntor was becoming a magnet for football fans disaffected with the experience at Hamburger SV's Volksparkstadion, where certain neo-Nazi groups had made their way on to the terraces.[80] Throughout the 1980s, the Millerntor continued to attract leftist fans and the skull and crossbones flag was first introduced to the terraces. Natxo Parra is the co-author of *St Pauli: Another Football is Possible*. Parra tells me that one of the key catalysts for FC St Pauli's emergence as a 'cult club' was the Viva St Pauli festival in 1991. The festival was held at Millerntor by a campaign group to raise funds for protesters' legal fees and police fines in a squatter dispute.

'The club was not directly involved in FC St Pauli becoming a cult club. There was no political connection at the board level; it was the terraces that led change,' Parra tells me. 'The club allowed the festival to go ahead in the stadium. The festival was a great success – punk and rock bands came from all over Europe to play and the organisers made more money than they needed.' Some of the punks even donated some of the proceeds to one of the churches in the area that had supported their cause. The club has had to strike a delicate balancing act between being a commercial entity and not 'selling out' or abandoning the principles that draw many of its fans. It has run festivals for refugees in Hamburg and also removed adverts for men's magazine *Maxim* from the Millerntor over complaints of the magazine's sexist depiction of women. 'If you talk to people in St Pauli, you will find two different viewpoints,' Parra explains. 'You will find people who say FC St Pauli should refuse commercialism, but you will also find people who understand FC St Pauli is a professional club and want it to continue to fight any form of discrimination, to fight for social values, while also performing on the pitch. This is a big challenge the club has to face. I am sure FC St Pauli will not lose its values.'

The club also marks Holocaust Memorial Day on 27 January. This ethos of inclusiveness and radical left-wing activism meant that FC St Pauli was something of a high-profile outlier for some time, not just in Germany but also within Europe. As such, it has attracted a significant international fanbase and inspired the foundation of fan clubs around the world. Rob Carroll is a founding member of the Yorkshire St Pauli fan group in England. He started following FC St Pauli in the early '90s as a German Studies student in Leeds. 'In Jumbo Records, a great little independent record shop that still exists, I spotted *Millerntor Roar!* amongst all the British football fanzines. I started buying them and found them more interesting to read than my course books,' Carroll tells me. 'At that time, the fans were mobilising against racism and also against the proposed "Sport Dome" redevelopment of the Millerntorstadion into a horrible all-seater complex with shopping mall. I followed the club's fortunes, then in 2001 I found myself changing trains in Hamburg on match day. I left my bag in the station lockers, walked to St Pauli through the sleet, purchased some warm club regalia in the Portakabin that was the club shop, then stood on the old *Nordkurve*, a muddy open terrace, in the driving snow. We beat Chemnitz, with songs in different languages struck up from all corners of the ground. Around me were punks, hippies, alternatives of all types. Everyone was having a beer, a smoke and a good time. Occasionally a waft of something stronger than tobacco floated across the terrace. In the distance, the famous *Gegengerade* [stand] was rammed with fans singing, dancing and celebrating the fact that we exist. We have a place where we can be ourselves. Unapologetically against all forms of racism, sexism and homophobia. I returned a few years later to the partially redeveloped stadium, felt the same feelings. Thirty thousand anti-fascists in one place. I knew I had come home.'

For Carroll, following English football had always been something of a toil, he tells me. 'From the hooliganism and mindless racism in the '80s, to the gentrification of the game into a billionaire's plaything, modern football is pretty rank. It has lost its soul,' he says. 'When you visit the Millerntor you can't avoid being stirred, by the atmosphere, by the fact that the result doesn't matter that much. What matters is that we exist and we have made a difference. In around 2010, I was at a music festival in my hometown, wearing a skull and crossbones St Pauli tee. Across the field, I saw someone else in a brown t-shirt. Our eyes met, we approached each other and had – for two middle-aged men – a pretty coy but sweet chat. We thought we were the only ones in Leeds, following a left-wing football club, mediocre on the field but world class off it. A few months later, work took me to New York. I watched a stream with the East River Pirates – the FCSP New York Fanclub – returned home, then located the UK St Pauli fan forum, asking whether there were any other people in Yorkshire. There were lots of us. We got together, became a community, created a space where we can watch football our way.' Carroll explains that Yorkshire St Pauli arranges tours to the Millerntorstadion and other away days, and streams matches. Yorkshire St Pauli helped inspire the foundation of several other FC St Pauli fan clubs around the UK. Its younger members set up 'Football for All', a social initiative in Leeds that offers free football sessions to some of West Yorkshire's most vulnerable and excluded, including refugees and asylum seekers.

Not far from St Pauli is the district of Altona, where the historic Altona 93 plays in the German regional division, *Regionalliga Nord*. The club is one of the oldest in Germany, established in 1893, and was a founding member of the German Football Association, the DFB. Altona 93 has something of a *gemellaggio* with like-minded south London club Dulwich Hamlet. The two clubs were formed in the same year and first played a friendly match back in Easter 1925. The Londoners won 4-1 as part of a tour of Germany that also included games in Gelsenkirchen and Düsseldorf. The match remained largely forgotten until a chance encounter between a Dulwich Hamlet fan and an Altona supporter led to a rekindling of the friendship. There have been friendly rematches since – at Dulwich in 2015 and at Altona in 2018 – as well as a number of supporters' games, and the link between the two clubs remains strong today. Michael Wagg is a writer and fan of both Dulwich Hamlet and Altona 93, and he has co-authored a novel inspired by the club friendship. 'I think there's a shared common value in relation to inclusivity – as a very active stance,' Wagg explains. 'I'm sure it's true for other clubs and other club friendships, and who knows what it is that keeps this particular bond so strong, but I sense a common spirit that fans from both sides celebrate: around fairness and openness; in reaching out to their communities and encouraging a sense of belonging; in tackling prejudice, and redressing the idea of what modern football can stand for; and in not taking the game too seriously! In my experience, this shared spirit is witty, welcoming, and left field.'

Jan Stöver edits a fanzine at Altona 93. Stöver explains that Altona 93 is a popular choice both for people from within Hamburg and it also attracts fans from across Germany and beyond. 'We like to think that we welcome all people to our matches as long as they are interested in the football and respect the ethical values we share at the Adolf-Jäger-Kampfbahn,' he tells me. Stöver explains that Altona 93's fanbase has no tight structures and aims to be as inclusive as possible. 'For example, we wouldn't be so keen on a *capo*, a drum or permanent clapping for organising our chants. Everyone should be free to start (and stop) a song whenever they like to do so.' Altona 93 fans have invited locally housed asylum seekers into the ground and collected clothes for them in the winter, as well as providing clothes for local people struggling with drug addiction.

Altona 93 fans organised an anti-racist fan football tournament called the *Cup der Angst – gegen die Festung Europa* (The Fear Trophy – Against Fortress Europe). It helped raise money for anti-racist initiatives and to support migrants in the area. 'By chance, the *Cup der Angst* was the first occasion the Tennis Borussia supporters presented their *Fußballfans gegen Homophobie* (Football fans against homophobia) flag outside Berlin,' Stöver adds. Dulwich Hamlet gifted Altona 93 with an anti-homophobia flag too, which has been flown to demonstrate that the LGBTQ+ community is always welcome at Altona. Altona fans have also shown solidarity for fans at other clubs that have had to deal with unwanted attention from supporters of right-wing groups. 'For fifteen years, our fanzines have informed football supporters about history and social issues,' Stöver adds. Altona 93 fan stickers include messages such as '*Gegen Rechts*' (Against the Right Wing) and 'Kick Fascism'. Fans have also got involved in supporting International Women's Day and are connected with other progressive fans across Germany. Another example of Altona 93's inclusive ethos is its support for *On The Ball*, an initiative that encourages football clubs to provide free women's hygiene products at their grounds. 'Altona 93 fans are becoming ever more organised in making sure we're as inclusive as possible,' Stöver concludes. 'We've seen more people volunteer to get involved with our social media and merchandising, and they're helping to spread our ethical values in the name of the club.'

Anti-fascism in former East Germany

Modern Berlin is one of the most vibrant and progressive cities in Europe. Yet the German capital sits in the heart of the former *Deutsche Demokratische Republik* (DDR/GDR – German Democratic Republic), East Germany. When the Berlin Wall fell in November 1989, many East Germans had been looking forward to freedom away from the institutions of the GDR, which had become an acute surveillance state. However, reunification with West Germany came at a long-term price for the regions of the former GDR. Many eastern companies and properties were privatised and sold off, the vast majority going to wealthier buyers from the west. The western regions also continued to attract the most investment and skilled labour, which led many from the east to head west for greater opportunities. There is still a huge gap in wealth between eastern and western Germany, even more than three decades after reunification. Political parties had been banned in the GDR era and there had been little inward migration to create a visibly ethnically diverse population, as had happened in the former West Germany. As early as September 1991 – less than a year after reunification – riots fuelled by neo-Nazis were recorded in the former East Germany when asylum seekers and workers from Vietnam and Mozambique were targeted, and hate attacks are much higher in the east of Germany than in the west.[81] Far-right and anti-migrant parties emerged and in recent years have performed better in the regions of the former East Germany than the west.

Football can become a forum for encounters between the new far right in the former GDR and anti-fascist fans. This was certainly the case in the spring of 2017 when far-right fans of Energie Cottbus visited SV Babelsberg 03. Babelsberg, near Potsdam, 35km south-west of Berlin, is most famous for its film studios. Here, Fritz Lang's influential 1927 sci-fi movie *Metropolis* was filmed, along with Nazi propaganda films during the Third Reich, and later Babelsberg became part of the GDR during the Cold War. It continues to be the site of one of Europe's largest and most influential film studios. Fans of Babelsberg's football club are well known to be progressive and left-leaning and, as part of the former GDR, have longer-standing rivalries with other former GDR clubs. Energie Cottbus, conversely, has elements among its fanbase that have long been associated with the far right. The club faced a growing challenge from a far-right presence in the stands even while on the pitch the team was performing better than most post-GDR teams in the unified Germany. It made it to the *DFB-Pokal* final in 1997 and spent three seasons in the Bundesliga at the start of the 21st century. However, the club – like the coal industry on which the town depended – slid into decline.

On 28 April 2017, a match between Energie and Babelsberg – meeting for the first time in more than two decades – descended into what is now known as the *Skandalspiel* (Scandal Game). Just 15 minutes into the *Regionalliga Nordost* match in the fourth tier of Germany's football pyramid, some visiting Cottbus supporters threw missiles on to the pitch. Chants of '*Arbeit Macht Frei*' (work makes you free), the slogan of the Nazi death camps, were heard coming from sections of the visiting support. Nazi salutes – illegal in Germany – were also reported. 'Ticks, Gypsies and Jews' was another chant among the 400 or so visiting Cottbus fans and a Celtic cross was sprayed on a wall in the town by visiting fans, also an offence in German law. The Friday night game had been deemed high-risk in advance and there was a heavy police presence. Play was stopped twice, and ten Cottbus fans were arrested for suspected bodily harm and breach of the peace.[82] Both clubs were fined by the region's football association (NOFV) as a result. However, Babelsberg refused to pay, which led to the NOFV beginning proceedings to eject the club from the league. The DFB interjected, and a compromise was agreed. Babelsberg would pay half its €7,000 fine, with the money going towards the funding of anti-discrimination projects.[83]

Energie Cottbus and many of its fans have been keen to reclaim their club from the far-right minority, and the club itself launched its *Energie Für Vielfalt und Toleranz* (Energie for Diversity and Tolerance) initiative as early as January 2015.[84] As a key club in the German region of Brandenburg, the club works with anti-racism organisations and schools to promote tolerance. The April 2017 incident at Babelsberg also inspired the formation of *Energiefans gegen Nazis* (Energie Fans Against Nazis) to represent normal fans who were also appalled by the actions of the neo-Nazi minority who follow the club. Its flag depicts the club crest smashing through a swastika. *Energiefans gegen Nazis* has a growing following on social media, and one of its aims is to change the perception of the fanbase. When Energie Cottbus returned to play Babelsberg in the 2018/19 season, *Energiefans gegen Nazis* displayed their flag for the first time. Reportedly, it was torn down twice.[85]

Back in Babelsberg, striker Daniel Frahn re-joined the club from Chemnitzer FC in early 2020, but large sections of the Babelsberg fan base were unhappy with the signing. The previous March while at Chemnitzer FC, Frahn had celebrated a goal against VSG Altglienicke by holding up a t-shirt that read '*Support Your Local Hools*', a reference to the Chemnitz HooNaRa (short for Hooligans, Nazis, Racists) group. The t-shirts had been sold as a fundraiser for the cancer treatment of HooNaRa founder Thomas Haller. Frahn later apologised.[86] However, a few months later, Chemnitzer FC sacked the

32-year-old former RB Leipzig captain. Frahn had been sidelined through injury for a match but rather than watch the game with his team-mates on the bench, he reportedly chose to sit with known far-right hooligans in the stands. At a time of rising tension and far-right violence in Chemnitz, the club said it felt it needed to make a stand against right-wing extremism.[87]

In Leipzig, Saxony, where the DFB was founded in 1900, another left-right chasm has emerged. While the city's most prominent team RB Leipzig has enjoyed a meteoric rise to the upper echelons of the Bundesliga and regular European football, thanks to huge investment, Leipzig's two other senior clubs have struggled. 1.FC Lokomotive Leipzig has a long history. It was founded as VfB Leipzig in 1893, was a founding member of the DFB in 1900 and won the first all-German national championship in 1903. The club re-emerged some time after World War II as the railway workers' team in the GDR era. After a decade or so named as VfB Leipzig, the club is now back as 1.FC Lokomotive – or 'Lok'. Across town, its bitter rival is Betriebssportgemeinschaft (BSG) Chemie Leipzig, the former chemical works team in the GDR era. While the railway team enjoyed the benefits of the East German state drafting in its best players – Lok finished runner-up in the 1987 European Cup Winners' Cup Final to Ajax, losing to a Marco Van Basten goal – Chemie represented the 'rest of Leipzig'.[88] Since German reunification, Lok has attracted a sizeable right-wing element who are on friendly terms with BFC Dynamo and Halleschen FC, among others. Meanwhile, Chemie has attracted a left-wing base and the club itself expects its fans to 'stand for non-violence and anti-racism'.[89]

Football in the GDR had been political to some extent, with clubs being representative of various state departments. However, in the post-unification era, it was not until the 21st century that left-versus-right politics began to enter the encounters between

Lok and Chemie. In 2002, Lok fans displayed a banner that read, 'Rudolf Hess, on the right wing for Lok' – Hess was deputy leader in Adolf Hitler's Nazi Party. In 2006, a group of Lok fans formed a human swastika in the stands at a youth match and have also used Anne Frank's imagery and the term 'Jew' intended to insult Chemie fans.[90] Violence has erupted at encounters between the two sides and in November 2017 far-right insults from Lok fans were audible on live TV. In 2018, two Lok youth coaches were sacked by the club after they had gathered a group of youth players together to perform a Nazi salute for a photo.[91] The club was swift to react, and it also stands against all forms of discrimination.[92]

Progressive, inclusive clubs in the former GDR, such as Babelsberg and Chemie Leipzig, are not outliers. In 1999, Roter Stern Leipzig (Red Star Leipzig) was formed with an anti-fascist ethos and attracts left-leaning fans in the city to its lower league matches. In cosmopolitan Berlin, in the multicultural district of Kreuzberg, FSV Hansa 07 has been running a football project for refugees called *Champions Ohne Grenzen* (Champions Without Borders) since 2012. Similarly, in the west of the city, Tennis Borussia, or 'TeBe', has gained a reputation for its inclusiveness, its anti-racism and anti-homophobia stance, and its support for migrants. 'Here, we say everyone can have their first love, but their second love should be TeBe,' Franzi Hoffmann from the club's board tells me. The multi-sports club was founded in 1902 and, at the time of writing, the men's football branch plays in Germany's fifth tier. In the early 1930s, TeBe lost almost a third of its members due to antisemitic Nazi laws forcing Jews out of the club. Conscious of its history, the club created a whole new constitution in 2001, which Hoffmann explains was to define TeBe not just solely as a football club, but also a club against homophobia, antisemitism, and to create a welcoming and inclusive environment for all. TeBe has been active in collecting money for refugees, for example, and organised free tickets for Syrians to attend the club's matches as well as flying its anti-homophobia flag. 'Even though Berlin is a multicultural place, many left-wing people found their place here at TeBe,' she says. 'West Berlin was always an island [in the GDR], it was always democratic. I came from the groundhopping scene and when I visited TeBe, it was the first time ever that I really felt part of a football club. And I didn't just want to watch football, I wanted to be part of it.' At the time of our interview, Hoffmann is one of just a few women in senior positions in German football. Others being, as you might expect, at FC St Pauli and SV Babelsberg 03.

So, has being a progressive club in Eastern Germany presented any problems for TeBe? 'Yeah, you sometimes get high-risk games,' Hoffmann continues. She recalls a period in the early 2000s, when anti-TeBe graffiti and threats were made against the club, and how fans would welcome them with throat-slitting hand gestures. 'We are probably an easy target,' Hoffmann says. In 2021, in place of a sponsor, TeBe wanted to display the name of a charity for victims of right-wing violence. The regional FA objected, arguing that such advertising would constitute a political statement, which is against its rules.[93] TeBe received support from fellow Berliners FC Internationale Berlin 1980, which had displayed the message 'No Racism' on its shirts for years.

Up in Rostock on the north coast, Internationaler FC (IFC) Rostock was formed in 2015, based on a previous incarnation of the club that existed until 1945. It describes itself as a 'left-wing, grassroots-democratic football club' and does not tolerate 'any glorification of National Socialism, its rhetoric and symbolism in our club, among our members on our home ground,' the club says.[94]

Clubs across Germany have taken steps to combat discrimination from the stands. German terms such as *Gegen*

Rechts (Against the Right Wing) and *Nazis Raus* (Nazis Out) now appear in left-leaning stands across the world. Football club ownership in Germany is very different from elsewhere with its 50+1 rule that ensures that club members always have the majority say in the running of the club. Some German clubs have football liaison officers and fan coaches to drive awareness of issues such as racism and antisemitism on the terraces. In December 2017, Eintracht Frankfurt, one of the early victims of Nazi race laws in the 1930s, announced that supporters of the far-right were not welcome at the club.[95] Werder Bremen has won awards for its work in the community, including social education and coherence projects, and tackling racism.[96] In Leer, near the Dutch border, Borussia Leer also believes that 'another football is possible'. The club has a clear socio-political position, creating an open, welcoming environment for all. Borussia Leer is 'against racism, nationalism, homophobia, sexism, discrimination and right-wing hate speech'.[97] Club members are involved in voluntary initiatives, and the club's structure is open and democratic.

In the Ruhr, *Fan-Projekt Dortmund*'s 'Kick Racism Out' campaign at Borussia Dortmund celebrated its 25th anniversary in 2021, making it one of the longest-running anti-racism campaigns in Europe. BVB had a particular challenge in the 1980s and '90s, with certain elements of its fanbase affiliated to the far right active and vocal on the terraces of the Westfalenstadion. One such element was the *Borussenfront* ultra group, headed by right-wing extremist Sirgfried Borchardt, who also went by the name 'SS-Siggi'. The spectre of right-wing fans has bubbled up repeatedly over the years in the BVB fan scene, mainly with an anti-immigrant agenda, according to Benjamin McFadyean, a regular at Westfalenstadion since the 1980s who also runs the Borussia Dortmund London Fan Club. 'Germany still struggles to integrate its immigrant population to this day to some extent, which is partly to do with the German language, which is notoriously difficult to learn; as anyone who has tried to learn it like me has found, it is not easy,' he tells me. 'Partly, it is also to do with the fact that refugees are not allowed to work whilst their status is being decided, which means that they have difficulty, having little money and little prospects.' McFadyean explains that this challenge can lead to disenfranchisement, misunderstandings and even conflict with local people, as has occurred over the years. The most extreme example occurred in Hoyerswerda in the former GDR in 1991, when immigrant hostels were attacked and even had petrol bombs thrown at them, thankfully without loss of life. There have been cases of conflict in parts of Germany where integration is particularly difficult for immigrants, although one notable exception is the Turkish population, which has been in Germany since the 1950s as *Gastarbeiter* (guest workers) to service then-West Germany's booming post-war economy and has assimilated well. 'BVB has worked tirelessly, including through *Fan-Projekt Dortmund* – a group of social workers independent of the club who act as a support mechanism for fans in Dortmund – and also to educate on issues like antisemitism and xenophobia, and to contain or work to turn around hate and acts of aggression,' McFadyean tells me. In 2017, BVB even released an anti-Nazi video on social media to spread the message that 'football and Nazis just don't go together' in response to the rise of anti-immigration parties in German elections.[98]

Even at an international level, German football plays a role in progressive politics. In June 2021, in response to a Hungarian ban on LGBTQ+ content in education or TV shows for under-18s, the mayor of Munich requested that Bayern's stadium be lit up in rainbow colours ahead of Germany's match there with Hungary at the European Championships. UEFA denied the request, deeming it political, but goalkeeper-captain Manuel Neuer was allowed to wear his rainbow armband. In response, a long list of

German clubs and media outlets displayed the rainbow flag in support of Munich. A protester managed to run on to the pitch and past the Hungarian team holding a rainbow flag.

Back in Hungary, Viktor Orbán declined to travel to the match. Given its stage and global audience, football once again found itself as the platform for a European culture war deep into the 21st century. Due to racist and homophobic activity by its fans during the delayed Euro 2020 championships, UEFA punished Hungary with a €100,000 fine and forced the country to play three UEFA competition matches behind closed doors. When England visited for a FIFA World Cup match in September 2021, the ultras roundly booed as the multicultural England team took the knee and racist abuse was aimed at England's black players.[99] In the return fixture at Wembley the following month, Hungarian fans displayed a banner against taking the knee and scuffles broke out with police after reports that a steward had been racially abused by a visiting supporter.[100]

While many German football clubs and authorities are highly active in tackling far-right elements, this remains a challenge for the sport in Hungary and many other countries of the former Soviet Bloc.

1 Goldblatt, David, *The Ball is Round: A Global History of Football* (London: Penguin, 2007, loc.5533/20696)

2 http://juedische-sportstars.de/index.php?id=187&L=2 (retrieved 21/02/2021)

3 https://kfv.letsdev.de/epoche-1933-1945/ (retrieved 21/03/2022)

4 http://juedische-sportstars.de/index.php?id=191&L=2 (retrieved 21/02/2021)

5 *Belfast News-Letter,* 8 January 1934 (p7)

6 https://fcbayern.com/us/club/fcb-club/kurt-landauer (retrieved 20/02/2021)

7 https://www.theguardian.com/football/2012/may/12/bayern-munich-anti-nazi-history (retrieved 17/06/21)

8 https://historisch.eintracht.de/events/8090 (retrieved 21/02/2021)

9 https://www.spvggunterhaching.de/verein/chronik/chronik-2/ (retrieved 14/03/2021)

10 https://www.schwatzgelb.de/artikel/2019/report/der-bvb-in-der-ns-zeit-eine-spurensuche (retrieved 02/11/21)

11 *Belfast Telegraph*, 1 April 1933 (p4)

12 https://olympics.com/en/athletes/werner-seelenbinder (retrieved 16/01/22)

13 *Western Daily Press*, 20 June 1933 (p12)

14 *Yorkshire Post and Leeds Intelligencer*, 10 September 1935 (p16)

15 *Daily Mirror*, 19 October 1935 (p3)

16 *Western Mail*, 17 October 1935 (p6)

17 *Ibid*

18 *Londonderry Sentinel*, 5 December 1935 (p5)

19 *Nottingham Evening Post*, 3 December 1935 (p8)

20 *Daily Mirror*, 5 December 1935 (p2)

21 *Ibid*

22 *Aberdeen Press & Journal*, 6 December 1935 (p4)

23 *Northern Whig*, 6 December 1935 (p10)

24 *Hartlepool Northern Daily Mail*, 1 October 1936 (p7)

25 *Western Mail*, 15 October 1936 (p4)

26 *Daily Herald*, 22 August 1938 (p9)

27 Hesse, Ulrich, *Tor! The Story of German Football* (London: WSC Books, 2003, p57)

28 Simpson, Kevin. E., *Soccer Under the Swastika: Defiance and Survival in the Nazi Camps and Ghettos* (London: Rowman & Littlefield, revised edition, 2020, loc.984/5410)

29 Simpson, Kevin. E., *Soccer Under the Swastika: Defiance and Survival in the Nazi Camps and Ghettos* (London: Rowman & Littlefield, revised edition, 2020, loc.287/5410)

30 Hesse, Ulrich, *Tor! The Story of German Football* (London: WSC Books, 2003, p62)

31 https://thesefootballtimes.co/2020/06/02/how-austrias-wunderteam-defied-the-nazis-for-one-last-act-of-greatness/ (retrieved 24/10/21)

32 *Ibid*

33 http://www.rsssf.com/miscellaneous/oostduit-recintlp.html (retrieved 24/10/21)

34 *Hall Vier*, Issue 7, August 2021 (p63)

35 https://www.historyworkshop.org.uk/aston-villa-the-offside-trap-and-the-nazi-salute/ (retrieved 07/03/21)

36 https://www.expressandstar.com/sport/football/wolverhampton-wanderers-fc/2016/10/25/wolves-legend-stan-cullis-remembered-the-early-years/ (retrieved 05/03/21)

37 Interview with author

38 *Yorkshire Post and Leeds Intelligencer*, 28 May 1938 (p23)

39 *Reynolds's Newspaper*, 22 May 1938 (p16)

40 *Daily Mirror*, 31 May 1938 (p27)

41 Bohemians FC official match day programme, 8 August 1981 (p14)

42 https://www.nationalgeographic.fr/histoire/2020/06/le-football-

instrument-de-propagande-et-de-resistance-pendant-la-seconde-guerre (retrieved 04/05/21)

43 *Halb Vier* Issue 6, (p13)

44 https://beyondthelastman.com/2019/11/06/a-game-of-survival-in-the-terezin-league/ (retrieved 15/05/21)

45 https://footballpink.net/2019-1-21-a-game-of-survival-in-the-terezin-league/ (retrieved 15/05/21)

46 https://beyondthelastman.com/2019/11/06/a-game-of-survival-in-the-terezin-league/ (retrieved 18/08/21)

47 http://www.holocaustresearchproject.org/revolt/gerron.html (retrieved 24/10/21)

48 *Bradford Observer*, 27 October 1941 (p4)

49 https://www.theguardian.com/football/2015/jan/22/erno-erbstein-hungary-holocaust-torino-superga (retrieved 08/07/21)

50 https://www.worldsoccer.com/blogs/bela-guttmann-curse-benfica-351924 (retrieved 09/07/21)

51 https://mazsihisz.hu/hirek-a-zsido-vilagbol/mazsihisz-hirek/a-fradi-hose-a-nemzeti-ellenallas-martirja (retrieved 09/05/21)

52 https://www.asroma.com/en/news/2019/1/holocaust-memorial-day-remembering-geza-kertesz-roma-coach-and-war-hero (retrieved 09/05/21)

53 https://www.theguardian.com/football/blog/2019/may/06/remembering-the-cream-of-jewish-footballing-talent-killed-in-the-holocaust (retrieved 09/07/21)

54 *Derry Journal*, 24 November 1939 (p5)

55 http://www.kladenskeosobnosti.cz/62-frantisek-kloz.html (retrieved 19/08/21)

56 http://www.bbc.co.uk/history/worldwars/genocide/jewish_deportation_01.shtml (retrieved 08/05/21)

57 https://www.nationalgeographic.fr/histoire/2020/06/le-football-instrument-de-propagande-et-de-resistance-pendant-la-seconde-guerre (retrieved 07/05/21)

58 https://www.france24.com/en/20150911-red-star-football-club-paris-saint-ouen-hollande-suburbs-immigration-psg (retrieved 08/05/21)

59 https://www.panenka.org/tiempoextra/una-estrella-roja-tercer-reich/ (retrieved 07/05/21)

60 https://www.futbolistamag.com/post/red-star-paris-football-for-all (retrieved 07/05/21)

61 http://dictionnaire.sensagent.leparisien.fr/L%C3%A9on%20Rossi/fr-fr/ (retrieved 08/05/21)

62 https://www.archyde.com/etienne-mattler-intractable-defender-of-sochaux-the-blues-and-the-fatherland/ (retrieved 08/05/21)

63 https://www.estrepublicain.fr/edition-belfort-hericourt-montbeliard/2020/03/04/foot-et-resistance-l-indomptable-etienne-mattler (retrieved 08/05/21)

64 https://www.theguardian.com/sport/blog/2009/nov/16/france (retrieved 29/05/21)

65 https://www.facebook.com/MenilFC/ (retrieved 20/10/21)

66 *Lincolnshire Echo*, 16 May 1940 (p1)

67 https://www.yadvashem.org/righteous/stories/netherlands-historical-background.html (retrieved 11/06/21)

68 https://www.gvvunitas.nl/538/geschiedenis/ (retrieved 11/06/21)

69 https://www.omroepwest.nl/nieuws/3627826/ADO-een-NSB-club-Onzin-Iemand-verzint-wat-en-iedereen-lult-elkaar-na (retrieved 11/06/21)

70 Simpson, Kevin. E., *Soccer Under the Swastika: Defiance and Survival in the Nazi Camps and Ghettos* (London: Rowman & Littlefield, 2020, revised edition, loc. 2701/5410)

71 https://beeldarchief.hcan.nl/de_volewijckers/atlas-van-een-bezette-stad-amsterdam-1940-1945/ (retrieved 11/06/21)

72 https://footballmakeshistory.eu/referee-in-the-resistance/ (retrieved 10/07/21)

73 https://www.joodsamsterdam.nl/leo-horn/ (retrieved 10/07/21)

74 https://sportgeschiedenis.nl/sporten/voetbal/unieke-foto-uit-de-tweede-wereldoorlog-voetballende-onderduikers-in-limburg/ (retrieved 11/06/21)

75 https://www.nd.nl/nieuws/nederland/736434/inzet-voor-verzet-belangrijker-dan-ajax (retrieved 11/06/21)

76 https://adodenhaag.nl/nl/nieuws/laatste-nieuws/overig/7602-ado-den-haag-keurt-gebeurtenissen-in-amsterdam-af (11/06/21)

77 https://changingthechants.eu/wp-content/uploads/2021/05/compendium5-8.pdf (retrieved 22/07/21)

78 https://www.heraldscotland.com/news/18246611.glasgow-st-pauli-football-fan-group-challenges-home-office-counter-terror-watchlist/ (retrieved 05/06/21)

79 Viñas, Carles and Parra, Natxo, *St. Pauli: Another Football is Possible* (London: Pluto Press, 2020, p31)

80 *Ibid*, p86

81 https://www.aljazeera.com/opinions/2018/9/29/how-east-germany-became-a-stronghold-of-the-far-right/ (retrieved 21/08/21)

82 https://m.tagesspiegel.de/berlin/potsdam-rechte-randale-bei-derby-in-babelsberg/19736920.html (retrieved 16/07/21)

83 https://thesetpieces.com/latest-posts/how-a-fourth-tier-club-are-leading-the-fight-against-racism-in-german-football (Retrieved 21/08/21)

84 http://www.fcenergie.de/vielfalt-und-toleranz.html (retrieved 16/07/21)

85 *Halb Vier*, Issue 3, August 2020 (p66)

86 https://www.sportbuzzer.de/artikel/frahn-entschuldigt-sich-fur-jubel-mit-neonazi-shirt-in-chemnitz/ (retrieved 16/07/21)

87 https://www.theguardian.com/football/2019/aug/05/chemnitzer-fc-sack-captain-for-openly-displaying-sympathy-for-neo-nazi-groups (retrieved 21/07/21)

88 https://www.spiegel.de/sport/fussball/lokomotive-leipzig-vs-chemie-leipzig-tradition-im-schatten-a-1179353.html (retrieved 20/07/21)

89 https://www.chemie-leipzig.de/verein/vereinsleitbild/ (retrieved 20/07/21)

90 https://www.thenation.com/article/archive/berlin-wall-germany-soccer/ (retrieved 20/07/21)

91 https://www.dw.com/en/lok-leipzig-youth-coaches-sacked-for-nazi-salute-photo/a-43672762 (retrieved 20/07/21)

92 https://www.lok-leipzig.com/verein/leitbild/ (retrieved 20/07/21)

93 https://www.kicker.de/trikot-streit-um-tebe-solidarische-selbstanzeige-des-fc-inter-berlin-869177/artikel.amp (retrieved 22/09/21)

94 https://www.ifc-rostock.de/index.php/der-verein/ueber-uns (retrieved 21/08/21)

95 https://www.fr.de/zukunft/storys/75-lektionen-mut/eintracht-frankfurts-praesident-peter-fischer-steht-auf-wenn-es-rechts-aussen-stuermt-90080377.html (retrieved 22/07/21)

96 https://www.efdn.org/blog/news/werder-bremen-wins-uefa-grassroots-award/ (retrieved 15/11/21)

97 https://www.borussialeer.de/selbstverst%C3%A4ndnis/ (retrieved 25/07/21)

98 https://www.irishnews.com/magazine/daily/2017/09/25/news/borussia-dortmund-s-anti-nazi-video-is-an-absolute-must-watch-1145437/ (retrieved 02/11/21)

99 https://www.telegraph.co.uk/football/2021/09/02/hungary-vs-england-world-cup-qualifier-live-score-latest-updates/ (retrieved 11/09/21)

100 https://www.theguardian.com/football/2021/oct/12/hungary-supporters-fight-with-police-inside-wembley (retrieved 19/10/21)

Chapter 4

Eastern Europe and the Balkans

THIS BOOK opens with the story of the 'Death Match' in Kyiv between FC Start and the Nazi *Flakelf* team in August 1942. It is possibly the most famous and lionised account of football against fascism. Yet, the match pitting the oppressed against the oppressor was just one of many such encounters during World War II; games even took place in labour camps. After the defeat of Nazism in 1945, the countries of Eastern Europe found themselves under the authority of another oppressive foreign regime – Soviet communism run from Moscow. Soviet influence would last four and a half decades until the fall of the Berlin Wall in 1989. During the communist era, football culture was overhauled to fit the Soviet ethos. Football clubs often became associated with workplaces. *Dinamo* or *Dynamo* was the team of the police. *CSKA* was the army team, while some were even more specific, such as railway sides *Lokomotiv*, or *Torpedo* from the automotive sector. Following the fall of communism, democracy has flourished in some parts of the former Communist Bloc and faltered elsewhere. Far-right politics has surfaced with economic uncertainty and a general lack of diversity in those countries and has often manifested in the stands. In 2019, England's black players were subjected to racist chanting and Nazi salutes in a Euro 2020 qualifying match in Sofia, Bulgaria, which caused officials to stop play twice. It was just one of a long line of incidents in Eastern European football, where Nazi symbols are not uncommon. 'In Eastern Europe, many countries just don't have laws or enforcement of laws around far-right symbols,' Cas Mudde tells me.

Michael Cole is an Early Stage Researcher on the FATIGUE Project, based at the University of Tartu, Estonia, and a doctoral fellow at the Centre for the Analysis of the Radical Right. His research interests include the relationship between football and far-right politics in Central and Eastern Europe, and the use of football as a political tool by right-wing populist leaders. 'One of the common threads that I've noticed in the countries that have emerged from communism is that it's really important for them to deal with pretty big questions regarding national identity and how that's defined and expressed, both in terms of who these nations *are* and also who they're *not*, even 30 years after independence,' Cole tells me. 'For example, in places like Poland, we see discussions around what constitutes a truly patriotic Pole; in the process of negotiating this, some of the symbols, ideas and slogans which have been adopted and used to say, "Look, this is who we are" have fostered a stronger sense of who is outside of that, who is not part of that. It's perhaps this way of seeing the world as a group of "us" on one side, and a group of "them" on the other, that seems to sit well with radical and extreme politics, particularly on the right.'

Football against fascism in Poland

Despite the prior annexations of Austria and Czechoslovakia by the Nazis, it was the invasion of Poland on 1 September 1939 that finally sparked World War II. Under the premise that it was reclaiming lost territory and protecting the German population held within it, the German military advanced into Poland from the west, overpowering the inadequate Polish defences with its advanced mechanised forces from land, sea and air. Britain and

France declared war on Germany in response on 3 September. The USSR, which had signed the Molotov-Ribbentrop pact of non-aggression with Germany just days previously, invaded from the east on 17 September. Poland was overrun and surrendered officially on 27 September. One of many footballers called to fight for Poland was former ŁKS Łódź and national team defender, Antoni Gałecki. Gałecki had been held in a POW camp in Hungary but escaped to fight again in the Allied north African and Italian campaigns before returning to Łódź after the war. Poland remained controlled by its ideologically opposed neighbours until, in June 1941, Nazi Germany turned on the USSR and invaded it, taking full control of Poland until early 1945. To the east, Adam Kogut, who had appeared for a number of Kraków clubs and won a cap for Poland, together with former Czarni Lwów player Tadeusz Kowalski and Marian Spoida, who had played for Warta Poznań and the Polish national side, were among thousands killed after being captured by the Soviets in the spring of 1940.[1]

During its six-year occupation, Poland was the only country under Nazi control where organised sports – including football – were banned. 'Football, in particular, had become so engrained into Polish culture and society, and intertwined with patriotism and nationalism, that the occupiers offered strict punishment to those found flouting the rules,' explains Ryan Hubbard, author of *From Partition to Solidarity, the First Hundred Years of Polish Football*.[2] Polish football had been on the up before the German invasion. Poland had eliminated Great Britain's amateurs *en route* to fourth place at the 1936 Olympic football tournament. Two years later, at the 1938 FIFA World Cup, the Poles had pushed Brazil to extra time in their first-round elimination, eventually succumbing 6-5. In the new reality of Nazi occupation, Polish football grounds were often used by the Nazis for munitions storage and logistics, as was the case at both main Kraków clubs, Wisła and Cracovia. Fellow Kraków club Garbarnia, Polish champions in 1931, saw its main stands demolished by the Nazis. In the meantime, football was forced underground. According to Hubbard, football took on a new identity as a form of rebellion and defiance. Games were arranged clandestinely, often attracting crowds of hundreds, with spotters placed around to keep an eye out for occupying forces. In May 1940, the first *Okupacyjne Mistrzostwa* (Championship of Occupied Kraków) was held in secret at Park Juvenia, a public space on the edge of the city. It featured eight clubs – Wisła Kraków, Cracovia, Garbarnia, Bloki, Sparta, Juvenia Kraków, Groble and Zwierzyniecki. There appears to be some inconsistency around German knowledge of the games at Juvenia. While there might have been some knowledge of matches taking place, officially, they should not have been.

The first round of matches featured what is still Kraków's longest-running rivalry, Wisła versus Cracovia. The derby is known to this day as the *Święta Wojna* (Holy War). The origins of this terminology appear to stem from describing the rivalry between two Jewish-founded clubs, Makabbi and Jutrzenka – Kraków had a sizeable Jewish community before World War II. When a Jutrzenka player joined Cracovia, another club with Jewish roots, he reportedly told his new team-mates ahead of a match against Wisła, 'Let's win this holy war', and the name stuck.[3] The Holy War derby was due to take place on 2 September 1939, but was cancelled due to the German invasion the day before. The two teams finally met on 5 May 1940, with Wisła running out 3-0 victors. Wisła won the first Championship of Occupied Kraków tournament in 1940 with seven straight wins, defending their title the following year. The club had lost defender Władysław Szumilas in 1941, accused by the Nazis of resistance activity. He became prisoner no.25538 at the Auschwitz death camp near Kraków and was shot dead. Similarly, Wisła winger

Antoni Łyko was incarcerated at Auschwitz as prisoner no.11780 for alleged links with the Polish resistance, which carried out sabotages in the area. Łyko had travelled with the Polish national side to the 1938 World Cup in France. On 2 June 1941, he was picked to play a match against a Nazi team at the camp, in which he appears to have performed well. The following night, he was in a party of 80 from Polish high society that the Nazis executed, and died barefoot with his hands bound.[4] The championship was put on hold in 1942 when Park Juvenia was closed, and Nazi crackdowns intensified. Competitive football returned in 1943 with 22 participants split into three groups, with a final round for the top two in each league. Again, the championship came down to Wisła versus Cracovia, with the decider descending into violence involving both players and spectators after a controversial penalty was awarded against Wisła. The SS, whose Kraków headquarters were nearby, became aware of the disturbance, but the local commander Hans Mitschke apparently dismissed the violence. 'Football fans are the same everywhere – let them fight,' he is reported to have said.[5]

Meanwhile, in the capital Warsaw, a clandestine football league was also up and running in the spring of 1940 at Mokotów Park, near the city centre. The organiser was former Legia Warsaw and Poland striker Józef Ciszewski and featured four clubs, including three created from the Polonia club. Ciszewski's team, Błysk, made up largely of university students, would also go on to field actors, journalists and even the vice-president of the Polish FA.[6] By September that year, Polonia hosted a 13-team tournament.[7] Legia had lost a player – Leonard Kowalski – to a Nazi bullet at Okęcie on the southern outskirts of Warsaw as early as September 1939. Anyone caught visiting his grave was threatened with arrest.[8] News of the clandestine matches spread by word of mouth and attendances at wartime games in and around Warsaw even topped a thousand. As in Kraków, club grounds had often been commandeered by the Nazis. It was safer to host matches in more remote playing fields, where Poles could avoid detection and have a better chance of escape in case of a raid. Mokotów Park itself was subject to a Nazi raid in 1941, with the referee narrowly escaping arrest. But, in the face of Nazi threats and daily round-ups across Warsaw, football continued underground, with football fans chipping in to pay for the trophy. Players and match officials also received a medal featuring an engraved mermaid – the symbol of Warsaw – on a ball. Polonia won the Warsaw wartime championship in 1942 and 1943.

By November 1940, the Nazis had confined the Jewish population of the Polish capital – which made up almost a third of the city's population – into a tiny area known as the Warsaw Ghetto. Among the estimated 80,000 Jews to have died in the Warsaw Ghetto was Jósef Klotz, scorer of Poland's first international goal in a 2-1 win against the Swedes in Stockholm in May 1922. Klotz had played for Jewish clubs in both Kraków and Warsaw in the interwar period. Former Cracovia and Poland international defender Stefan Fryc, who had appeared at the 1924 Olympic Games in Paris, was also executed by the Nazis in the Ghetto. Further football resistance came in the form of the *Szare Szeregi* (Grey Ranks), a division of the Polish Underground Army that included players from the ambitious pre-war club, Junak Drohobycz. These players helped smuggle at-risk Poles out of the country and into neighbouring Hungary. Some players also crossed the border, joining with Romanian and Hungarian soldiers to become part of the Carpathian Brigade. This division included former Legia Warsaw and Polonia players. 'Coached by former Junak striker Tadeusz Krasón, the men played over 20 games from Budapest, through Yugoslavia, Syria and Palestine, and even as far as Egypt,' according to Hubbard.[9] The Carpathian Brigade went on to fight in Italy, and many settled in the UK after the war rather than return to their devastated homeland. One player, Jan Wasiewicz, turned out for Hibernian in Scotland, while another, Stanisław Gerula, become the first Pole to play at Wembley in the 1952 FA Amateur Cup Final with Walthamstow Avenue FC. Several decades after the original Carpathian Brigade saw action, a new organisation adopted that name as ultra groups from across Hungary got together to form the Carpathian Brigade of ultras in 2009, instantly recognisable in their black shirts. In the modern era, Hungarian and Polish ultras enjoy close relationships.[10]

As happened elsewhere in Nazi-occupied Europe, matches took place between Germans and locals in Poland. At Rybnik in the spring of 1943, a team of Poles beat a team drawn from the SS. In July the following year, another team of Poles beat a Wehrmacht team 4-2 in Lwów (Lviv). Just a few days later, on 1 August 1944, the people of Warsaw rose up against their Nazi oppressors. Several Polonia players featured in the Warsaw Uprising. The club's Stadion Polonii was even the scene of a clash between Poles and Nazis that resulted in the death of 12 partisans. Without Soviet support the Warsaw Uprising failed, and much of Warsaw was subsequently razed to the ground by the Nazis. Polonia lost several players during the war, from the initial defence of Poland in September 1939 and in resistance acts throughout the war.[11] Legia players Henryk Martyna and Marian Łańko took an active role in the uprising, as did club official Stanisław Gburzyński. The club had already lost Klemens Frankowski, who was arrested and killed for his resistance activity.

The Soviet Red Army marched into Poland in early 1945, liberating Auschwitz in January. According to camp survivor Primo Levi's account, one of the celebrations of the Allied victory over Nazi Germany, which was confirmed on 8 May 1945, was a football match between Poles and freed Italian prisoners in Katowice.[12]

Kraków's Holy War and Polish football today

Michael Cole spent a year in Kraków as a visiting researcher. Although he attended home matches of both Wisła and Cracovia while there, he noticed a marked difference when walking around the city as derby day approached, he tells me. 'A lot of graffiti was appearing, some of which was very specific to football, but alongside that there was graffiti that struck me as quite clearly antisemitic. You'd see in huge letters *anti-Jude* – *"Jude"* being the German word for Jew – or sometimes just *"AJ"* on the wall along with a picture of the Star of David with a line drawn right through it,' Cole explains. 'I was pretty surprised by this, bearing in mind this history of Poland, the Jewish history, the proximity to Auschwitz. It just shocked me that this was happening.' Cole investigated this graffiti further, speaking to other researchers and historians, and was surprised to learn that these antisemitic messages were apparently an accepted part of the football culture in Kraków around derby day. 'It was accepted that Wisła fans would use the term *Jude* to insult Cracovia fans, and people didn't really notice it any more; it was so much a part of what was going on in the city,' Cole continues. 'It brought up all these negotiations again about what it means to be Polish, and how Polish identity is understood and defined, and it seems to be all the same kind of problems going back to the pre-war period.'

Cole explained that in the pre-war period, Polish Jews suffered discrimination as they did in many other countries in Europe. Wisła even banned 'non-Polish' players while Cracovia supported Jewish and foreign players, which gained the club a reputation as a 'Jewish club', and that has stuck to this day as a key part of the club's identity. One of the club's ultra groups calls itself the *Jude Gang* (Jewish gang), which Cole adds is part of the reason there is so much '*anti-Jude*' graffiti around the city. 'From my research, the idea of "the Jew" in Polish football is something of a bogeyman, so it takes on whatever particular meaning the fans of a club decide to give it,' Cole continues. 'So, for certain fans, when they use what on the face of it is antisemitic language, it's aimed at attacking Cracovia fans. It's a term that's used in other cities as a way of insulting rival fans, too. This idea of calling your opponents "Jews" as the worst insult you can use shows that there is definitely an underlying sense of antisemitism going on, otherwise why would it be considered such an insult?' I asked Cole whether there were comparisons with Tottenham Hotspur, whose fans 'reclaimed' its Jewish identity – so-called due to the high Jewish population traditionally associated with that part of north London – after receiving insults from some opposing fans in the 1970s. 'It's a similar idea to Tottenham or Ajax in Amsterdam. The justification is taking what was initially used as an insult against the club or its fans and trying to "re-own" this name,' he says.

Stowarzyszenie Nigdy Więcej (Never Again Association) is Poland's leading anti-racist organisation. It was founded in the 1990s as a response to rising Nazi skinhead violence in Polish cities, taking place in various settings, from the streets to rock concerts and football. The group monitors racism and discrimination of all forms in Poland and has worked with numerous bodies, including the Council of Europe, the European Union and Football Against Racism in Europe (FARE). The group worked with UEFA ahead of Euro 2012, hosted jointly by Poland and Ukraine, to implement the 'Respect Diversity' programme of awareness-raising activities. Never Again also organises football tournaments for inclusive and progressive football fan groups from Poland and other countries. Rafał Pankowski heads up Never Again's Monitoring Center. He tells me that the Nazi skinhead subculture was a relatively new phenomenon in Poland in the 1990s, which emerged around the same time that Nazi insignia started appearing at Polish football grounds.

'Polish football had been strong in the 1970s and '80s, but by the 1990s, it was very weak, both at the national team level and the club level,' Pankowski explains. 'Attendance figures dropped, and it became easier for a radical or extremist minority to dominate the culture and subculture around football. People just didn't bother going to football any more, so there were no longer 50,000 people at the game, there was maybe 1,000, and if you bring 200 skinheads to the stadium, you are more or less in control.' Pankowski is keen to emphasise that most Polish football fans are only interested in the football and not the politics of a vocal minority. Despite some fantastic new stadiums in Poland thanks to Euro 2012, many Polish football fans are put off going to the stadium because of a 'nasty subculture' they might witness at league matches, preferring instead to follow on television.

According to Pankowski, in recent years the far right in Poland has revisited the Polish nationalist ethos of the 1930s and much of its symbolism, along with other international symbols of white power, such as the Celtic cross. The radical Polish nationalism of the 1930s could be violent and antisemitic, both themes that have returned, Pankowski says. In addition, Pankowski informs me that images of Janusz Waluś, a Pole who is serving a life sentence in South Africa for the killing of South African Communist Party (SACP) secretary-general Chris Hani in 1993, have appeared at Polish football stadiums in recent years. Pankowski believes that the use of Waluś's image by the far right in Poland has more to do with his victim having been a black man rather than a communist.

Pankowski explains the paradox that, while Polish football is relatively diverse and multicultural on the pitch, on the terraces one can witness xenophobic and racist behaviour just metres from the field of play. 'I'm not saying that every football fan is a racist fascist, of course, but I'm afraid the far right is very strong and even if not everybody supports it, the far-right presence in the stadium is intimidating enough to make any opposition difficult,' Pankowski adds.

The far right in Poland uses football as a tool for mobilising support; for example, a young far-right candidate polled a tiny percentage of the national vote in a recent election yet was the first choice among football fans. The Polish far right galvanises for Poland's annual National Independence Day rally on 11 November, which has attracted the far right from across Europe.[13] 'Poland for the Polish' is a familiar cry. According to Pankowski, that doesn't just mean the exclusion of ethnic minorities, but also the LGBTQ+ community. 'There have been a lot of homophobic banners and statements in Polish stadiums in recent years, and – as in the 1990s – we've seen a lot of passivity from the football establishment towards it,' he adds. Given the weight of apparent indifference towards the vocal minority of the far right in Polish football, is there even space for progressive opposition, as in Germany with FC St Pauli, or Rayo Vallecano in Spain? 'No, that's very difficult, I don't think there is an equivalent at all yet, but over the years, we will try and try, and we will succeed at last,' Pankowski insists.

One example of a progressive club in Warsaw is AKS (Alternative Sport Club) Zły, which means 'bad' in Polish. The club is based in the Praga district of the capital and was founded in 2015 as an independent and inclusive society. Swearing is outlawed in the club's stadium to attract families, and the club is open, democratic and multicultural. With both women's and men's teams, AKS Zły also believes in gender equality at the club where 'football comes first'.[14] Makabi Warszawa was a Jewish football club that had been founded in 1915 and dissolved under Nazi occupation in 1939. Its original ground stood where Poland's national stadium stands today. The club was re-founded in 2014. A year later, the club played newly formed AKS Kraków in what is believed to be the first Polish-Jewish football match in Poland since the war.[15]

So what does the future look like for football in Poland? 'We're in a situation, not just in Eastern Europe but across the world, where we're seeing an increase in polarisation. And that does mean a higher support for the far right, but I think that we're seeing a positive response from people on the left,' Michael Cole concludes. 'In Poland, for example, where things like homophobia, antisemitism and other forms of racism are deemed acceptable in society because we have political leaders who use this kind of language, it's no surprise that we see this kind of behaviour in football stadiums and may continue to do so. But it's important to point out that clubs do quite a lot of good work in the community, and there is a big sense of community built around these clubs, so I think it's important to emphasise this and focus on the positive elements of what it means to be associated with a club while continuing to try to combat and deal with these big issues.'

Russia's difficult history

In August 1939, having failed to secure strategic agreements with Britain and France, Soviet leader Joseph Stalin sent his foreign minister Vyacheslav Molotov to sign a non-aggression pact with his German counterpart Joachim von Ribbentrop. Nazi Germany invaded Poland from the west just days after the deal was struck, with the Soviets advancing into Poland from the east. And so it remained until June 1941 when Hitler, frustrated by his failure to secure a surrender from Britain, turned his mind eastwards to break the deadlock. He broke the non-aggression pact and invaded Soviet territory, gambling on a swift advance to Moscow within four months, named *Operation Barbarossa*. The Soviets were caught unaware but regrouped and resisted. The Great Patriotic War had begun. Initially, the

Germans moved quickly, securing the Ukrainian capital Kyiv by the end of September, where this book began. But then the Nazi advance became bogged down at certain key cities, which resisted fiercely, such as Stalingrad and Moscow. In the north, Leningrad – modern-day Saint Petersburg – was surrounded and besieged from September 1941 until January 1944. Victims of the siege of Leningrad included the former Russian international striker Sergey Filippov and midfielders Mikhail Yakovlev and Aleksei Uversky, who had all appeared in Russia's first Olympic football team at Stockholm in 1912. Soviet domestic football was cancelled on 24 June 1941 and would remain so until much of Russia had been liberated from the Nazis. The whole population was expected to contribute to the defence of the nation. Even 12-year-old Lev Yashin, future goalkeeper of the USSR and regarded as one of the greatest stoppers of all time, chipped into the war effort, working in an armaments factory.

One of the most epic battles of World War II and a significant turning point in the momentum against the Axis came at Stalingrad, modern-day Volgograd. For six months between August 1942 and February 1943, troops and civilians fought at close quarters as the Nazis and their allies tried – and ultimately failed – to take one of the USSR's industrial centres. Being named after the Soviet leader, Stalingrad also had symbolic significance for the Nazis. By the time Soviet troops retook the city, an estimated two million soldiers and civilians were dead, 100,000 Axis troops surrendered and the city itself was in ruins. The leading football club in Stalingrad, Traktor, had been founded by workers of the Dzerzhinskiy tractor factory in 1929 and by 1937 was competing at a national level. During the defence of Stalingrad, Traktor players refused the chance to evacuate to Siberia. At least seven fought on the front line, and two lost their lives. Club captain, defender Konstantin Belikov, was a key standout, running at least 30 missions and reputedly holding back a Nazi advance single-handedly for 40 minutes until reinforcements arrived. There was even an armed division made up of athletes defending the city under the command of Major-General Gleb Baklanov. His division was made up of not just footballers from Moscow, Leningrad and Kyiv, but also boxers, rowers, skiers and swimmers.[16]

To celebrate International Workers' Day on 1 May 1943, and to boost national morale as the Great Patriotic War continued, Belikov and Traktor goalkeeper Vasily Yermasov suggested a football match. Traktor's own ground had been badly damaged, but a stadium in the south of the city, the Azot, was repairable. The challenge remained to find a team of men who could last 90 minutes. Mines that lay on the route to the Azot were cleared, and holes on the pitch were filled by the Traktor players themselves. Players from Spartak Moscow were called up and flown down to Stalingrad for the match, held on 2 May 1943. An estimated crowd of more than 12,000 turned up for the free event. The match ball was dropped from a swooping fighter plane on to the pitch, and Traktor players received medals for their part in the defence of Stalingrad. Remarkably, Traktor won the encounter with a single goal from Alexander Moiseyev, set up by skipper Belikov.[17] News of the encounter in the ruins of Stalingrad even made the news in the UK just days later. The match had symbolic significance for the Soviets to send a message – both internally and externally – that life would go on after the Nazi occupation. Stalingrad was renamed in 1961 following the dictator's death, and Traktor Stalingrad is now called Rotor Volgograd.

In the north of Russia, football would play a similar role in restoring morale and an air of normality. Leningrad side FC Zenit's players even competed as Moscow Zenit in the Moscow Championship in 1943 as their city was still under siege. The FC Zenit players only returned to Leningrad in early 1944 after the near-900-day blockade was broken. That year's USSR Cup represented a return to domestic football normality, even though the Red Army was still in action, driving the Nazis back west. FC Zenit, at the time not even the strongest club in Leningrad, defeated Dynamo Moscow, Dynamo Baku and Spartak Moscow to meet the Red Army side CDKA (later CSKA) in the final in Moscow. FC Zenit came from behind to triumph 2-1 and claimed the first USSR Cup since the resumption of football in the Soviet Union. FC Zenit's victorious team were awarded gold Swiss watches with an engraved five-pointed star on the back, along with leather coats, sugar and medals 'For the Defence of Leningrad'. The club would have to wait another 40 years for its next cup final.[18]

In December 1945, George Orwell, a veteran of the Spanish Civil War, wrote an article in which he famously compared 'serious sport' to 'war minus the shooting'.[19] He had been inspired to write the piece by the recent tour to Britain of the Dynamo Moscow team. It also provided the Soviets with a chance to raise funds for the rebuilding of Stalingrad. The champions of the USSR were the first visiting side from their country, and few in Britain knew anything about them. The objective of the tour was to celebrate the peace that the two countries had fought so hard for. However, on a political level, relationships were in a parlous state. The Russians, who revered English football, debuted in front of more than 70,000 against Chelsea at Stamford Bridge and were carried off by supporters at the end of an entertaining 3-3 draw. From London, Dynamo moved on to Cardiff, where the team was presented with a miner's lamp before the Soviet side dispatched their hosts Cardiff City 10-1. Back in London, Arsenal were Dynamo's next opponents. But the Gunners were light of several players who were still overseas on military duty, so they drafted in England winger Stanley Matthews, future England international Stan Mortensen and Chelsea's Joe Bacuzzi, prompting Soviet radio to refer to Arsenal as an 'All-England' team. The contest took place at Tottenham's White Hart Lane ground because Highbury was still under the control of the Ministry of Defence. Dynamo won a controversial game 4-3 in thick fog officiated by a Russian referee and English linesmen, who required a translator to confer on several challenging decisions. Dynamo drew 2-2 with Rangers at Ibrox, while proposed matches at Aston Villa and Racing Club in Paris never materialised as the Russians were summoned home, returning unbeaten. Football – along with other sports – would become a feature of Soviet propaganda for the next four and half decades.

The Soviet Union could not survive clamour for change from its component republics and satellite states after the fall of the Berlin Wall in November 1989. By Christmas 1991, the USSR no longer existed. Each component state went its own way, including the largest and most powerful of them all, Russia. As is common in other post-communist states in Eastern Europe, a far-right element emerged and found a platform in Russia's football stadiums. As was the case in other European countries, English hooliganism of the 1970s and '80s became the go-to inspiration for would-be Russian football ultras in the post-Soviet era. Hooliganism arrived relatively late – it wasn't until 1999 that a Russian match was stopped for the first time due to fan violence.[20] The Russian ultra culture that would emerge was different, however. In contrast to the beery pre-match punch-up between rival fans dressed in fashionable sports brands in 1980s England, Russian ultras at the turn of the new century were bulking up and arranging fights in remote locations.

Russian ultras announced themselves on the international stage in Marseille at Euro 2016, when an organised group of around 200 Russians targeted England fans in the port area, ending in violent skirmishes. At the England-Russia match itself at the Stade Vélodrome, some Russians managed to charge the England fan-occupied stand at the end of the match. Various far-right flags were reported to have been on display.[21] The shameful incidents in Marseille turned the spotlight on the darker side of Russia's football culture ahead of the country's hosting of the 2018 FIFA World Cup. Running up to the start of the 2018 tournament, a major study by the FARE network and the Moscow-based SOVA Center found that the number of far-right banners, such as the use of the Celtic cross and runic symbols, was in decline. However, it noted a sharp increase in discriminatory chants, such as monkey sounds, and a rise in homophobic behaviour. The report also commended the Russian Football Union for its fan-monitoring efforts.[22]

Meanwhile, in Ukraine, statues of the martyrs of the 'Death Match' can be found around Kyiv. Decades after that significant game united the country against an aggressor, so football again played a role when Ukraine found itself in conflict with Russia in 2014. Ultras from rival Ukrainian clubs put their differences aside to protest against the presidency of Viktor Yanukovych, when he pivoted away from closer relations with the European Union and looked to Russia. Ukrainian ultras from across the country have also taken up arms in defence of their nation, as seen in 2022 when volunteers joined the front line to help repel a brutal Russian invasion, described by its president Vladimir Putin as a 'special military operation'. Asking around, I found very little evidence of any left-wing ultra groups at a time when many of Ukraine's ultra groups are ensconced to the right, politically. One standout is Arsenal Kyiv. Like its London namesake, Arsenal Kyiv emerged from a historical armoury. Their fans are particularly noted for their anti-fascist stance, along with FC Lviv fan group Citizens 61.[23]

Football resistance in the Balkans

By the late 1930s, many of Yugoslavia's football clubs had working-class origins. They were closely aligned with political activism, which often caused a headache for the authorities. In 1939, Zagreb club Gradanski was dissolved at the behest of the state due to the publicly subversive nature of some of its members at a time when some communist parties were outlawed in Yugoslavia. By then, many young Yugoslavs had been inspired to support the Spanish Republic. Some even headed to Spain to fight against Franco, including many players, such as Radnički Belgrade's Mirko Kovačević. At home, clubs raised funds to support the players' and supporters' families while they were away with the International Brigades. Those who headed to Spain via the Adriatic port of Split often posed as fans visiting matches at the workers' club Radnički športski klub (RŠK) before slipping out on ships to Iberia.[24] One prominent Yugoslav to fight in Spain was the former SK Jugoslavija and BSK Beograd defender Boško Petrović. Petrović had been capped once for Yugoslavia in a 3-2 defeat to France at the Parc des Princes in Paris. He had also trained as a pilot at the Air Academy of Novi Sad and, in 1936, slipped into Spain illegally from France on a false passport with the Spanish name 'Fernández García'. He was engaged in fighting in the summer of 1937 over the Sierra de Guadarrama, downing five enemy planes in a month of active service before he himself was shot down near Madrid in July and killed. Petrović is commemorated in his native Serbia with a plaque at the Partizan Belgrade stadium, and several streets bear his name.[25] While Yugoslavia was on friendly diplomatic terms with Nazi Germany at the outset of hostilities, a scheduled match between the two nations in Belgrade in October 1939 was cancelled on the recommendation of local police for fear of local demonstrations, even though the German team was already in the city.

Down Croatia's Dalmatian coast, nestled between forested mountains on one side and the azure of the Adriatic Sea on the other, Split is an idyllic spot. The Romans certainly thought so and established a prominent city here that still survives in the heart of Split. The city's main football club, Hajduk Split, was founded by four Croatian students on 13 February 1911, while they were away studying in Prague. The word *hajduk* can translate as 'brigand' in English and harked back to an age when Croatians were fighting against the Ottomans in the Balkans. Croatia became part of the newly formed country of Yugoslavia after the collapse of the Austro-Hungarian Empire following its defeat in World War I. The Yugoslavian Football Association was formed in 1919 and a year later entered its first tournament, the Olympic Games in Antwerp, where the team was eliminated in the first round, losing 7-0 to Czechoslovakia. A decade on, Yugoslavia was one of just four European nations to undertake the long journey to Uruguay for the first World Cup, where the team beat Brazil on the way to the semi-finals, losing to eventual champions and hosts Uruguay.

By the time World War II broke out in 1939, the Yugoslavian government had pursued a policy of neutrality and found itself out of the conflict. However, surrounded by Axis forces, on 25 March 1941, Yugoslavia's prime minister signed the Tripartite Pact to join Nazi Germany, fascist Italy and Japan against the western allies. Within two days, the Yugoslavian government suffered a coup. In response, Germany invaded on 6 April and divided the country once more. Clubs with patriotic names, such as Belgrade club Jugoslavija, were forced to rebrand, in Jugoslavija's case, to SK 1913.[26] The Gestapo and their local allies cracked down on opponents, some of whom were footballers, such as former SK Jugoslavija player Milutin Ivković. Serbian Ivković starred for the national side at the inaugural FIFA World Cup in 1930 and won 39 caps at right-back. He trained as a doctor after his playing career and also edited the communist youth magazine *Mladost*, and helped the *Komunistička partije Jugoslavije* (KPJ – Yugoslavian Communist Party). He was arrested and shot in May 1943 at the Jajinci prison camp. His body was never found.

Croatia soon became a puppet state for the Nazis under the right-wing *Ustaša*, who immediately set about replicating the Nazis' reign of terror over the local Jewish and Roma population. The Independent State of Croatia (NDH – *Nezavisna država Hrvatska*) even sent a football team to play against Germany in Vienna just two months after the Nazi invasion of Yugoslavia. Germany won 5-1, with two goals coming from future World Cup winner Fritz Walter. The NDH side included the talented 24-year-old midfielder Svetozar Danić of the Zagreb club, HŠK Gradanski. Upon returning to Zagreb the next day, Danić was arrested by the Ustaša, denounced as a communist, and two days later was shot dead in the infamous Dotrščina forest, where thousands of anti-fascists, communists and intellectuals met their fate during the war.[27]

Parts of Croatia's Dalmatian Coast, including the city of Split, were annexed by Mussolini's Italy in 1941. Richard Mills, author of *The Politics and Football in Yugoslavia: Sport, Nationalism and the State*, tells me that the Italian football authorities tried to entice Hajduk Split into *Serie A* with the offer of a new stadium and planes laid on to transport the team – although the plan was to rebrand the club with an Italian name, AC Spalato. But Hajduk refused and instead chose to disband rather than join the occupiers. Mills says that Hajduk's refusal to co-operate was in stark contrast to the stance taken by many of the other leading clubs in Yugoslavia. Hajduk was reformed on 7 May 1944 on the Adriatic island of Vis, where the partisan resistance had their headquarters and was occupied by the Allies. Many of the players had endured a ten-day hike and sail from Split, giving German soldiers the slip *en route*. 'They decided that this club should be reformed, and it should serve as a kind of propaganda arm of Josip Broz Tito's partisan movement,' Mills explains. 'And this all goes rather well. Hajduk is rebranded as the team of the National Liberation Army of Yugoslavia and performs very strongly against British armed forces sides that are packed with professional footballers.' One of these matches in 1944 was billed as the Yugoslav National Liberation Army XI against the British Services XI in Bari in newly liberated Italy. The British Army team featured England defender Stan Cullis and future England winger Tom Finney. Although Hajduk lost the match 7-2, it marked the first time that the new Yugoslav anthem was played in public, along with the unveiling of the new socialist flag of Yugoslavia – a red, white and blue horizontal tricolour with a red star over the top. Hajduk's kit was all white with a simple red five-pointed star as a crest. For the Bari match, the shirt featured the new flag of Yugoslavia. The match was attended by more than 40,000 spectators. Later in the war, Hajduk toured the liberated Mediterranean and played matches in Italy, Egypt, Lebanon, Palestine and elsewhere.

Hajduk was not the only club in the city to resist the Ustaša and the Nazis. Members of RŠK signed up for the partisans in the summer of 1941. Many of them would die or be taken prisoner within the first few days, having encountered both Croatian and Italian fascist forces in the Dalmatian mountains. According to Mills, RŠK lost more than 100 members and 71 members of NK Mosor, which was near Split at the time and has now been absorbed into the expanded city, perished in the conflict.[28] Juraj Vrdoljak is a Croatian sports journalist. 'For a lot of the upper classes, it was a case of keeping your head down during the Nazi rule, but for the working-class – and most footballers were working-class – they joined the resistance immediately in 1941,' he tells me. 'Players of both Hajduk and Radnički joined the resistance, and over time many other people joined them. Radnički suffered huge losses but reformed again after the war.' Just as football had been a critical propaganda vehicle for the Ustaša at the start of its regime, so the sport took on an important role for Tito and the resistance. Photos of the Bari match appeared in leaflets dropped by the RAF over occupied Yugoslavia.[29] By 26 December 1944, it was safe enough in Split for the British Army to play Hajduk – billed as 'Yugoslavia' – in front of 8,000, even though the conflict was being fought just 30km away. The home side won 1-0, prompting a pitch invasion at the final whistle. Elated locals carried the Hajduk players from the field on their shoulders.[30]

In the north of Croatia, Zagreb's leading club before the war was Gradanski, with five Yugoslav championships to its name. During World War II, Zagreb had become the centre of Ustaša authority until its fall in May 1945. With the new communist regime in place, football would take on a whole new complexion in the future Yugoslavia, and Gradanski became Dinamo Zagreb. Along with Hajduk Split and the two newly formed clubs in the Serbian capital – Crvena Zvezda (Red Star) and Partizan Belgrade – Dinamo Zagreb would make up the new 'big four' in Yugoslav football from 1945 until the country disintegrated in the 1990s. Dinamo's Maksimir Stadium became the scene of one of the most infamous moments in tensions between Croats and Serbs in May 1990, when the ultras of Dinamo Zagreb and Red Star Belgrade clashed. The following year, the region collapsed into conflict, leading to what is known in Croatia as the 'Homeland War', which ultimately resulted in Croatian independence.

Dr Andy Hodges spent several years in Zagreb studying the *ultrà* scene and wrote a book about his observations, called *Fan Activism, Protest and Politics: Ultras in Post-Socialist Croatia*. 'Football fans in Croatia and the Balkans more generally should be taken seriously as political actors, because they're highly organised and they've been responsible for organising demonstrations that are larger than the largest trade union demonstrations in the history of Croatia,' he tells me. 'There are these deep ideological divisions in Croatian society at the moment, and there have been for quite a few years now. In part, they relate to the Homeland War following the secession from socialist Yugoslavia, but these divisions in some sense also go back to World War II and the people who were in Partisan families – so they were fighting as part of the anti-fascist resistance – and people who were in the Ustaša families, the Croatian nationalists who were collaborating with Nazi Germany. These divisions resurfaced in the 1990s partly because they were being talked about again following the censorship during socialist Yugoslavia. And these divisions do have a big impact on football fans and how they organise themselves.'

Dinamo Zagreb's main *ultrà* group is called the 'Bad Blue Boys'. The group's logo, which draws inspiration from British bulldog imagery, can be found painted on walls in neighbourhoods around the city. 'If you look at the ways in which the Bad Blue Boys organise themselves, it's actually closer to the Italian ultras,' Hodges tells me. 'So, they have organised social spaces in the city centre, they have membership cards, they have a strict hierarchy, they put on a pyrotechnic show, and they also nod in the direction of the English or British hooligan tradition.' Hodges informs me that many of the Bad Blue Boys fought on the frontline during the Homeland War and apparently even had a tank with their name written on it. However, the Bad Blue Boys is a broad church of beliefs, and its members should not be stereotyped as nationalist or right wing. Across the city is NK Zagreb, which – at the time of writing – competes in the fourth tier of Croatian football. Although the club has a much smaller fanbase than Dinamo, the club has a passionate and vocal ultra group called 'White Angels', which identifies strongly with the left. 'These left-wing groups, although they are organised around progressive principles, they still want to be seen as participants in the ultras scene, which has a hegemonic masculinity built into it,' Hodges explains. Hodges observes that 'banter' between ultra groups in Zagreb is very politicised and helps cement identity within respective groups.

Back down the coast in Dalmatia, Split can also claim to be the entry point of ultra culture in Europe, not just into Croatia but the whole continent. Yugoslavian fans travelling to the 1950 World Cup in Brazil observed the passionate sound and colour of the fans there in the *torcida* (crowd). When some of those fans returned to tell the story of what they had seen, a group of those who supported Hajduk Split founded Europe's first organised fan group and called it *Torcida*. Their culture of songs and *tifo* spread across Europe, most notably in neighbouring Italy. 'While Bad Blue Boys have a historical, deep connection with the national category of Croatia and they have a military aesthetic, Hajduk Split's Torcida are a bit more anarchist, a bit more diverse,' Hodges concludes.

Greece's partisan footballers

At the outbreak of World War II, Greece was under its own authoritarian dictatorship headed by prime minister Ioannis Metaxas. Metaxas wanted to remain neutral while Nazi Germany was making significant advances throughout Europe in 1939 and 1940. On the other hand, Mussolini wanted to make conquests of his own and already occupied Greece's neighbour Albania. On 15 August 1940, the Italians attempted to antagonise Greece into confrontation by torpedoing the Greek navy warship *Elli* on the island of Tinos. An ultimatum followed on 28 October 1940: surrender or face invasion. Metaxas refused, and the Italians crossed the border from Albania, while Italian bombers pummelled the city of Patras. Mussolini expected an easy victory. However, the Greeks rallied and, within six weeks, had driven the Italians back across the Albanian border. It was the first significant reverse of the war for the Axis and also dragged the Germans into a theatre of war that they had not expected to be involved in. Critically, it took troops, supplies and logistical resources away from Hitler's planned invasion of the Soviet Union.

Some football in Greece – such as the domestic City Cup – was played right up to the day before the Italian invasion. Then, Greece's football players and clubs took on a whole new role in the defence of the nation, and stadiums were used as makeshift hospitals or storage depots. Going into the abandoned 1940/41 season, AEK Athens had been the dominant side, winning the previous two Greek championships. Prior to AEK's prominence, Olympiacos, Aris and Panathinaikos had dominated the league. Some of these clubs' players would play prominent roles in the upcoming defence of Greece. Even before the Italian invasion, Greek football teams were involved in fundraising for the anticipated conflict. In July 1940, the ancient city of Thessaloniki hosted the Army Cup to raise money for the Greek army featuring local sides Aris, Iraklis and PAOK, who lifted the trophy after defeating both rivals. Similarly, a cup competition was held in Athens in September to help fund the air force. It featured the Greek capital's leading sides and was won by Panathinaikos.

In 1936, Panathinaikos' top scorer had been Mimis Pierrakos with 18 goals in just ten games, firing his team to a second-place finish in the league. Pierrakos signed up for the army on the day of the Italian invasion and was sent to the front as a radio operator. He helped capture a downed Italian pilot near the Albanian border, but, just as he was writing home about the incident, he was killed by Italian shell fire. His remains were recovered in 1950 by his brother Stefanos – also a Panathinaikos player – and returned to Athens, where his bones were buried in the family grave, wrapped in the Panathinaikos club flag. While the Greeks repelled the Italian invasion, Hitler needed to secure his southern flank and in April 1941, shortly after Metaxas himself had died, the Germans invaded. Despite the intervention of the British, Australians and New Zealanders, the

Germans proved too strong for the Greek forces. By 27 April, the Nazis occupied Athens. Resistance went underground while the occupiers stripped Greece of its food supply, leaving much of the country to starve. Greek football writer George Tsitsonis tells me that by the eve of World War II, football in Greece had become the country's sporting passion. 'It's no surprise then that the game was used by the government to help drum up support and funds for war efforts,' he explains. 'Greek football during the pre-war period was still amateur in its organisation. Despite this and the ensuing widespread poverty caused by occupation, the Greek love of football never abated.'

As in parts of Republican Spain, charity matches were held in Greece to raise funds for the reconstruction of destroyed towns. However, one proposed charity match between Panathinaikos and AEK at Panathinaikos's Leoforos Stadium is remarkable more for the fact that it did *not* take place. The two Athens giants planned to raise money for the Sotiria hospital, but then the Germans intervened, demanding a cut of the match proceeds and installing an Austrian to officiate the match. The players of both sides disagreed and refused to play. Many of the 15,500 spectators smashed up the stadium's wooden benches in anger. As in many other parts of Nazi-occupied territory, matches took place between locals and their overlords. The Italians and Germans had their own league on the island of Samos, where they also took on local sides Vathilos and Apollo. In Kalamata, a local side lost 3-2 to a German team, which placed a machine gun menacingly close to the pitch.[31] 'The German invasion caused pain and suffering for the entire populace and sport was the furthest thing from the mind of most. However, football continued to be played,' Tsitsonis explains. 'The game took the form of one-off matches pitting locals against the occupiers or friendlies between the country's bigger sides to raise funds for charity and reconstruction efforts. Even though the majority of people in Greece were starving, Greeks continued to find their way to local stadiums to watch these matches. It was a testament to their love of the game.'

One club that never played a match against Nazi invaders was Olympiacos from Piraeus.[32] During the resistance, Olympiacos's midfield maestro Nikos Godas became a captain in the Hellenic People's Liberation Army (ELAS). Like many among the Greek resistance, Godas was a communist, and he fought around his hometown of Piraeus and Perama. He also defended Greece's electricity infrastructure from sabotage by the Germans as they retreated in 1944.[33] Godas had also played brilliantly in wartime competitions, such as the Christmas Cup of 1943, where Olympiacos thumped Panathinaikos 5-2. After the Germans left in October 1944, the Greek communists fought against rival factions and their former allies, the British, who backed the new Greek government. Godas was imprisoned for three years for his role as a communist and consistently refused to sign a declaration of repentance that could have spared his life. He was executed on 19 November 1948, aged 27. For his execution, he insisted on wearing the red-and-white striped shirt of Olympiacos and not a blindfold, so that the last thing he saw was the shirt of his beloved football club. Speaking to Olympiacos supporters, I learn that Godas is celebrated most for his performance in the Christmas Cup match – widely regarded as a footballing masterclass – and for insisting on wearing the Olympiacos jersey at his execution. Olympiacos's fanbase nowadays has moved away from its working-class, leftist roots and contains a fairly wide spectrum of politics, fans tell me. Those on the left idolise Godas, while those on the right acknowledge his performances but choose to remember him as a communist. A number of other Olympiacos players were involved in the Greek resistance struggle between 1941 and 1944. Christoforos Raggos was injured in the initial conflict with Italy and could not play

Statue commemorating the 'Death Match' in Kyiv, Ukraine (Credit: Michael Page)

St Ambroeus's Armata Pirata fan group, Milan (Credit: St Ambroeus FC)

In memory of Carlo Castellani, Municipal Stadium, Empoli (Credit: Municipality of Empoli, Franco Castellani, and Empoli FC)

L'AMMINISTRAZIONE COMUNALE PER ONORARNE LA MEMORIA DENOMINÒ QUESTO STADIO A CARLO CASTELLANI GIOCATORE DI CALCIO NELL'EMPOLI E NEL LIVORNO DAL 1925 AL 1938 DEPORTATO IN GERMANIA MORÌ A MAUTHAUSEN L 11.8.1944

Quartograd, Naples. The t-shirt reads 'Against Modern Football' (Credit: ASD Quartograd)

The crest evolution of Club Esportiu Júpiter of Barcelona reflects the changing times since its formation in 1909 (Credit: Natxo Torné)

Independiente de Vallecas fans in Madrid (Credit: Andrew Gillen)

*The 1937 Copa España Libre-winning Levante FC team
(Credit: Museo Levante UD)*

The Copa España Libre trophy (Credit: Museo Levante UD)

'Love Rayo, Hate Racism' graffito in Vallecas, Madrid (Credit: Paul Reidy)

Académica de Coimbra line up in student gowns for the 1969 Portuguese Cup Final (Credit: Formidável)

Poststadion, Berlin, where Hitler is reputed to have watched his only football match – a German defeat to Norway in the 1936 Olympics (Credit: Author)

Eugène Maës of Red Star (Paris), the first player to score five goals in a single game for France in 1912, was denounced for anti-German comments during the Nazi occupation of France and died in a concentration camp (Credit: Redstar.fr and Gilles Saillant)

Antoni Łyko of Wisła Kraków was accused of being linked to the Polish resistance during World War II and died at Auschwitz (Credit: National Digital Archives, Poland)

'Polish Woodstock' in 2019 – the Never Again Association aims to build bridges through football (Credit: Never Again Association)

FC Zenit in the 1944 USSR Cup Final (Credit: FC Zenit/ФК «Зенит»)

Clapton CFC's away kit was inspired by the colours of the flag of the Spanish Republic (Credit: Nick Davidson)

LOVE
PEACE
NO RACISM
NO SEXISM
NO VIOLENCE
NO HOMOPHOBIA

The steps at Whitehawk FC, Brighton (Credit: JJ Waller)

Graffito at progressive Dublin football club, Bohemian FC (Credit: Gerard Farrell)

football again, while Michalis Anamateros lost his life towards the end of the war.

During the Nazi occupation of Athens, Panathinaikos's Leoforos stadium was looted, and its ground was used by the Germans for their troops to play in. However, the stadium director Antonis Vrettos made rooms available to members of the resistance.[34] Many connected with Panathinaikos joined the resistance, including former player Michalis Papazoglou, who had suggested the club's shamrock emblem. During the war, he was part of a resistance group headed by Polish-born Greek athlete Jerzy Iwanow-Szaijnowicz. The Germans were yet to withdraw from Athens in 1944 when Vrettos raised the blue-and-white flag of Greece over the Leoforos ground, the first in Athens to do so, which itself was an extremely bold act of defiance.

Athens club AEK, which won the last two Greek titles before the Italian invasion, also saw its stadium looted. AEK defender Spiros Kontoulis joined other AEK players on the Albanian front, sustaining a leg injury driving the Italians back into Albania. He was arrested by the Nazis while visiting his mother near Piraeus in April 1944 and was shot trying to escape his transportation to an execution site.[35] Football re-started in 1946, with Aris from Thessaloniki winning its third title. Modern-day AEK Athens fans have *gemellaggi* with like-minded fans of AS Livorno and Olympique de Marseille in a 'Triangle of Brotherhood' and are famously anti-fascist. In 2013, 20-year-old AEK midfielder Giorgios Katidis scored a late goal to give his side the lead in a match against Veria and celebrated by performing what appeared to be a Nazi salute. The move stunned Greek football and AEK terminated Katidis's contract for the rest of the season, despite Katidis claiming he did not know what the gesture meant. Meanwhile, AEK's largest fan group, Original 21, made it clear Katidis was no longer welcome, and would not be forgiven for making the Nazi salute.[36] Katidis had captained Greece at Under-19 level, but the Hellenic Football Federation (EPO) effectively ended his international career with a life ban from all national teams. The EPO said Katidis's gesture was a 'severe provocation' and 'insults all the victims of Nazi bestiality'.[37]

Over in Cyprus, another by-product of the Greek civil war was a new football club – AC Omonoia Nicosia. In 1948, at a time when the Greek government was being supported by the British and Americans against the Greek communists, the authorities required athletes in Cyprus to sign statements condemning left-wing activity in Greece. Many left-leaning athletes refused. When the board of Cyprus's leading football club, Apoel, telegrammed the Greek athletics authorities criticising the communists, some Apoel players and staff left to found Omonoia, which means 'concord' in English. Apoel and Omonoia now contest Cyprus's fiercest football rivalry. Omonoia's ultras, Gate-9, founded in 1992, continue the left-leaning tradition, waving Che Guevara flags in the stands, and also have *gemellaggi* with other left-wing football clubs.

Modern Greek football is dominated by three big clubs – Olympiacos, Panathinaikos and AEK – and the rivalry between the three is intense. 'Greek football could take a lesson from history in order to show that these clubs are more alike than we have been led to believe,' Tsitsonis concludes. 'Each of these teams had players who went on to help with the war effort, either as soldiers or as part of the resistance after the German occupation. Their individual acts of heroism have sadly flown underneath the radar. It would be of great benefit for the health of Greek football if these stories were told in a much more comprehensive fashion. Names such as Godas, Vrettos, Papazoglou and Kountoulis should be better known. They have enriched Greek football history thanks to the way they helped defend their nation.'

1 https://sport.onet.pl/ii-wojna-swiatowa-polscy-sportowcy-ktorzy-zgineli-w-latach-1939-1945/ectp3rt (retrieved 02/08/21)

2 Hubbard, Ryan, *From Partition to Solidarity, The First Hundred Years of Polish Football* (Leicester: RAH, 2019 (p113)

3 https://bleacherreport.com/articles/60684-wisla-krakow-vs-mks-cracovia-the-holy-war (retrieved 14/05/21)

4 https://futbolretro.es/antoni-lyko/ (retrieved 02/09/21)

5 Hubbard, Ryan, *From Partition to Solidarity, The First Hundred Years of Polish Football* (Leicester: RAH, 2019, p116)

6 https://legia.com/historia-1941-1950/ (retrieved 21/05/21)

7 https://thesefootballtimes.co/2016/07/26/czarne-koszule-a-history-of-polonia-warsaw/ (retrieved 21/05/21)

8 https://legia.com/historia-1941-1950/ (retrieved 21/05/21)

9 Hubbard, Ryan, *From Partition to Solidarity, The First Hundred Years of Polish Football* (Leicester: RAH, 2019, p.128)

10 https://www.theguardian.com/football/2021/oct/13/why-hungary-is-infected-by-ultras-who-are-almost-impossible-to-control-wembley-violence (retrieved 19/10/21)

11 https://www.kspolonia.pl/klub/historia/okres-ii-wojny-swiatowej, p1200091835 (retrieved 21/05/21)

12 https://footballmakeshistory.eu/football-in-primo-levis-work/ (retrieved 30/05/21)

13 https://www.buzzfeednews.com/article/lesterfeder/march-led-by-authoritarian-group-in-poland-draws-tens-of (retrieved 01/08/21)

14 https://www.opendemocracy.net/en/can-europe-make-it/in-bad-guys-lair-aks-z-y-and-their-alternative-fo/ (retrieved 02/08/21)

15 https://www.jweekly.com/2015/03/20/playing-soccer-as-a-jew-in-warsaw/ (retrieved 03/07/21)

16 *Yorkshire Evening Post*, 8 March 1943 (p4)

17 https://www.rbth.com/arts/2015/05/27/traktor_vs_spartak_the_football_match_on_the_ruins_of_stalingrad_46415.html (retrieved 27/06/21)

18 https://spbvedomosti.ru/news/sport/palto-i-sakhar-pobeditelyam-kak-zenit-zavoeval-kubok-sssr-v-1944-godu/ (retrieved 25/06/21)

19 https://www.orwellfoundation.com/the-orwell-foundation/orwell/essays-and-other-works/the-sporting-spirit/ (retrieved 26/06/21)

20 https://www.theguardian.com/news/2018/apr/24/russia-neo-nazi-football-hooligans-world-cup (retrieved 25/06/21)

21 https://www.theguardian.com/football/2016/jun/12/uefa-open-disciplinary-proceedings-russia-england-marseille-euro-2016 (retrieved 25/06/21)

22 https://farenet.org/wp-content/uploads/2018/05/FINAL-SOVA-monitoring-report_2018-6.pdf (retrieved 19/09/21)

23 http://www.futbolgrad.com/ukrainian-ultras-where-two-wings-collide/ (retrieved 01/10/21)

24 Mills, Richard, *The Politics and Football in Yugoslavia: Sport, Nationalism and the State* (London: I.B. Tauris, 2018, loc1049/8977)

25 https://www.marca.com/futbol/2017/03/31/58dd782f468aebb82f8b45ef.
html (retrieved 28/06/21)

26 Mills, Richard, *The Politics and Football in Yugoslavia: Sport, Nationalism and the State* (London: I.B. Tauris, 2018, loc1205/8977)

27 https://telesport.telegram.hr/kolumne/nogomet-narodu/vatreni-kojeg-su-strijeljali/ (retrieved 19/06/21)

28 Mills, Richard, *The Politics and Football in Yugoslavia: Sport, Nationalism and the State* (London: I.B. Tauris, 2018, loc1262)

29 *Ibid*, loc1544

30 *Ibid*, loc1664

31 https://www.ekirikas.com/athlitika_omogeneia/arthro/to_elliniko_podosfairo_sta_xronia_tou_polemou-1107666/ (retrieved 01/07/21)

32 https://www.olympiacos.org/en/olympiacos-history (retrieved 01/07/21)

33 https://www.gazzetta.gr/football/superleague/article/1293921/nikos-godas-min-moy-desete-ta-matia-gia-na-vlepo-ta-hromata-vids-pics (retrieved 02/07/21)

34 https://www.pao.gr/en/history/events/ (retrieved 02/07/21)

35 https://www.aek-live.gr/to-telos-toy-iroa-spyroy-kontoyli-kai-oi-quot-alles-quot-kaisarianes/ (retrieved 02/07/21)

36 https://www.vice.com/el/article/59k53x/akrode3ia-kai-e3edra-h-periptwsh-ths-aek (retrieved 25/11/21)

37 https://www.ekathimerini.com/sports/149372/life-ban-from-national-teams-on-katidis-for-nazi-salute/ (retrieved 25/11/21)

Chapter 5

Latin America

IN THE 1950s and '60s, Latin America became a key theatre of the Cold War as the opposing ideologies of communism and capitalism clashed. For nearly half a century between the 1950s and the 1980s, much of Latin America was taken over by right-wing dictatorships. Paraguay fell under the brutal military regime of Alfredo Stroessner in 1954. Five years later, the Cuban Revolution of 1959 – when Fidel Castro and his followers overthrew the Fulgencio Batista government and installed a communist regime – spooked many on the right in Latin America, along with the US administration. Fearing the spread of communism throughout Latin America, many governments began to crack down on leftist activism. Successive Latin American countries fell to right-wing military dictatorships, including Brazil (1964), Argentina (1966), Peru (1968), Bolivia (1969,) and Chile and Uruguay (1973). These military dictatorships often colluded with each other to exchange exiled opponents, and engaged in kidnappings, torture and disappearances as part of a covert programme known as *Operation Condor*.

Ironically, this period coincided with the pinnacle of some of these countries' national team performances – as in the case of Brazil and Argentina – and the political potential of football as a high-profile platform was not lost on the dictators. Dr Pete Watson is a lecturer on Latin American studies, and he tells me that since the very earliest days of football's introduction into the continent by the British community, Latin American politicians have sought to align themselves closely with the sport for political gain. 'In the early days, being associated with football is a way for politicians to show that they're part of something modern, of cultural importance and the elite,' Watson explains. 'And then over time with increased urbanisation and migration to cities like Buenos Aires, Rio de Janeiro, São Paulo, Montevideo and Lima, for example, football becomes a way for politicians to control these workers and reduce the spread of socialist or trade union movements that might have had the intention of undermining the traditional power base of many of the elites in Latin American society.'

Football and the far right in Brazil

Football had become a key part of Brazilian identity at home and abroad as a way of nation-building and integrating the country's diverse population since the 1930s during the presidency of Getúlio Vargas. Brazil had been very late to abolish slavery in 1888 and even as recently as the 1920s, Rio de Janeiro club Vasco da Gama had been forced to fight back against the other elite clubs in the city excluding it on the basis of its diverse membership. Following the disaster of the 1950 *Maracanaço*, when Brazil had lost 2-1 to a late Uruguayan goal to miss out on winning its first World Cup at home, Brazil rebuilt to win back-to-back World Cups in Sweden (1958) and Chile (1962). In England, in 1966, Brazil – and Pelé, in particular – were on the receiving end of some rough treatment from their opponents and exited at the group stage. Back home, the Brazilian military and United States alike were concerned about the radical reforms pursued by the democratically elected socialist government of João Goulart. This dissatisfaction led to the *Golpe de 64* (Coup of 64), which saw Goulart's government toppled by members of the Brazilian military. Two decades passed before democracy returned to Brazil, during which time thousands of people were illegally detained, many were tortured, and at least 434 people were killed or disappeared.[1] Throughout the dictatorship, football became a key propaganda tool, particularly before, during and after the 1970 World Cup, and footballers would also play a key role in accelerating the return of democracy in the 1980s.

In 1969, General Emílio Médici was nominated by his peers in the military to become president of Brazil. Médici was a genuine football fan and supporter of Rio de Janeiro club Flamengo, where he attended matches and even reportedly influenced the transfer of his favourite player, Dário, from Atlético Mineiro to Flamengo in 1973. The non-selection of Dário for the national team, the *Seleção* (selection) in 1970, would change the course of Brazil's World Cup preparations and highlight the proximity of football and the regime. Brazil coach João Saldanha was fired weeks ahead of the 1970 tournament in Mexico after his relationship with star player Pelé broke down. Saldanha – a communist – had also been vocal in his criticism of General Médici's continued pressure to include Dário. Saldanha pointed out that he did not get to choose Médici's ministers, so Médici should not get involved with his team selection.[2] Saldanha was replaced by Mario Zagallo, himself a World Cup winner with Brazil in 1958 and 1962. Brazil's *Jogo Bonito* (beautiful game) would blow away all-comers in the heat of Mexico. Brazil beat Italy 4-1 in the final exhibiting some of the best football ever seen and on brilliant colour TV for the first time. Brazil was awarded the Jules Rimet Trophy to keep for claiming a third world title. 'General Médici made huge political capital out of the 1970 World Cup win, claiming it was a victory for the nation and a vindication for the military project,' Watson adds. The team was feted across Brazil, a national holiday was declared and Médici himself was photographed lifting the trophy, aligning himself personally with the win. Yet moves to bring a more disciplined approach to the Brazilian national team's style of play to reflect the regime's 'order and progress' message in the 1970s at the expense of the individual flair for which it was known backfired as the national team fell short at the 1974 and 1978 World Cups. In addition, public discontent was starting to grow.

On 3 June 1978, in Brazil's first World Cup group match in Mar del Plata, Brazil trailed Sweden 1-0 before prolific Atlético Mineiro striker Reinaldo pounced on a deep cross to level. In his celebration, Reinaldo stopped dead and raised his clenched right fist briefly before embracing his team-mates. The raised right fist would become his goal celebration trademark and also cause consternation for the Brazilian dictatorship. He was advised by the military-run Brazilian Sports Federation not to display the gesture, which it associated with socialism. In interviews and in his biography, Reinaldo has said the regime was out to undermine him, and that he felt isolated as almost no one in Brazil was speaking up against the regime.[3] Nicknamed *O Rei* (The King) by fans of Atlético Mineiro, Reinaldo was not selected for the following World Cup in Spain in 1982 due to injury, when Brazil really could have done with an out-and-out striker.

Reinaldo was a few years ahead of his time because in the early 1980s a new and impactful movement emerged in São Paulo – Corinthians Democracy. Conditions were easing slightly in Brazil with the arrival of the 1979 Amnesty Act, which provided amnesty to most political prisoners and enabled some exiled opponents to return to the country. It also provided the chance for the formation of new political parties and, eventually, to free elections. At influential São Paulo-based side Sport Club Corinthians Paulista – named after the English amateur side that had inspired its founders on a 1910 tour to Brazil – players were already demonstrating how democracy could work and encouraging its fans to follow its lead. Led by star playmaker

Sócrates and supported by defender Wladimir and striker Walter Casagrande, *Democracia Corinthiana* started as a new way of running a football club. Corinthians' president Waldemar Pires and publicist Washington Olivetto were supportive, and everything in the running of team affairs – from when to train, which players to sign, to whether players should stay at home or in hotels ahead of match day – were put to a 'one member, one vote' system.

On 15 November 1982, for the first time since the military had taken over nearly two decades earlier, Brazilians had the chance to elect a state governor. Corinthians, with its large working-class fanbase, had a huge platform to encourage people to vote – many for the first time. A few months earlier, the *Conselho Nacional de Desportos* (CND – National Sports Council) had allowed clubs to use the back of their shirts to advertise. Corinthians did not yet have a sponsor for the back of the shirt above the number, so the players got together and decided to include the message '*Dia 15 Vote*' (Vote on the 15th) on both its home and away shirts. On 27 October, Corinthians took to the field against São Bento in the first of five matches in the run-up to the election day in which the team wore their *Dia 15 Vote* message. Crucially for Corinthians Democracy, the players had not encouraged fans to vote for any particular candidate, just to make sure that people voted in the first place. In the state of São Paulo, the candidate for the *Partido do Movimento Democrático Brasileiro* (PMDB – Brazilian Democratic Movement Party), which had only reformed the previous year, won with 44 per cent of the vote. Across the state, 10.6 million people out of 13.1 million had voted.[4]

In 1983, in a *Paulista* derby against São Paulo at the Morumbi, Corinthians players walked on to the pitch with a banner that read '*Ganhar ou perder, mas sempre con democracia*' (Win or lose, but always with democracy). Corinthians' persistent activism earned them a rebuke from the CND, warning that they would intervene if they continued. Instead, Corinthians went on to claim the Paulista state championship in 1982 for the first time in three years and retained it a year later. The following year, Sócrates was vocal in a push for the right for the public to vote for the president of the country, not just state governors, as the military looked for ways to transition control. As part of the *Diretas Já* (Direct Elections Now) movement, Sócrates spoke to a huge crowd in São Paulo pledging that if the so-called Dante de Oliveira bill, named after its author, did not pass, he would leave the country. When the proposals were rejected by congress, Sócrates followed through on his threat and signed for Fiorentina in Italy. Corinthians Democracy faded away without its talisman and, on the pitch, Corinthians went into decline. In 1985, the military did finally hand over power to a civilian president, José Sarney, who initiated moves towards political freedom and a new constitution.

Yet Sócrates was not done with his messaging. At the Mexico '86 World Cup, he appeared in Brazil's opening game with Spain wearing a headband that read, *'Mexico sigue en pie'* (Mexico still stands), which referred to Mexico's recovery from a massive earthquake the year before. 'Corinthians Democracy was a response to the tentacles of militarisation and control that was present in all aspects of Brazilian society, and Brazilian football clubs were no different,' Watson explains. 'There were seeds of people looking for something different. Remember, it had been nearly 20 years of military dictatorship when Corinthians Democracy emerged. These very public demonstrations encouraging people to go and vote and saying things need to be democratic gave more Brazilians a greater belief that their vote would make a difference and they would not be in danger from the dictatorship which had, let's remember, tortured and imprisoned a lot of political opponents.' Watson concludes:

'I think it's important to see that footballers like Sócrates, Wladimir and Casagrande could have some impact on giving the wider public – who do look at the football pages and listen to the radio – confidence, and I think a lot of Brazilian political analysts undervalue that impact of the football culture on the political climate at that time.'

The dictatorship ended in 1985 with a transition to civilian government while the 1979 amnesty ensured that no one from the military was prosecuted for their role in tortures, disappearances and killings. Sócrates died in 2011, but the legacy of Corinthians Democracy lives on. In March 2019, Brazil's right-wing president Jair Bolsonaro wanted to hold a celebration to mark the 55th anniversary of the 1964 military coup that overthrew Goulart's democratically elected government. A judge barred the celebration and Bolsonaro's decision was met with widespread protests. Among those in the protest were Sport Club Corinthians Paulista, whose official Twitter feed issued a photo of a blood-splattered shirt with the words *Democracia Corinthiana* where the *Dia 15 Vote* message would have been. The tweet text included just a clenched fist emoji and #DemocraciaCorinthiana hashtag.[5] Bolsonaro, a former army officer, understands the power of football and several high-profile Brazilian professionals came out in support of his 2018 election campaign. Bolsonaro was named after the former Palmeiras and Santos player Jair da Rosa Pinto and has also appeared in public wearing a number of different clubs' shirts. Brazil was hit particularly hard by the Covid-19 pandemic, which drew heavy criticism for Bolsonaro's handling of the crisis. Corinthians' supporter group *Gaviões da Fiel* (Faithful Hawks) joined other fan groups on the streets of São Paulo in May 2020, including anti-fascist fans from rival club Palmeiras. Like the Corinthians of the early 1980s, the fans carried a huge banner that read '*Somos pela democracia*' (We are for democracy).

In Rio de Janeiro, some Flamengo fans also took to the streets, as did fans of Cruzeiro and Atlético Mineiro in Belo Horizonte. Football fans across the country were putting aside their differences and joining together to make themselves heard. When Brazilian deaths from Covid-19 passed 500,000 in June 2021, the fans were back on the streets. A 2015 study found that 76.6 per cent of Brazilians – around 150 million people – support a football club, which illustrates the sport's power,[6] and it is estimated there are around 60 anti-fascist *torcidas* (supporters' groups) in Brazilian football.[7] Football activism in Brazil has risen since the turn of the 21st century, driven partly in response to the *Estatuto do Torcedor* (Statue of the Fan) in 2003. The statute was designed to protect fans, but also led to higher ticket prices. Just as Brazil's turn came to host high-profile tournaments – such as the Confederations Cup in 2013, the FIFA World Cup in 2014 and the Olympic Games in 2016 – so football became a theatre of political protest. With political displays banned in the stadium, the streets have become the forum for protest. But are these fan protests actually making an impact? Andrew Downie is the author of *Doctor Socrates: Football, Philosopher, Legend*, a biography of the former Corinthians and Brazil captain. He says that fan groups are now more present at political demonstrations, but also fears that Brazilian fans' capacity to create a strong united voice might prove to be a false dawn. 'I think the fan groups are very welcome, but I don't know how much influence they have on their clubs,' Downie tells me. 'Corinthians is in a class of its own because of its history. To be sure, Corinthians fans have always been fiercely proud of the Corinthians Democracy movement.'

Rio de Janeiro club Vasco da Gama has a long history of fighting racism. In the 1920s, the club won the *Campeonato Carioca* with a racially and socially diverse team. At the time, football was a sport enjoyed by the social elites in a country that had been the last in the Americas to ban slavery. In 1924, Rio de

Janeiro's elite clubs demanded that Vasco drop 12 of its players on account of their social and educational background or risk exclusion from their proposed new association. Vasco refused, and the club was barred entry to the new *Associação Metropolitan de Esportes Athleticos* (AMEA – Metropolitan Athletic Sports Association). Vasco's president, Dr José Augusto Prestes, struck back with what is known as the *Reposta Histórica* (Historical Response). Prestes was unwilling to 'sacrifice' his players and his letter is now considered a watershed moment in Brazilian sport that opened up opportunities for black, dual-heritage and working-class footballers. In April 2021, to mark the 97th anniversary of the Historical Response, Vasco launched a special all-black kit. The club is also helping to raise funds for a mural that celebrates Vasco's black goalkeeper Barbosa, who was made a scapegoat for the *Maracanaço* – Brazil's 1950 World Cup defeat to Uruguay. It's not just in the big cities of Brazil's south where fan groups are becoming politically active. In the northern city of Salvador, fans of Esporte Clube Bahia are taking a stand on issues such as indigenous rights, racism, LGBTQ+ rights, sexual harassment and the environment.[8]

Chile and the long shadow of Pinochet

For Chileans, there is another September 11. It came 28 years before the attacks on the World Trade Center in 2001. On this date in 1973, the democratically elected Marxist government of Salvador Allende in Chile was overthrown by a CIA-backed military coup led by General Augusto Pinochet. Allende, holed up in the La Moneda presidential palace as the Chilean Air Force strafed the building, apparently shot himself rather than surrender. Pinochet's coup topped off a decade that had seen successive Latin American countries fall to right-wing military dictatorships. To secure his power base early, Pinochet rounded up thousands of his opponents in the Estadio Nacional.

Chile's national stadium had hosted the 1962 World Cup final, a tournament in which Chile had finished third, and was an immense source of national pride. Now, however, the Estadio Nacional was a detention centre for tens of thousands of students, trade unionists and activists. Changing rooms were used as torture cells. The infamous *Escontilla No.8* (Doorway No.8) is left empty as a memorial.

Adam Brandon has spent more than a decade living in Chile and analysing its football. 'To this day, space remains empty in the Estadio Nacional as a memorial for those who were tortured there,' he explains. 'There's a mural there that reads "A people without memory is a people without a future."' Other sports arenas throughout the country were used as detention and torture centres, including Estadio Chile, which was renamed in 2003 after its most famous victim, the protest singer Victor Jara. Sports arenas – especially football stadiums – served the dual purpose for the new regime of being spacious enough to detain large numbers of people as well as having a symbolic place in the heart of communities, according to Brenda Elsey, author of *Citizens and Sportsmen: Fútbol and Politics in Twentieth-Century Chile*. 'Football had become very associated with the left by the early 1970s. Almost all the football clubs had voted out a lot of the most conservative people that held positions in Chilean football's governing bodies,' she tells me. 'After the coup in 1973, there's opposition, but it's totally squashed out between 1973 and 1983 by doing a couple of things: firstly, replacing all of the football governance leaders with military men and elections are forbidden for all the top positions. Secondly, a lot of the former leaders who were union people go into exile, so they're not in the country to resist but they are able to do a lot of solidarity work outside Chile.'

Just over a week after Pinochet's coup, the Soviet Union (USSR) – which had supported Allende – broke off diplomatic relations with Chile. The timing was awkward, as the USSR and Chile were due to take part in a two-legged play-off to decide a qualification spot for the World Cup in West Germany the following year. The Soviets had topped their European qualifying group and had been losing finalists in the European Championships two years earlier. Chile had taken a replay against Peru to reach the play-off, so the Soviets were favourites. However, in the build-up to the first leg in Moscow's Lenin Stadium on 26 September, the Soviet press went quiet on the match, barely mentioning it in the news or even broadcasting it.[9] For the Chileans' part, the team had special dispensation to leave the country and were not able to communicate with any friends and family in Chile for the entire two weeks they were away. Chilean winger Leonardo Véliz reflected later that he was worried his bag would be checked as he was carrying music by left-wing musicians, including Victor Jara.[10] The Moscow leg finished goalless. The second leg was scheduled for the Estadio Nacional in Santiago on 21 November. Yet, instead of playing Chile on that date, the USSR team was beating Mexican second division outfit Irapuato 3-0. The Soviets refused to play at the Estadio Nacional, which it said had been turned into a concentration camp for Allende's supporters. The Chileans refused to postpone the game while the Soviets declined to play at another venue in Chile. In the end, the Chilean side kicked off at the Estadio Nacional without the USSR present, jogging the ball up the field, where skipper Francisco Valdes walked the ball into the empty net for the 'winner'. The referee blew his whistle at that point and Chile had qualified for the World Cup in West Germany at the USSR's expense. Chile instead played a full match against Brazilian side Santos, losing 5-0.

While the dictatorship never touched the players themselves, some family members were impacted. Forward Carlos Caszely's mother was abducted and tortured by the regime and Caszely himself refused to shake Pinochet's hand before the team set off for West Germany.[11] Although there were fears that the Soviets' exclusion would lead to a sympathetic boycott at the World Cup from the USSR's communist bloc partners, this did not materialise, with East Germany, Yugoslavia, Poland and Bulgaria all attending. Chile lost its opening match 1-0 to hosts West Germany at the Olympiastadion in West Berlin. It was a tempestuous affair in which Caszely became the first player to be sent off in a World Cup tournament. Four days later, Chile lined up against East Germany, communist allies of the Soviet Union. Alan McDougall is the author of *The People's Game: Football, State and Society in East Germany*. He informs me that the East German sports media had referred to the 'fascist junta' and the murders in the Estadio Nacional in the build-up to the World Cup. 'Even some fairly anti-communist West German newspapers criticised the decision to kick out the Soviet Union after the refusal to play in the Estadio Nacional,' McDougall explains. 'From what I've seen, there wasn't any pre-match comment from East Germany's coach, Georg Buschner, or the players on the Chile situation in June 1974, but I'd expect anything to have followed an anti-Pinochet line evident in some East German sports media.' Chile's final group match against Australia at the Olympiastadion in Berlin was a damp 0-0 draw. At the start of the second half, eight Chilean student demonstrators managed to plant a flag in the centre circle with the words '*Chile Socialista*' (Socialist Chile) on it. The protesters were removed by police and plain-clothed security, but the Chilean team was booed throughout.

In May 1973, several months before the coup, Santiago-based Colo-Colo had become the first Chilean side to reach the final of South America's premier club tournament, the *Copa Libertadores*, with Caszely leading its attack. Colo-Colo, the 'people's club', lost to a powerful Independiente side from Buenos Aires in its prime over three matches, after a decider was required. Once Pinochet took power, he appointed former director general of the police, Eduardo Gordon Cañas, president of the national football association, the *Asociación Central de Fútbol* (ACL) – nowadays known as the *Asociación Nacional de Fútbol Profesional* (ANFP – National Professional Football Association). Newspaper *La Tercera* reported that 300 million pesos would be made available for Colo-Colo's new stadium.[12] 'There's no evidence that Colo-Colo accepted any money from Pinochet,' Brandon tells me. 'It's a common insult to hear fans of Colo-Colo's main rivals Universidad de Chile say that they're the club of Pinochet, but from what I can see and the people I've spoken to it's heavily disputed.' During the dictatorship, new clubs emerged – such as two-time Copa Libertadores finalists Cobreloa from a major mining company. Cities in the extreme north and south of Chile, such as Arica, Iquique, Valdivia and Puerto Montt, all got teams. 'The theory is that the dictatorship encouraged football as it was seen as a distraction,' Brandon continues. 'I've also heard that *El Superclásico* between Chile's two leading clubs – Colo-Colo and Universidad de Chile – was often played on 11 September to distract from the chat and protests about how Pinochet and his allies ousted Allende from government. The date is always a big flashpoint to this day.'

In 1976, Colo-Colo made Pinochet honorary club president, a post he would hold until he relinquished power in 1990. This connection would forever link the club with the regime in the minds of many Chilean football fans. As for Caszely and Pinochet, the two would meet again in 1985, with Caszely wearing a red tie. According to Caszely, Pinochet called him over and said he would cut his red tie, making a cutting motion with his fingers, to which Caszely said he had more red ties at home and his heart would always be red.[13]

The memories of what occurred at the Estadio Nacional in late 1973 were still fresh in 1977 when Scotland embarked on a three-match tour of South America, which included a game against Chile at that ground. The match divided opinion, with some believing that football and politics should not be mixed, while various bodies, including the Trade Union Congress (TUC), British Foreign Office and various Scottish Members of Parliament, opposed the fixture. In an editorial in the *Aberdeen Press and Journal* four months ahead of the planned match, James Hunter described the decision to go as an 'insult to the memory' of those who died in the Estadio Nacional concentration camp and an 'affront' to those Chileans who had fled Pinochet's regime to settle in Scotland.[14] Scotland won the game, dubbed 'the match of shame' by some, 4-2 as part of its warm-up ahead of the World Cup in Argentina the following year, a tournament that would bring its own fair share of controversy.

Argentina's Dirty War and the 1978 World Cup

Every Thursday, a group of women meet at the *Plaza de Mayo* (May Square) in central Buenos Aires, where they gather in front of the presidential residence, *La Casa Rosada* (the Pink House). The women, wearing their distinctive white headscarves, have been gathering there since 1977 demanding answers to questions about what happened to their disappeared children in the 1970s and '80s during Argentina's 'Dirty War'. Some estimates put the total deaths during the Dirty War (1975–83) at more than 30,000.[15] Many others were tortured and new-born babies stolen from their imprisoned mothers. As early as March 1977, more than a year before the World Cup was due to kick off, Argentine investigative journalist Rodolfo Walsh wrote an open letter to the junta claiming 15,000 people had gone missing, 10,000 had been imprisoned and 4,000 were dead. Just after posting his letter, Walsh was gunned down in the street and his body taken away. *Las Madres de la Plaza de Mayo* (The Mothers of the Plaza de Mayo) and many *abuelas* (grandmothers) too have helped continue to shine a light on, and demand answers concerning, a dark period in Argentina's history during which the country hosted – and won – the World Cup.

Argentina had been awarded the right to host the 1978 World Cup way back in 1966. The country was yet to host the tournament, even though its neighbours in Uruguay, Brazil and Chile already had. In the decade between being awarded the tournament and the takeover of a military *junta* in a coup on 24 March 1976, the country had more or less descended into civil war, with bombings and kidnappings becoming an almost daily occurrence. Coup leader General Jorge Videla assumed the Argentine presidency and extended his crackdowns on both left-wing guerrillas and supporters of deposed president Isabel Perón. Media was forbidden to report or comment on the disappearances. The junta even engaged a New York-based public relations agency to help with its global image.[16] One of the junta's preferred tactics was to throw their opponents from planes into the waters of the River Plate, sometimes while they were still alive. It did not take long for opposition to the Videla government to hit the terraces. A banner supporting the left-wing guerrilla group *Los Montoneros* was displayed among Huracán fans visiting Estudiantes for a fixture in May 1976. The banner was removed but police moved into the stand at half time and one fan was shot dead.[17] The very first protest by *Las Madres de la Plaza de Mayo* was held on 20 June 1977 at *El Gasómetro*, the legendary former stadium of Club Atlético San Lorenzo de Almagro, one of Argentina's 'Big Five' football clubs. San Lorenzo's fans have an activist temperament, and many believe the land on which *El Gasómetro* stood before it was demolished in 1981 was sold to the government under duress.[18] Other sports associations became caught up in the politics. One by one, 20 members of a left-leaning rugby team in La Plata were kidnapped and disappeared between 1975 and 1978.[19]

Despite the ongoing domestic trouble in Argentina, FIFA had confirmed as early as February 1975 that the country would be allowed to host the 1978 World Cup by turning down an offer from the Netherlands and Belgium to host the tournament jointly.[20] The World Cup would become a massive propaganda opportunity for the junta and a huge amount of money was spent on the organisation of the tournament, despite the ongoing economic turmoil that Argentina was experiencing. A special body was created just to get the tournament ready on time – the *Ente Autárquico Mundial* (EAM – Overarching World Cup Entity). However, the EAM's chairman, General Omar Actis, was shot dead while on his way to his very first press conference. Rhys Richards is the author of *Blood on the Crossbar: The Dictatorship's World Cup*, which examines Argentina '78 in detail. He tells me that, for Argentina's military junta, hosting the 1978 World Cup provided both opportunities and risks. 'Sceptics within the military would cite the precarious economic climate in the country, with inflation soaring, as a reason to abandon the tournament. However, head of the navy Emilio Massera succeeded in convincing *de facto* president General Jorge Videla that hosting the World Cup was an opportunity to strengthen the dictatorship's control over its citizens, as well as legitimising the regime internationally. The dictatorship was eager to promote the stability of Argentine society and the ability of the administration to host one of the world's biggest events,' he explains.

Footballers were not exempt from the regime's oppressive approach. In 1977, Claudio Tamburrini was playing in goal for the lower league professional side Almagro in Buenos Aires. He was also studying philosophy at university, where he became involved with left-wing political groups. On 23 November, Claudio received a visit from two men at his home who forced him at gunpoint to get into a car. He was driven out of the city to Mansión Seré, a historic house that had been commandeered by the military, where he was interrogated and beaten. The men wanted names and information, and Tamburrini was subjected to electric shocks and waterboarding. Tamburrini and his cellmates managed to open the cell window and – naked, bound at the ankle and handcuffed – succeeded in climbing down to ground level using blankets tied together. Tamburrini stayed in a number of safe houses before slipping out of the country into Brazil and went on to build a new life in Sweden. Tamburrini's autobiography of his escape was turned into a film, *Crónica de una fuga* (*Chronicle of an Escape*) in 2006.[21]

Overseas, opposition to the Argentine World Cup picked up. An Amnesty International poster featured a football made out of barbed wire carrying the words 'Football Yes, Torture No'. A report by Amnesty International carried out by Lord Avebury, a British peer, made comparisons between how the military junta viewed the propaganda benefits of the World Cup and the way Hitler had used the 1936 Berlin Olympics to 'whitewash the evils of the regime', the *Birmingham Daily Post* reported.[22] In Paris, a body was set up called The Committee for the Boycott of the World Cup in Argentina (COBA) to raise awareness of the atrocities taking place in Argentina. 'COBA produced a lot of propaganda, particularly cartoons in magazines that linked football with right-wing dictatorships – blood and skulls and jackboots, and so on – that were very poignant, so there was a fairly organised movement there,' explains Dr Pete Watson. Some opponents to French participation at the World Cup went to further extremes. On 23 May 1978, French national team coach Michel Hidalgo was nearly the victim of a kidnapping attempt just two days before he and his team were due to fly out to the tournament. Hidalgo and his wife were driving near their Bordeaux residence when another car forced them off the road and four men got out to confront him. Hidalgo managed to fight off the only armed assailant, whose gun it later turned out was not loaded.[23] Eventually an anonymous caller claimed the failed kidnapping was an attempt to draw attention to the 'hypocritical complicity of France', which was the leading supplier of military equipment to the Argentine junta.[24]

In the Netherlands, two comedians – Bram Vermeulen and Freek de Jonge – launched a campaign to raise awareness of the atrocities that were being committed by the junta in Argentina. The two took their 'Blood on the Goalpost' cabaret show on tour across the country calling for the Dutch to boycott the tournament. They performed 25 shows in four months in conjunction with a media campaign and petitioned Dutch politicians and the Dutch FA (KNVB) take action. The Dutch government wanted the KNVB to decide whether to go or not, while the KNVB – like other European football associations at various points in history – did not want to mix sport and politics.[25] De Jonge and Vermeulen were joined by a crowd of protesters as the Dutch team boarded the plane at Schiphol Airport in Amsterdam bound for Argentina. The calls for a boycott had not succeeded, even with the support of players such as Oeki Hoekema of ADO Den Haag. The Dutch had been losing finalists at the previous World Cup in 1974 and were keenly fancied again to do well, even without Johan Cruyff, who decided not to go to Argentina due to a kidnapping ordeal that he and his family experienced in Barcelona rather than because of any opposition to the hosting of the World Cup in Argentina.[26]

In West Germany, 1974 World Cup-winning midfielder Paul Breitner refused to travel to the World Cup on political grounds. Goalkeeper Sepp Maier was also aware of the situation and signed an Amnesty International petition against the torture of the Videla regime.[27] Unlike Breitner, Maier did travel to Argentina and even hoped to join the *Madres de la Plaza de Mayo* in a protest but was advised against it.[28] The players and press who flew into Ezeiza Airport in Buenos Aires travelled into the city and drove past a concrete wall that blocked their sight of the poverty of the *villas miserias* (shanty towns).

Argentina's team had not been immune from the politics. 'Leopoldo Luque scored a number of goals in the tournament. The body of one of his close friends had turned up in a river,' Dr Pete Watson explains. 'René Houseman talks about how the area he grew up in – one of the *villas miserias* – had been destroyed by the military and a lot of the poor people moved out because [the regime] wanted to get rid of these examples of poverty or a lack of success when the public eye was going to be on them.'

Most significantly from a selection point of view, coach César Luis Menotti had chosen Huracán left-back Jorge Carrascosa to be his captain, but Carrascosa had become disillusioned with football in general – from refereeing to its politicisation.[29] Like Saldanha before him in Brazil, Menotti was a politically left-leaning coach working on the national side of an autocratic right-wing regime. Unlike Saldanha, Menotti kept his job. 'I think that for the junta, it was good from an external point of view to have a manager in charge who had socialist ideas,' Argentinian football journalist and podcaster Nacho Dimari tells me. 'They could show the world that there were no problems regarding that issue. His relationship did not impact the junta, of course, because he limited himself to managing the national team.'

For the tournament opener between 1974 champions West Germany and Poland, General Videla dispensed with his army uniform and wore a suit to tone down the optics of militarism. He was fairly hands-on during the tournament, pressuring the players to perform and even visiting the Peruvian dressing room along with former US Secretary of State Henry Kissinger to wish them well in a game that Argentina needed to win by four clear goals to proceed to the final due to the second-round group set-up. Argentina won 6-0. Among other incidents, opponents pointed to the fact that Peru fielded an Argentinian-born goalkeeper (even though he made some fine saves), but a fix was never proven. Peru had nothing to play for but pride and even hit the post. While the match was going on, at the exact moment that Leopoldo Luque scored Argentina's crucial fourth goal, a bomb went off outside the home of the Secretary of the Treasury, Juan Alemann, in the Buenos Aires neighbourhood of Belgrano. Alemann had been openly critical of the cost of hosting the World Cup and later revealed that he suspected the blast to be a message from within the military establishment.[30]

Intimidation tactics came into play when the hosts took on the Netherlands in the final. The Dutch team coach was battered by Argentinian fans *en route* to the Estadio Monumental. The *Oranje* players were then left waiting for their opponents on the pitch in front of a baying crowd and kick-off was delayed as the Argentinians complained to the officials about the cast on René van de Kerkhof's arm. The Argentines won 3-1 after extra time, although the story could have been different had Rob Rensenbrink's last-minute shot not rebounded off the posts with the scores level at 1-1. Even the goalposts at the Estadio Monumental held a hidden message. The ground staff had painted black bands around the base as a sign of remembrance for the disappeared, unbeknownst to the junta.[31] Argentina erupted at the final whistle, and even Claudio Tamburrini left his suburban safe house to join the victory celebrations in the streets. The FIFA World Cup trophy belonged to Argentina, but the Dutch players refused to shake Videla's hand.

One of the most notorious detention and torture centres was at the *Escuela de Mecánica de la Armada* (Navy Mechanics School), just 2km from the Estadio Monumental in Buenos Aires, where the World Cup Final was played. In other cities, too, there were torture centres within earshot of football stadia. Many survivors recount stories of being able to hear the euphoric cheers of the crowds as matches were going on interspersed with the screams of torture victims within their building. According to Dr Pete Watson, in one account a captive was taunted by her captors by being driven around to see the victory celebrations on the street. She recounts how she could have shouted for help but would probably have been ignored by the crowds. Domestic opposition was fairly low throughout the tournament as the junta were on high alert. The *Montoneros* did attempt to jam television and radio signals while Argentina's matches were being broadcast, but that was fairly limited in its reach. For a few minutes, some listeners would hear the *Montoneros'* message in their transmission. 'It's a very chilling time and it's a really problematic historical point of FIFA that their landmark competition is going on when tens of thousands of people are being tortured or disappeared during the time of the junta,' Watson concludes. 'It's a black period for Latin American football and FIFA as well.'

The dream photo for Videla of Argentina captain Daniel Passarella lifting the World Cup in front of a noisy and grateful home crowd covered in tickertape may have come true, but in many ways the tournament backfired, with global attention focusing on Argentina's human rights record. 'Opening Argentina's doors was not without risk. The news of the disappeared people, labelled "subversives" by the dictatorship, was spreading and their mothers had their voices heard internationally for the first time, thanks to the presence of the international press,' Rhys Richards explains. Videla was replaced as head of the junta in 1981. The failed attempt to take over the Falkland Islands/Islas Malvinas by force from Britain in 1982 led to the downfall of the military dictatorship and the following year it collapsed. 'The dictatorship's use of the Argentine national team was a tactic throughout their rule,' Richards adds. 'During the Malvinas/ Falklands War, then under the leadership of Leopoldo Galtieri, they organised a telethon to raise money for their soldiers. The phones were manned by celebrities, including Diego Maradona.

It would later be discovered that the money raised by the telethon was misappropriated by the dictatorship. As the war was lost, and the nation humiliated, it hastened the path to democracy and signalled the end for the dictatorship.'

So, how is the 1978 World Cup viewed inside Argentina with the benefit of hindsight? Nacho Dimari explains, 'You have two different points of view: the sporting one and the political one. For the first one, the players focused on winning the cup and Menotti was very important in that step. He got his players to concentrate on the sporting campaign – and he succeeded,' Nacho adds. 'The political one is a stain in our history as a country.'

After the return to democracy, military leaders were put on trial, with Claudio Tamburrini just one of the many witnesses. In its first World Cup after the fall of the dictatorship, Argentina triumphed in the sunshine of Mexico '86, thanks mainly to the genius – and a little of the hand – of Diego Maradona, who was left out of the 1978 squad. Tamburrini has since played again for Almagro in a friendly in remembrance of the victims of the dictatorship.[32] In March 2021, to mark 45 years since the military coup, Argentina's 1978 World Cup-winning goalkeeper Ubaldo Fillol – who was once threatened by the EAM's Carlos Lacoste to get him to renew his contract with River Plate with his father beaten up as part of the intimidation – planted a tree in tribute to the *Madres* and *Abuelas* of the Plaza de Mayo.[33] In May 2021, the Argentine government sent hundreds of DNA testing kits to its embassies across the world to help identify the estimated 30,000 victims of the dictatorship. Among those encouraging people to submit DNA was Diego Maradona's son, Diego Armando Maradona Jr. He urged people in his homeland of Italy to take DNA tests to help the Argentine government trace children stolen from their parents in the Dirty War.[34] Videla died in prison in 2013, serving time for his crimes during Argentina's darkest era.

Uruguay's 'Mundialito'

Uruguay flourished during the post-World War II period, enjoying the highest income per head in the whole of Latin America by the early 1950s, driven mainly by its wool trade. However, as the decade went on, demand fell and the economy deteriorated, leading to years of political and economic instability. This friction sparked protests from students and trade unions against job losses. The violence escalated when a left-wing guerrilla group called the *Tupamaros* initiated political kidnappings and assassinations in the late 1960s. The Uruguayan government called on the military to take on the *Tupamaros*, which they succeeded in doing, but in the face of continued economic uncertainty, the military seized complete control in early 1973. In moves that would be echoed in neighbouring Argentina later that decade, Uruguay's military limited the power of political opposition and unions, wrested control of the media and captured, tortured and disappeared many opponents. At one point, Uruguay is thought to have had the highest ratio of political prisoners per head of population anywhere in the world.[35]

In a footballing context, things were also in a dire state. At the 1974 World Cup in West Germany, Uruguay finished bottom of their first-round group, having picked up just one point. Four years later, the *Celeste* (Sky Blues) failed to qualify for the World Cup for the first time since 1958, meaning that Uruguayans had to look on enviously while their noisy neighbours across the River Plate celebrated winning their first World Cup trophy. Football had already been a platform for public opposition. In 1976, Defensor, led by communist-sympathising coach Professor José Ricardo de León, broke the traditional duopoly of Peñarol and Nacional to win its first league title. Its fans sounded the first audible calls for change.[36] However, football could provide the circus the Uruguayan dictatorship needed, with 1980 marking 50 years since the first FIFA World Cup, held in – and won by

– Uruguay. The regime gained FIFA approval to host the *Copa de Oro de Campeones Mundiales* (Gold Cup of World Champions) – or *El Mundialito* (Little World Cup). Uruguay invited all previous winners of the tournament to the Estadio Centenario in Montevideo, where the first competition had been held. The *Mundialito* was scheduled for 30 December 1980 to 10 January 1981, at the height of the European club season. An emerging Italian media magnate called Silvio Berlusconi handled the TV distribution. Uruguay was joined by holders Argentina, three-times winner Brazil, Italy and West Germany. England declined, citing fixture congestion at home, so the Netherlands – twice runners-up in 1974 and 1978 – stepped in. Uruguayan football had already taken an upswing that year with Club Nacional de Football, one of Uruguay's powerful duopoly along with Peñarol, winning its first *Copa Libertadores*. Now, it was up to the national team to restore some pride.

At least, that was the plan. A month before the *Mundialito* kicked off, the military regime had offered the people a plebiscite, suggesting a two-party democratic system headed by a pre-approved president. The goal was to endorse the 1973 coup and abolish the 1967 constitution. The regime expected to win the vote and the *Mundialito* would show the new Uruguay to the world. If Uruguay won the tournament, the regime could expect the same patriotic uplift that the Videla dictatorship in Argentina had enjoyed two years previously. However, to the regime's surprise, the people rejected the suggestion, with 57 per cent voting against the proposed new constitution and opposition in Montevideo as high as 63 per cent.[37] The *Mundialito* went from a celebration of a new Uruguay to a lightning rod for public dissent against the regime.

Uruguay won both its group games against Italy and the Netherlands 2-0 and advanced to the final to take on an impressive Brazilian side. With echoes of the *Maracanaço* – when

Uruguay beat Brazil at the 1950 World Cup in Rio de Janeiro to deny the hosts a first World Cup – the *Celeste* won 2-1 with a late Waldemar Victorino goal. Uruguay's coach for the *Mundialito* was Roque Máspoli, who had played in goal in the 1950 World Cup victory. Despite the heroics on the pitch, events off the pitch would concern the regime most. The Uruguayan crowd were heard to sing, *'Se va a acabar, se va a acabar, la dictadura militar'* (the military dictatorship is going to end, it's going to end), much to the chagrin of acting president Aparicio Méndez. In addition, the Brazilian side featured the influential Sócrates, who was well aware of the political situation in Uruguay and encouraged his team-mates to focus solely on the football. The tournament is barely remembered in Uruguay, let alone outside it. Afterwards, crackdowns continued on socialists and communist supporters, especially on the university campuses. The economy deteriorated further, and the military reluctantly ceded to a transition to return to a civilian government under Julio María Sanguinetti, who was elected president in November 1984. Largely forgotten, the *Mundialito* is not recognised by FIFA and the 18-carat gold trophy itself sat in a bank safe for decades before being rediscovered in 2018.

As in neighbouring Argentina, the years of military dictatorship still resonate on the football field four decades on from its demise. In June 2021, José Gavazzo, an army colonel who had been a leading actor in the military dictatorship and was serving a sentence under house arrest for his role in disappearances in both Uruguay and Argentina, died aged 81. The following day, players of Villa Española took to the field against Peñarol with a banner that read, *'Ni Olvido Ni Perdón'* (Neither forget or forgive). Villa Española forward Santiago *'Bigote'* (Moustache) López wore a t-shirt that read *'Te fuiste sin hablar, COBARDE'* (You left without speaking, COWARD). López disclosed that he wore the message as there were still relatives of the disappeared who could not find their family, and that football was an important platform to highlight the issue.[38]

According to Dr Pete Watson, football's role is changing in South America. 'I think one of the most interesting facets of how football is used politically in South America is that it's moving away from just being a rhetorical device to gain popularity and obscure national problems,' he explains. 'Football's now becoming increasingly deployed as part of health and education campaigns, peace processes, and as a way of reducing crime and violence in cities and rural areas. So football is being recognised as a potentially really powerful political and social tool for leaders across the continent.'

1 https://www.hrw.org/news/2021/06/22/first-conviction-dictatorship-crimes-brazil (retrieved 29/06/21)

2 https://thesefootballtimes.co/2018/06/17/brazil-1970-and-the-most-beautiful-football-in-history/ (retrieved 28/03/21)

3 https://pressfut.com/post/reinaldo-o-pantera-na-luta-contra-o-racismo-e-a-ditadura/ (retrieved 19/06/21)

4 https://www.ocuriosodofutebol.com.br/2015/09/corinthians-e-sua-camisa-dia-15-vote.html (retrieved 20/06/21)

5 https://twitter.com/Corinthians/status/1112386822380945408?s=20 (retrieved 21/06/21)

6 https://www.brazilfoundation.org/project/bom-senso-futebol-clube/ (retrieved 05/12/21)

7 https://brasil.elpais.com/esportes/2019-12-25/torcidas-antifascistas-se-multiplicam-nas-arquibancadas-do-futebol-brasileiro.html (retrieved 05/12/21)

8 https://www.theguardian.com/football/2019/nov/13/bahia-progressive-football-club-brazil-prices-fans-political-issues-love (retrieved 08/08/21)

9 *Aberdeen Evening Express*, 26 September 1973 (p18)

10 https://www.theguardian.com/football/2015/sep/09/chile-military-coup-general-pinochet-leonardo-veliz (retrieved 27/02/21)

11 https://www.lacuarta.com/espectaculos/noticia/caszely-torturas-madre-pinochet/615704/ (retrieved 05/04/21)

12 https://www.diarioantofagasta.cl/deportes/107528/la-historica-y-estrecha-relacion-de-colo-colo-con-la-dictadura-de-pinochet/ (retrieved 28/03/21)

13 https://www.lacuarta.com/espectaculos/noticia/caszely-torturas-madre-pinochet/615704/ (retrieved 05/04/21)

14 *Aberdeen Press and Journal*, 11 February 1977 (p10)

15 Hylland, Christopher, *Tears at the Bombonera* (Worthing: Pitch Publishing, 2021, p55)

16 *Aberdeen Evening Express*, 3 June 1978 (p13)

17 Wilson, Jonathan, *Angels with Dirty Faces: The Footballing History of Argentina* (London: W&N, 2017, p192)

18 Hylland, Christopher, *Tears at the Bombonera* (Worthing: Pitch Publishing, 2021, p74)

19 https://www.theguardian.com/sport/2021/apr/05/rugby-argentina-dirty-war-la-plata-1978-world-cup (retrieved 25/04/21)

20 *Aberdeen Press and Journal*, 10 February 1975 (p20)

21 https://www.bbc.co.uk/sounds/play/p09g8pll (retrieved 05/06/21)

22 *Birmingham Daily Post*, 26 May 1978 (p1)

23 http://papelitos.com.ar/nota/intento-de-secuestro-de-michel-hidalgo?z_language=en (retrieved 25/04/21)

24 *Aberdeen Press and Journal*, 25 May 1978 (p24)

25 https://npokennis.nl/longread/7808/argentinie-1978-had-oranje-dit-wk-beter-kunnen-overslaan (retrieved 24/04/21)

26 https://www.theguardian.com/football/2008/apr/16/newsstory.sport15 (retrieved 24/04/21)

27 Glanville, Brian, *The Story of the World Cup* (London: Faber & Faber, 2018, p216)

28 Wilson, Jonathan, *Angels with Dirty Faces: The Footballing History of Argentina* (London: W&N, 2017, p194)

29 https://www.clarin.com/deportes/Carrascosa-Menotti-Mundial_1978-renuncia_0_B1Z4ui5Pml.html (retrieved 25/04/21)

30 http://papelitos.com.ar/nota/una-bomba-en-la-casa-de-juan-alemann?z_language=en (retrieved 25/04/21)

31 https://www.theguardian.com/football/in-bed-with-maradona/2017/jul/05/1978-world-cup-argentina-political-protest-goalposts (retrieved 05/06/21)

32 https://www.bbc.co.uk/sounds/play/p09g8pll (retrieved 05/06/21)

33 https://www.iamnoticias.com.ar/2021/03/24/fillol-con-el-panuelo-de-fondo-un-arbol-plantado-y-la-memoria-intacta/ (retrieved 05/06/21)

34 https://www.theguardian.com/global-development/2021/jun/11/maradona-jr-pleads-for-dna-donors-in-search-for-argentinas-stolen-babies (retrieve 26/06/21)

35 https://www.britannica.com/place/Uruguay/The-struggle-for-national-identity (retrieved 31/05/21)

36 Goldblatt, David, *The Ball is Round: A Global History of Football* (London: Penguin, 2007, p626/975)

37 http://www.marca.com/reportajes/2011/12/el_poder_del_balon/2012/12/07/seccion_01/1354842065.html (retrieved 31/05/21)

38 https://www.ole.com.ar/futbol-internacional/bigote-lopez-villa-espanola-jose-gavazzo_0_i1rm0MEmx.html (retrieved 28/06/21)

Chapter 6

Britain

AS WE saw in Chapter Three, football fans in Britain had been active against fascism since at least 1935, when the Nazi Germany side came to play England at White Hart Lane. The following year, a planned march by the British Union of Fascists under its leader Oswald Mosley through the heart of the Jewish East End of London was abandoned after tens of thousands of locals – both Jewish and non-Jewish alike – blocked attempts by the police to clear their path. The event, known as the Battle of Cable Street, is now commemorated in a huge mural in Stepney. Three years later, war broke out.

Most domestic football was halted in September 1939, but British footballers would go on to play their part in the downfall of Hitler and Mussolini over the following six years. Even in the spring of 1939, when the British and French governments were still pursuing a policy of appeasement while continuing to arm themselves, it was clear to many that war was coming. During a match at Bolton Wanderers' Burnden Park, 28-year-old club captain Harry Goslin addressed the crowd with a megaphone. 'We are facing a national emergency,' he told the nearly 23,000 in attendance, adding that the Nazi danger could be met. 'This is something you can't leave to the other fellow,' he added. 'Everybody has his share to do.' His words clearly resonated, as the *Bolton Evening News* reported queues of people at the local Territorial Army hall after the match.[1] Goslin, who represented England in wartime matches and had played 107 consecutive games for Bolton Wanderers, was evacuated from Dunkirk after being credited with destroying four German tanks in France. He also saw action in north Africa and Italy. He died in December 1943 from wounds sustained from mortar shrapnel while advancing through Italy with the British Central Mediterranean Force.

Football was a key part of the recruitment process and within seven months of the Nazi invasion of Poland, 629 professional footballers had enlisted in the armed forces, while many others joined factories. In all, 80 British professional footballers were killed during the war.[2] Football would play a crucial role in maintaining morale and fitness both among the forces and the general population. Stan Mortensen, the first and, so far, only man to score a hat-trick in the FA Cup Final (1953), was lucky to survive the war. He was the only member of his crew to survive when their bomber crashed. Stanley Matthews and Eddie Hapgood, the captain when England were urged to give their infamous Nazi salute in Berlin in 1938, also joined the Royal Air Force (RAF). Another player to be evacuated from Dunkirk in 1940 and go on to fight in Italy like Goslin was Middlesbrough's Wilf Mannion, who would become part of England's first World Cup squad in 1950. Future England international Nat Lofthouse worked down the mines digging coal, as did Len Shackleton and Jackie Milburn. In London, Arsenal had been England's leading club in the 1930s. During the war, 42 of its 44 professionals along with many of the club's wider staff signed up to help the war effort. Ten Arsenal players would lose their lives at home or abroad during the conflict and many retired after the war.[3]

While Britain had officially declared war on Germany in September 1939 after the invasion of Poland, the Germans had not turned their attention westward in the first few months of the conflict, a period known as the 'phoney war'. Although the English season was officially cancelled, there was football in the form of Wartime League and also the Football League War Cup. The cup was a nine-week national tournament that culminated in a Wembley final on 8 June 1940, with West Ham beating Blackburn Rovers 1-0 in front of 43,000 people. The scorer of the only goal, Sam Small, was building ambulances for the war effort when not playing football. Just a month later, the Battle of Britain – Germany's attack on British air defences – began. Yet the Football League War Cup continued, with Preston North End beating Arsenal in the 1941 final after a replay. The cup was contested annually until 1945, with Bolton Wanderers winning the final competition against Chelsea. Later that year, Chelsea would be the first to play the visiting Dynamo Moscow team that came to build post-war bridges between the emerging Soviet-led Communist Bloc and the West.

Britain's global standing went into decline after World War II, as did England and Scotland's status as leading football nations. England lost 1-0 to the US at the 1950 World Cup and followed up that shock with a first home defeat to continental European opposition in 1953, when Hungary's 'Mighty Magyars' won 6-3 in the 'Match of the Century'. Just to prove this was not a one-off, the Hungarians inflicted a 7-1 defeat on England back in Budapest just six months later. Britain's economic decline, combined with inward migration from its former colonies, created resentment in some quarters, which in turn led to increased incidents of racism and the re-emergence of British fascism. In the 1970s, football stadiums became a key recruiting ground for the right-wing National Front (NF), with incidents reported at Leeds United and London clubs Chelsea, West Ham and Millwall, among others. Throughout the 1970s and 1980s, at Chelsea, for example, black players were regularly subjected to racist language and chants of 'Sieg Heil' from sections of the crowd, and Nazi insignia was also spotted. One account in the *Sunday Mirror* from October 1980 reports a Union Flag with the letters 'SS' sewn into it unfurled by Chelsea fans at Watford.[4] On Boxing Day that year, a group of Chelsea fans attacked a mosque on an away day to Luton.[5]

John Williams is Associate Professor at the University of Leicester in England. He attended the 1982 FIFA World Cup finals in Spain and is the author of several books on football, including hooliganism. He tells me that the Chelsea connection was also particularly strong with the England national team in the early 1980s, when the National Front was very active – for example, during the World Cup finals in Spain. 'Some squaddies [soldiers], based overseas, were also keen adherents. The NF was holding impromptu "meetings" before and after England matches, handing out stickers, comparing "smelly" Spaniards with "alien" communities back home,' Williams explains. 'This was the period when black England players were booed by some racist followers, or the goals they scored were discounted by sections of England's support because they were not "real" Englishmen.' I asked Williams how anti-fascist movements, supporters' groups and the authorities countered the far right in and around football during this period. 'To be honest, not very well,' he says. 'There was some local activism, of course, but football is peculiarly partisan and lacking a collective presence of voice, and without the ease of the mobile phone and social media contacts of today, it was often difficult for rival fan groups to get together to oppose racism and the NF at someone else's ground. Rock Against Racism had none of these problems, of course, and it was much more successful.'

While the music scene took a direct approach to tackling racism, the Football Association maintained a policy of keeping politics out of the game during this period. However, the FA was at odds with Margaret Thatcher's government – which was presiding over a period of social discontent, with riots in major cities and the miners' strike – over how to deal with England's hooligan problem. When Mrs Thatcher asked the FA what it was doing about its hooligans, the FA chairman Ted Croker boldly stated that 'these people are society's problems' and that 'we don't want your hooligans in our sport, Prime Minister'.[6] In 1986, the Centre for Contemporary Studies – an independent social research body – published a report warning that football authorities and the government in Britain had 'slept too soundly' in the face of the rise of fascism in and around football in the 1970s.[7] The report, which highlighted the need for more action to be taken, particularly around racist abuse from the terraces, was published just a year after the Heysel Stadium disaster, in which 39 people were killed when a wall collapsed. Some groups had emerged in the 1970s to challenge the rise of the far right on the terraces. By 1978, the Anti-Nazi League had attracted the largest gathering of anti-fascists to a rally in London since the 1930s.[8] The organisation leafletted football grounds in the late 1970s to counter the activity of the National Front. The anti-fascist movement had a significant cheerleader in Nottingham Forest's two-time European Cup-winning manager Brian Clough. Forest's right-back was England's first black international, Viv Anderson, who had received plenty of racist abuse from the terraces. In a match against Norwich City in 1981, Nottingham Forest distributed anti-Nazi posters that read, 'Forest are magic, NF Nazis are tragic', with Clough stating that he would help in any way he could to stop the National Front.[9]

Following the success of the England national side at the Italia '90 World Cup, the advent of the Premier League and the Taylor Report, which recommended all-seater stadiums after the Hillsborough tragedy, English football took an upward turn. When an element of England fans rioted at Lansdowne Road, Dublin, in a friendly between the Republic of Ireland and England in February 1995, police cited neo-Nazi groups as the source.[10] The Dublin riot was very much at odds with a sport that was smartening up its image and becoming a strong international brand with the strength of the Premier League in the run-up to Euro '96, which was being held in England. This was also around the time of the dawn of *Cool Britannia*, Britpop and the coming of Tony Blair's New Labour government in 1997. The dark days of the 1980s looked a long way behind in the rear-view mirror in the colourful promise of the mid-late 1990s. English hooliganism's day was done. Or was it? Euro 2000 saw more trouble caused by some England fans in Charleroi, Belgium, which led to Blair apologising for their behaviour to his fellow European leaders. More sophisticated means were developed to identify troublemakers and prevent them from travelling to or attending matches. As Marseille 2016 showed, the English hooligan problem was still there. In addition, the racist abuse aimed at England's black players on social media after the Euro 2020 final penalty shootout defeat to Italy proved there was still work to do, although the public support shown to the players far outweighed the abuse.

In recent decades, English football has been far more proactive in combatting discrimination in and around the game. In 1993, Let's Kick Racism Out of Football – now known as Kick It Out – was launched by the Commission for Racial Equality and the Professional Footballers' Association to tackle all forms of discrimination. In 2013, the organisation made a mobile phone app available to fans to report any incidents of discrimination they witnessed in confidence. At club level, Chelsea FC launched its *Say No to Antisemitism* project around Holocaust Memorial Day in 2018. At fan level, groups such as Football Lads and Lasses Against Fascism have emerged in recent years.

The rise of the modern progressive football club

Not everyone has been happy with the Premier League. Many traditional fans in England have moved down the leagues for a more affordable, 'authentic' experience of football, even in the lower reaches of the non-league, where spectators can drink alcohol within sight of the pitch and stand where they please. British football fans have also ventured abroad and brought back elements of the European ultra culture to their grounds to add atmosphere. In the 21st century, this has led to new cultures emerging on many of the terraces across Britain, many of which are left-leaning. Cas Mudde says that some clubs attract fans who have those values, which he has observed particularly in the third club in a city, such as Unterhaching in Munich or Partick Thistle in Glasgow. 'What you see at the moment is smaller teams that are particularly progressive, sometimes anti-fascist. I don't think that's due to the prevalence of far-right sentiments in the stadiums, but almost more to the gentrification of top-flight football,' he says. In England, at least, there are some notable examples.

Clapton Community Football Club

Clapton Football Club from east London was one of football's early evangelists, becoming the first English side to play overseas when it travelled to Belgium in 1890 to trounce the club now known as Royal Antwerp 8-1. By the first decade of the 21st century, the club was playing in the lower reaches of England's regional tiers with very low attendance figures. Then something changed around 2012. Groups of football fans looking for an alternative football experience in an area where even lower-league football at Leyton Orient would cost £20 started appearing at Clapton's Old Spotted Dog ground. They started to invite their friends and other like-minded people and then, after resolving a dispute with Clapton FC's owner, launched as Clapton Community Football Club in early 2018.

'It started as a very humble support group, just trying to raise awareness of the club and trying to encourage people back into the ground,' Clapton CFC member Robin Cowan tells me. It worked and soon several hundred new supporters were coming along to support the club and put their own mark on the atmosphere. In the terraces, these fans found a space to express themselves and their voice against racism, homophobia and misogyny. In 2018, the club made the international press with its new away shirt, based on the red, yellow and purple of the flag of the Second Spanish Republic to coincide with the 80th anniversary of the end of the Spanish Civil War. The shirt features the three-pointed star of the International Brigades and the war cry ¡No Pasarán! (they shall not pass) on the collar. Cowan tells me that the shirt was inspired by the story of a volunteer from the nearby Newham area who went to fight in Spain for the International Brigades. 'We talked about opening up a competition to get different people to design shirts and this one idea really was the outstanding choice, just for the detail,' Cowan explains. 'East London had one of the highest volunteer rates in Britain for the International Brigades, so it's something that we are proud of and links us directly to the area the club is from, too.' Clapton CFC volunteers worked flat out to service international demand for the shirt, which was made in Italy by ethical sportswear firm Rage Sport.

Clapton CFC enjoys a big international support and has built links across Europe with other anti-fascist clubs. As well as playing against CE Júpiter in Barcelona, the club appeared in a match for Roter Stern Leipzig's (Red Star Leipzig) 20th anniversary. Cowan explains that east London has always been a hub of polarised political activity. Forest Gate had been the base of the British Union of Fascists and the area also saw National Front activity in the 1980s. 'At Clapton, we are really conscious that we're in a very diverse and very working-class area. I just think it's really, really important at the start just to kind of make a point, and the anti-fascist point was the clearest message we could send out,' he concludes.

Dulwich Hamlet

South of the river in the leafy suburb of Dulwich, another movement has sprung up over the last couple of decades. Listed in *The Guardian* in 2015 as a 'hipster's favourite football club',[11] Dulwich Hamlet's supporters have been campaigning on core issues for years, including the salvation of their own ground. I used to live not far from the Champion Hill stadium and went a few times each season, including to Dulwich Hamlet's landmark friendly with Britain's top-ranking LGBTQ+ football club, Stonewall FC, in 2015. Michael Wagg, who we met back in the section on Altona 93 and who has co-written a book inspired by the relationship between the two clubs, has been a Hamlet fan since around 2010. According to Wagg, the hipster tag is wide of the mark. 'It's become, in my view, fairly lazy shorthand, but in my experience far more significant and reflective of the culture around the club are the initiatives, often fan-led, which work actively with the south London community and beyond,' he tells me. For Wagg, the Stonewall FC fixture is a good example: an anti-homophobia friendly match instigated by a lifelong supporter, which saw a crowd of nearly 400 gather and raise £2,000 for the Elton John AIDS Foundation. Wagg adds that around the same time, Dulwich Hamlet fans were active in support of workers taking industrial action at both the Ritzy cinema in Brixton and the Dulwich Picture Gallery, while there was a large collection made for the Southwark Foodbank. Looking further afield, a group of fans from the club's Supporters' Trust teamed up to collect donations and deliver van loads of vital supplies to the refugee camps in northern France. More recently, the Supporters' Trust has organised bike collections for The Bike Project and winter coat collections for Wrap Up London. It has also raised money for LGBTQ+ charities from the sale of rainbow scarves, and for the local King's College Hospital Charity from the sale of face masks.

Other recent Hamlet fan-led initiatives have included a partnership event with Love Football Hate Racism and Fans for Diversity; and a series of thoughtful, in-depth online discussions inspired by the Black Lives Matter movement, hosted by the *Forward The Hamlet* podcast and striker Danny Mills, which explored the lived experience of players from both the men's and women's teams. On the playing side, the introduction of the Dulwich Hamlet Women's teams, merged from AFC Phoenix, as a central part of the club has been a recent important step, not least in welcoming more women and girls to Champion Hill. 'Outside of any political or social tags, I think these examples – and there are many others – are expressive of a commitment among much of the fanbase to try to help make a real difference where it's needed,' Wagg explains. 'The same spirit that sees the Hamlet support – part of which is known as "The Rabble" – singing reworded, sometimes mildly obscure pop, with wit and vim, also sees it challenging all racist, sexist, homophobic or transphobic behaviour, and working hard to make Champion Hill a welcoming and safe place for everyone.' Wagg concludes, 'On a lighter note, when there's a goal kick, rather than the usual yell to accompany it, personally I'd much rather hear The Rabble's alternative and random refrain – borrowed from visiting Belgian fans some years ago – *Ooshka beat, olé olé*!'

Visitors to Champion Hill and other grounds will spot stickers about the place, some of which may well have been designed by the Trade Union Football and Alcohol Committee (TUFAC). The non-profit sports society creates stickers, t-shirts, posters and more, featuring slogans and images from the history of anti-fascism, such as the famous Spanish Republican fighter

Marina Ginestà. For TUFAC, football was a key inspiration. 'We all went away together on an "infamous" lost weekend in Hamburg in 2017,' TUFAC founder Albert tells me. 'We all love football, beer and anti-fascism. We also like t-shirts and stickers. The idea just grew, using our age and experience as a force for good.' The TUFAC team naturally gravitates towards the world's leftist clubs, such as FC St Pauli, Rayo Vallecano and AS Livorno. 'Football is a reflection of our society, for good and bad,' Albert continues. 'The fascists thought they had it to themselves for too long. Football must be a force for good and a force for change. That's our *raison d'être.*'

Whitehawk FC, Brighton

Brighton has long been the LGBTQ+ capital of the UK, with around one in eight residents identifying as gay, lesbian or bisexual,[12] and it is also home to the country's largest Pride festival. This inclusive culture on the south coast has also filtered through to its local football clubs. Nearby Lewes CFC was the first football club in England to pay its women's team the same as its men's. But it's another football club in the eastern end of the Brighton & Hove urban area that has been attracting a lot of attention in recent years. Nestled in a lee of the South Downs, overlooked by windswept trees standing at awkward angles and the slow-moving silhouettes of dog walkers, is the Enclosed Ground, home of Whitehawk FC. When I first visited in 2017, I was greeted on entry by Half Man Half Biscuit's 'Joy Division Oven Gloves' playing over the PA system, which was a positive sign and a step back from the traditional pre-match crowd-pleasers. The attendance in the sixth tier of English football that day was nudging 300 and what was most remarkable was the complete absence of swearing. The fans created a family-friendly environment with European-style chanting and the rattling of keys at set pieces, which the fans call 'key moments'.

It was in the 2009/10 season when Whitehawk FC, until then a regular non-league club, started to attract a more diverse crowd of supporters. Former Brighton & Hove Albion midfielder Darren Freeman became first-team manager, supported by former West Ham defender George Parris in the first season. Freeman led the club to three promotions in four seasons, plus an infamous FA Cup run in the 2015/16 season. This kickstarted Whitehawk's now-famous 'party atmosphere', and with it came the inclusive message. Today, this atmosphere is all persuasive, and there's a new generation of students from nearby Brighton and Sussex Universities joining the chorus, according to Kevin Miller, the club's vice chair, head of commercial and marketing, and matchday PA.

'I suppose the core fan base – the "ultras", it's an ironic term – reflect the city as a whole: tolerant, inclusive and accepting of all,' Miller explains. 'The club adopted the ultras' "footballforall" mantra and a few years ago allowed them to put the inclusive statements on the main stand steps.' Miller believes that the non-league set-up enables local clubs to foster a real connection with their fanbase as familiar faces gather at each home game, which blurs the lines between club and supporter. This connectivity between club and community became particularly acute during the Covid-19 pandemic. Whitehawk FC ran a number of virtual initiatives with other clubs, including Guernsey FC, Raith Rovers and Dulwich Hamlet, raising thousands of pounds for various food banks and mental health charities during the pandemic. Hawks' first match back in 2021 after a winter of lockdowns included a 'Community Day' of Whitehawk FC fans versus Guernsey FC's mainland-based supporters and featured former England and Liverpool goalkeeper David James. James appeared as a brand ambassador for energy firm Utilita, whose 'Football Rebooted' campaign aims to repurpose more than a million pairs of football boots and spare them from landfill. Despite being located in the largely affluent South East of England, the Whitehawk Estate was one of the most deprived areas in the UK as recently as the 1990s. Whitehawk FC set up 'Hawks In The Community' in partnership with local youth centre the Crew Club, running programmes for people of all generations, which is helping to drive positive change in the area.

Whitehawk FC's stance on diversity and inclusion reflects the ethos of Brighton & Hove as home to a large LGBTQ+ community, Miller tells me. In early 2019, the club was approached by broadcaster and diversity champion Dr Sophie Cook and former Brighton & Hove Albion player Guy Butters with an idea to put together an LGBTQ+ game against an all-star team of ex-Premier League stars. So, during Pride weekend of 2019, the 'Rainbow Rovers' – a team of LGBTQ+ players from around the country – beat a team of ex-pros 5-2. The ex-pro team included Paul Walsh, Keith Gillespie, Lee Martin and Lee Hendrie. Rainbow Rovers is now amalgamated into the wider Whitehawk FC stable. 'Rainbow Rovers shirts have sold around the world, and the club are rightly proud of what we've achieved, and with the full backing of the sport's governing body, the Football Supporters Association, Kick it Out, Football v Homophobia, and so many more, we can take the message of tolerance and inclusion around the country,' Miller adds.

Miller believes that non-league football offers more freedom for expression and less factionalism as fans are free to mingle. 'It's been interesting to see students at the ground for the first time, brought up on the Premier League and unaware of the freedoms that non-league can offer,' Miller concludes. 'We try to be as inclusive as possible. The ultras even have a no-swearing policy, and you'll often hear them shout their indignation at an official's decision with the chant, "The Referee's a Referee!" and with the drums, the "key moments", the disco ball dangling from the home stand end, "The Din", the atmosphere created sums up the joys of the beautiful game at this level – warm, friendly, a little rough around the edges, but with a heart of gold.'

Meeting Pier Pressure: Eastbourne Town's ultra group

Down in the Southern Combination Football League Premier Division, the ninth tier of English football, there's a group of fans clad in yellow and blue huddled under a corrugated iron stand. 'It's full of old people and seagulls, oh, Eastbourne Town is wonderful!' they sing. This is Pier Pressure, one of the local ultra groups. There are worse places to watch football than Eastbourne Town FC. The club plays in the serene grounds of The Saffrons, a central location in Eastbourne. With the attractive Italianate tower of Eastbourne Town Hall at one end, the visitor almost gets the feel of being in a Victorian country club. Eastbourne Town FC is the oldest football club in Sussex, founded in 1881 as Devonshire Park FC. All the atmosphere is generated at one end, with the drums and flags of supporters' groups Pier Pressure and The Beachy Head Ultras, both named after local landmarks.

Alex Brown co-founded Pier Pressure in 2015. Brown concedes that Eastbourne is a geographically unusual place for an ultras group. 'Whilst there are three FA-chartered non-league sides in Eastbourne, there is only one football league club in East Sussex – Brighton & Hove Albion – 20 miles away,' he tells me. Another challenge in the area is that many local football fans support teams in the North West, such as Liverpool or Manchester United. 'I've never understood this, Paris Saint-Germain are geographically closer to Eastbourne,' Brown adds. The lack of local professional football clubs in the area led Brown and his friends to support their local side. 'We settled on the idea of supporting Eastbourne Town based on its location – on the same road as the train station – as this was the easiest meeting point for a group of friends spread across Eastbourne and its surrounding towns and villages.'

Brown explains that Eastbourne is a seaside town with a large amount of social deprivation, but it is also a traditionally Tory-voting town and there is huge disparity in wealth in the area. 'Politically, we align ourselves to the left and we are outspoken about this,' Brown continues. 'We have supporters and detractors within the club and have been threatened with bans on numerous occasions relating to banners that we have displayed and the use of pyrotechnics at games. We have come to an agreement with the club that any political messaging on banners or stickers that we produce should be attributed to the ultras group, which is entirely a separate entity from the club.'

Brown says that Eastbourne Town FC is the most traditional of Eastbourne-based clubs so perhaps not the most obvious choice for a left-wing ultras group to support. 'To be honest, we completely overlooked this fact when we first pitched up to a game in the autumn of 2015, armed with a packet of chimney cleaners we set light to, in lieu of having any smoke bombs,' Brown explains. 'Whilst the club was cautious about our support at first, we have been welcomed with open arms by most.' And Pier Pressure certainly contributes to the experience; group members produce the matchday programmes for the club and maintain the website and social media accounts. 'So, as well as running the ultras group, we volunteer for the club,' Brown says.

So why have non-league clubs like Eastbourne Town, Dulwich Hamlet, Whitehawk and Clapton attracted like-minded, left-wing fans? 'I think the reason non-league has experienced a resurgence in interest in the last decade is based in part on the internet and the community you are able to cultivate through social media,' Brown argues. 'And, also, the disillusionment with modern football, many feel priced out by Premier League clubs and are seeing the benefit and sense of community you gain from supporting a local team.' Brown explains that continental European clubs like FC St Pauli and Rayo Vallecano were not on Pier Pressure's radar when they were starting up their section. Instead, they were inspired by what they saw going on down the road in Whitehawk and in London at Dulwich Hamlet and Clapton. 'We were inspired by this and sought to replicate it, using the ultras group as a vehicle to express our politics and beliefs, and meet new people through doing so,' Brown adds. 'It's definitely worked, and I have met some of my closest friends through the club.'

A core group have known each other for years through playing in various bands together in the south coast punk scene. 'Our approach to running the ultras group is born out of the mentality of those punk days; it's very idealistic and everything is self-funded and produced in a very DIY way. We even funded the new stand at The Saffrons, which we spend our Saturdays in,' Brown says. 'I feel that political groups within English football are very much a niche and almost a bit of a novelty,' Brown continues. 'Weekly, we will get requests on social media to send out stickers or pin badges that we have self-produced and there is almost an ignorance to the fact that we are an ultras group and not a brand. We're not for sale; everything we do is to promote interest in our political beliefs, and hopefully people will support the club and join as a by-product of that. The response to these requests is always the same, *come to a game – see what we're about and show some support.* They rarely do.'

Politics in British football today

Domestic football in England remains largely apolitical at senior club level compared to Italy, Spain or Germany. In Scotland, the standout fixture of Rangers versus Celtic still carries the weight of a century and a half of inter-community rivalry within

Glasgow and beyond. At international level, we see that both the English and Scottish national sides have been drawn into political controversies when their respective football associations did not want sport and politics to mix – England in the 1930s when facing Germany and Italy, and Scotland's World Cup journey in 1978. Domestically, racism, antisemitism and homophobia remain a challenge to football authorities and clubs. In 2022, Tottenham Hotspur revealed the findings of a three-year fan engagement programme and encouraged its fans to 'move on' from using the Y-word in reference to the club's historical Jewish connections. More than nine in ten (94 per cent) Spurs fans surveyed acknowledged that the term could be considered racist abuse towards Jewish people.[13]

Andrew Lawn is the author of *We Lose Every Week: The History of Football Chanting*. He explains that incidents of racist chanting were falling in UK grounds until the European Union referendum of 2016, since when there has been an increase. While hard to enforce rules against racist chanting, he believes that fans self-policing the terraces is the answer, although there is still a problem with homophobic chanting. 'I do think that society is getting more attuned to this stuff, and we will get better. As a society, we're getting more progressive and this should filter through to the stands,' he says. 'I think you'll get more and more polarity between clubs, where fans who are more progressive and less willing to engage in the toxic stuff will congregate at clubs like Dulwich Hamlet, Eastbourne Town, Clapton, and then you'll get more left-wing and right-wing clubs.'

Once upon a time, European ultras drew inspiration from England's boisterous terraces – and some even absorbed the hooligan fashion and attitude that went with it; now, new cultures from the continent are infusing the game across the UK. Within the non-league structure, new cultures have emerged, in part inspired by European left-leaning ultra movements, such as those at FC St Pauli and Rayo Vallecano, but with a uniquely British flavour of song and wit.

1 https://www.theboltonnews.co.uk/sport/18019365.harry-goslin-bolton-wanderers-captain-led-side-war/ (retrieved 04/07/21)

2 https://www.iwm.org.uk/history/10-facts-about-football-in-the-second-world-war (retrieved 29/06/21)

3 https://www.arsenal.com/news/ve-day-75-arsenal-and-second-world-war (retrieved 04/07/21)

4 *Sunday Mirror*, 12 October 1980 (p21)

5 *Daily Mirror*, 6 February 1981 (p32)

6 https://www.fourfourtwo.com/features/how-90s-saved-english-football (retrieved 04/07/21)

7 *Dundee Courier*, 28 May 1986 (p3)

8 *Reading Evening Post*, 21 June 1978 (p8)

9 *Daily Mirror*, 4 April 1981, (p30)

10 *Sunday Tribune*, 19 February 1995 (p12)

11 https://www.theguardian.com/football/blog/2015/nov/06/the-joy-of-six-hipsters-favourite-football-clubs (retrieved 05/07/21)

12 https://theculturetrip.com/europe/united-kingdom/england/articles/why-is-brighton-the-gay-capital-of-the-uk/ (retrieved 08/12/21)

13 https://www.bbc.co.uk/sport/football/60330719 (retrieved 14/02/22)

Conclusion

THE COUNTRIES I focused on in this book have witnessed some of the most extreme examples of football clubs, players and fans standing against fascism and the far right. In the days when fascist or far-right regimes ruled over nations, this defiance could range from the simple but brave act of refusing to salute to active political campaigning. In times of war, defiance could range from taking up arms, saving the lives of the persecuted, or just staying alive in appalling conditions in camps designed to dehumanise and kill. In an age when the far right and far-right populism appears to be making a comeback, football is once again a theatre of the culture war in many countries around the world. Authorities have tried with varying degrees of success to curb racism, homophobia, sexism, xenophobia, antisemitism and other forms of discrimination, but it is often the fans themselves who have taken the most impactful stance.

Progressive football is not just limited to the traditional large footballing cultures of Germany, Spain or Italy, for example. In the 1990s, Norway was suffering from a spate of racist incidents in domestic football. In 1995, a fan of Oslo club Vålerenga travelling to play Brann in Bergen was spotted in a t-shirt with the slogan 'white power'. So the people in charge of Vålerenga's multicultural youth team decided to make a stand against the extreme-right elements within the club's fanbase. The club's initiative aimed at grassroots children's football even gained support from the country's prime minister. In one of its tournaments, a Muslim girls' team entered. In the late 1990s, the club carried the slogan '*Vålerenga mot rasisme*' (Vålerenga against racism) on its shirt.[1] 'Norway is a fairly small, transparent society. However, the far right was a problem, especially from the late 1980s and mid-90s,' Vålerenga fan Lars Schou informs me. Schou explains that anti-fascist manifestations have always far outnumbered fascist ones in the post-war years. However, by the 1990s, they did occasionally break into running battles between anti-fascist and neo-Nazi gangs. Schou says that within the Vålerenga supporter base, the *Klanen* (Clan) fan group was instrumental in making sure that right-wing elements knew they were not welcome. In 1997, spearheaded by young striker John Carew, the club enjoyed promotion back to the Norwegian top division and won the cup at a time when public interest in domestic football was on the rise. 'I remember this very fondly as it felt for the first time ever that the general public actually liked us [Vålerenga],' Schou continues. 'Just two years before, my mother had been embarrassed that I even went to the games because of the stigma of being labelled a bully or a racist.'

Schou is quick to point out that Vålerenga is not a 'left-wing club', like FC St Pauli. 'It's mostly an apolitical club and party politics is mostly left out of the stadium. But the club and the fans had to draw the line somewhere. Bigotry was not welcome any more. We have fans from all walks of life, but mostly working and lower middle class. And with that you get people who are both lefties and more on the right, as you do in the stands at most clubs,' he tells me. Vålerenga is also active outside football and runs a social project called *Jobbsjansen*, which helps young people who drop out of school to find work. Aside from Vålerenga, Norwegian football fans have become more activist in recent years, Schou explains, largely due to social media. 'All of a sudden the podcasts and Twitter brought different types of fans together and we learned that not everyone who supports that other team are idiots, that we agree on a few fundamental things.' Schou says that there is a natural scepticism in Norwegian fan culture towards modern football. When the World Cup was awarded to Qatar, many fans decided to do something about it. The potential for the Norwegian national side to boycott Qatar 2022 due to the Gulf state's human rights record was suggested and gathered widespread support. Schou was part of a group of fans that came up with an anti-sportwashing initiative called *Vår Fotball* (Our Football) that included a number of pre-made statutes that fans can encourage their clubs to adopt.[2] 'And it worked. Vålerenga, Fredrikstad, Brann, Strømsgodset, Tromsø, Lillestrøm, Molde, Start and Haugesund all passed anti-sportswashing statutes – sometimes unanimously – at their annual general meetings,' Schou says. 'More clubs will probably do so next year. This coincided with the boycott Qatar thing, so it was helpful, but perhaps also frustrating because it made the whole debate about Qatar in particular and not sportswashing in general.' However, the Norwegian Football Federation (NFF) rejected the boycott of Qatar 2022.[3]

In Belgium in the 1980s, there was a big problem in domestic football with certain far-right groups and many clubs had hooligan firms, but by the 1990s hooliganism had faded away. A new generation of progressive, non-violent fans emerged, some of whom were not happy with the way football was going. In 1996, Standard Liège fans founded the Ultras Inferno group, bringing a left-wing political edge to a traditionally apolitical establishment. Mario Bronckaerts is a life-long Standard fan who represents supporters' groups in meetings with the club's directorship. 'You have young people in the 1990s who want to change something about capitalism, because we have a lot of challenges with poverty in Liège,' he tells me. 'The ultras run activities, such as food and clothing banks, and that is pretty unique in Belgium. I can't think of another club in Belgium where fans do this.' A recurring theme among leftist clubs, from Livorno to Nicosia, is the image of Che Guevara among the stands. Bronckaerts explains that Guevara's face also appears on Standard fans' flags. 'For the ultras, Che Guevara's image represents the left against capitalism and also the freedom fighter, because ultras want to be free and against modern football. Football is for the people, and it has to stay for the people.' Bronckaerts believes that Standard fans' *tifos* are among the best in Europe, and explains that sometimes they are political, depending on the circumstances, but often they are critical of the board or matches arranged for TV scheduling, such as Monday night football. Ultras Inferno has *gemellaggi* with other leftist clubs in Europe, including Omonoia Nicosia.

In Turkey, a leading fan group of Istanbul club Beşiktaş called *Çarşı* – from the Turkish word for 'market' – has gained a reputation for its activism. Founded in the early 1980s, the group regularly stood against the capitalist advances in a changing Turkey, whether against dam constructions that would destroy sites of historical significance or, famously in 2013, the demolition of Gezi Park to make way for urban development when Istanbul was already short of green public spaces. *Çarşı* members have also protested against racism and neo-Nazis in their time. John McManus is the author of *Welcome to Hell? In Search of the Real Turkish Football*. He tells me that football is intensely political in Turkey, but often not in a way that fits into any particular ideology or party affiliation. 'Beşiktaş have a reputation for being left-wing due to their supporters' group, *Çarşı*. But I always prefer to characterise their stance as more anti-establishment than left-wing – it just happens to be that the establishment in Turkey has historically been conservative,' McManus explains. 'But it's also important to remember that *Çarşı* do not speak for – or stand in – for Beşiktaş fans more broadly. There are millions of Beşiktaş fans, many of more conservative bents.'

McManus adds that the 'Big Three' clubs, as Galatasaray, Fenerbahçe and Beşiktaş are collectively referred to in Turkey, are all essentially part of the establishment, having been around for over a century. Most rivalries between fans of these three giants stem from specific incidents, such as previous fights or perceived injustice, rather than politics. However, football's ability to mobilise as a progressive force for change in Turkey has been hampered by the increasingly authoritarian stance of Turkish president Recep Tayyip Erdogan. 'Perhaps up to and including the years around the 2013 Gezi Park protests, football was a space where fans could express themselves politically,' McManus continues. 'But since then, laws and tactics to suppress dissent – which were stepped up significantly after the failed coup attempt in 2016 – have effectively silenced a lot of fan action deemed critical of the government, as is the case in nearly all sectors of society. There was a brief flicker of politics in Istanbul stadiums during the disputed 2019 mayoral election in Istanbul, where some crowds chanted briefly in favour of Ekrem Imamoglu, the opposition challenger to the AKP [Erdogan's party]. But really, we're talking about a few chants. In recent years, the apparatus of intimidation deployed by those in power has been broadly effective at silencing dissent in football stadia, as elsewhere in Turkey.'

Following the example of trailblazers like FC St Pauli and Rayo Vallecano, progressive football cultures have emerged all across the globe. In Dublin, one of Ireland's oldest football clubs is 100 per cent member-owned Bohemians FC. The club has a significant charitable arm, The Bohemian Foundation, launched in 2016. It has provided training sessions for inmates at Mountjoy Prison, and worked with the elderly, migrants and schools in deprived areas of Dublin. The club's shirt has provided a great campaigning platform, carrying the message 'Refugees Welcome' one season. Its 2020/21 away shirt was sponsored by Dublin band and Bohemians fans Fontaines DC, which raised €15,000 for a homeless charity.[4] In the US Major League Soccer (MLS), Portland Timbers fans have a long history of anti-fascism and anti-discrimination. In 2019, several members of the club fan group Timbers Army were suspended from the ground for displaying flags containing the symbol of the Iron Front, an anti-Nazi paramilitary group from 1930s Germany. For the MLS, displaying the flag – three downward-facing arrows pointing to the left – contravened its ban on political symbols.[5] Timbers Army is co-ordinated by an independent supporters' trust called 107IST. Supporters do a lot of great work in their local community, including raising money for school playgrounds and football fields, and rallying volunteers for food banks, youth groups and conservation efforts.[6]

Across the world, football continues to be a microcosm for all spectrums of society. A century after football first became a platform for both fascists and anti-fascists, deep into the 21st century the sport remains a key political and ideological battleground. Football is being used to bring together communities in Warsaw, Berlin, Oslo, Milan and many other cities. While for most football clubs and fans, politics does not feature as a reason for their engagement with the sport, for some, it is a core part of their identity, wherever they are on the political spectrum. Sport is political. It always has been and always will be. Politicians who would rather sport and politics didn't mix have learned nothing from history. While some politicians have been able to exploit the sport for populist or propaganda reasons, football can also be used as a force for good: to educate, to include, to break down barriers and come together.

1 https://www.dagsavisen.no/kultur/2013/07/30/fargerik-fotball-en-del-av-valerenga-historien/ (09/10/21)

2 https://www.vaarfotball.no/english/ (retrieved 13/10/21)

3 https://www.france24.com/en/live-news/20210620-norway-decides-against-qatar-world-cup-boycott (retrieved 13/10/21)

4 https://tribunemag.co.uk/2021/07/how-dublins-bohemians-are-bringing-fan-owned-football-into-europe (retrieved 04/09/21)

5 https://www.espn.com/soccer/portland-timbers/story/3935328/timbers-army-fans-suspended-for-iron-front-flag (retrieved 06/09/21)

6 https://107ist.org/107ist/what-why (retrieved 07/09/21)

Acknowledgements

I'D LIKE to thank the following people for their time and insight, without whose input this book simply could not have been possible.

Professor Peter J. Beck, Dominic Bliss, Adam Brandon, Mario Bronckaerts, Alex Brown and Pier Pressure, Rob Carroll and Yorkshire St Pauli, Franco Castellani (son of Carlo), Michael Cole, Robin Cowan and Clapton CFC, Empoli FC and the Municipality of Empoli, Filipe d'Avillez, Nacho Dimari, Mark Doidge, Andrew Downie, Gian Marco Duina and St Ambroeus FC, Robbie Dunne, Brenda Elsey, Gerard Farrell, FC Zenit, John Foot, Marco Giani, Andrew Gillen, Wayne Girard, Joaquín Maidagan Goldenzweig and Independiente de Vallecas, Tom Griffiths, Beñat Gutierrez, Dr Andy Hodges, Luca Hodges-Ramon, Franzi Hoffmann, Mikel Huarte, Ryan Hubbard, Christopher Hylland, Leandro Iamin, Tobias Jones, Andrew Lawn, Kenny Legg, Nick Lloyd, Ricardo Martins, Alan McDougall, Benjamin McFadyean, John McManus, Steve Menary, Kevin Miller and Whitehawk FC, Richard Mills, Andy Mitchell, James Montague, Andrés Morales, Matthias Moretti and CS Lebowski plus fan Alex, Cas Mudde, Museo Levante UD, Denys Nachornyy, Mick Page, Rafał Pankowski, Natxo Parra, Miguel Pereira, ASD Quartograd, Alejandro Quiroga, Red Star FC, Paul Reidy, Rhys Richards, Francesco Sani, Lars

Schou, Ronald Schut, Séan Scullion, Kevin E. Simpson, Bradley Stafford, Jan Stöver, Jacob Sweetman, Peter Szegedi, Natxo Torné, George Tsitsonis, Jurryt van de Vooren, Juraj Vrdoljak, Michael Wagg, Tom Wardle, Trade Union Football and Alcohol Committee (TUFAC), Dr Pete Watson, Dr Stuart Whigham, Aidan Williams, Professor Jean Williams, John Williams.

I'd also like to thank the editorial and design team at Pitch Publishing for bringing this book to fruition.

Bibliography

Ball, Phil, *Morbo: The Story of Spanish Football* (London: WSC Books Ltd., 2002)

Beck, Peter J., *Scoring For Britain: International Football and International Politics, 1900-1939* (London: Frank Cass Publishers, 1999)

Bliss, Dominic, *Erbstein: The Triumph and Tragedy of Football's Forgotten Pioneer* (London: Blizzard Media, 2014)

Bolchover, David, *The Greatest Comeback: From Genocide to Football Glory, The Story of Béla Guttmann* (Hull: Biteback Publishing, 2017)

Campomar, Andreas, *¡Golazo! A History of Latin American Football* (London: Quercus, 2014)

Dougan, Andy, *Dynamo: Defending the Honour of Kiev* (London: Fourth Estate, 2013)

Downie, Andrew, *Doctor Socrates: Footballer, Philosopher, Legend* (London: Simon & Schuster UK, 2017)

Dunne, Robbie, *Working Class Heroes: The Story of Rayo Vallecano, Madrid's Forgotten Team* (Worthing: Pitch Publishing, 2017)

Foer, Franklin, *How Football Explains the World* (London: Arrow Books, 2005)

Foot, John, *Calcio: A History of Italian Football* (London: Harper Perennial, 2007)

Glanville, Brian, *The Story of the World Cup* (London: Faber & Faber, 2018)

Goldblatt, David, *The Ball is Round: A Global History of Football* (London: Penguin, 2007)

Hesse, Ulrich, *Tor! The Story of German Football* (London: WSC Books, 2003)

Hodges, Andrew, *Fan Activism, Protest and Politics: Ultras in Post-Socialist Croatia* (London: Routledge, 2020)

Hylland, Christopher, *Tears at the Bombonera* (Worthing: Pitch Publishing, 2021)

Hubbard, Ryan, *From Partition to Solidarity, The First Hundred Years of Polish Football* (Leicester: RAH, 2019)

Jones, Tobias, *Ultra: The Underworld of Italian Football*, (London: Head of Zeus, 2019)

Kuper, Simon, *Ajax, the Dutch, the War* (London: Orion, 2011)

Martin, Simon, *Football and Fascism: The National Game Under Mussolini* (Oxford: Berg, 2004)

McManus, John, *Welcome to Hell? In Search of the Real Turkish Football* (London: W&N, 2018)

Mills, Richard, *The Politics of Football in Yugoslavia: Sport, Nationalism and the State* (London: I.B. Tauris, 2018)

Molinelli, Edoardo, *Cuori Partigiani: La Storia Dei Calciatori Professionisti Nella Resistenza Italiana* (Rome: Red Star Press, 2019)

Montague, James, *1312: Among the Ultras: A Journey with the World's Most Extreme Fans* (London: Penguin, 2020)

Mudde, Cas, *The Far Right Today*, (Cambridge: Polity Press, 2019)

Simpson, Kevin. E., *Soccer Under the Swastika: Defiance and Survival in the Nazi Camps and Ghettos* (London: Rowman & Littlefield, 2020, revised edition)

Testa, Alberto and Armstrong, Gary, *Football, Fascism and Fandom: The UltraS of Italian Football* (London: A&C Black, 2010)

Usall, Ramon, *Futbolítica: Històries de Clubs Políticament Singulars* (Barcelona: Ara Llibres, 2017)

Villalobos Salas, Cristóbal, *Fútbol y Fascismo* (Madrid: Altamerea, 2020)

Viñas, Carles and Parra, Natxo, *St. Pauli: Another Football is Possible* (London: Pluto Press, 2020)

Wagg, Michael, *The Turning Season: DDR-Oberliga Revisited* (Worthing: Pitch Publishing, 2020)

Wilson, Jonathan, *Angels with Dirty Faces: The Footballing History of Argentina* (London: W&N, 2017)

Online resources

Anne Frank House

Arolsen Archives

BBC.co.uk

BleacherReport.com

Britannica.com

British Newspaper Archive

Farenet.org

Fifa.com

FootballPink.net

Gallica.bnf.fr

Golazzo: The Totally Italian Football Show

History.com

Imperial War Museum

National Archives

NationalFootballMuseum.com

Nigdywiecej.org

Marca.com

Oorlogslevens.nl

RSSSF.com

The Blizzard

TheseFootballTimes.co and *These Football Times* Podcast

The Gentleman Ultra
Voetbalmonument.nl
Nick Lloyd/Walking Museum of Spanish Civil
  War in Barcelona

Official websites of football clubs and national football
  associations cited

Films

Futebol de Causas
Estadio Nacional
Pelé, Argentina and the Dictators
Mundialito

Newspapers and other websites cited in text